African Video Movies and Global Desires

Ohio University Research in International Studies

This series of publications on Africa, Latin America, Southeast Asia, and Global and Comparative Studies is designed to present significant research, translation, and opinion to area specialists and to a wide community of persons interested in world affairs. The editor seeks manuscripts of quality on any subject and can usually make a decision regarding publication within three months of receipt of the original work. Production methods generally permit a work to appear within one year of acceptance. The editor works closely with authors to produce a high-quality book. The series appears in a paperback format and is distributed worldwide. For more information, contact the executive editor at Ohio University Press, 19 Circle Drive, The Ridges, Athens, Ohio 45701.

Executive editor: Gillian Berchowitz
AREA CONSULTANTS
Africa: Gillian Berchowitz
Latin America: Brad Jokisch, Patrick Barr-Melej, and Rafael Obregon
Southeast Asia: William H. Frederick

The Ohio University Research in International Studies series is published for the Center for International Studies by Ohio University Press. The views expressed in individual volumes are those of the authors and should not be considered to represent the policies or beliefs of the Center for International Studies, Ohio University Press, or Ohio University.

African Video Movies
and Global Desires

A GHANAIAN HISTORY

Carmela Garritano

Ohio University Research in International Studies
Africa Series No. 91
Athens

To obtain permission to quote, reprint, or otherwise reproduce
or distribute material from Ohio University Press publications,
please contact our rights and permissions department at
(740) 593-1154 or (740) 593-4536 (fax).
www.ohioswallow.com

Printed in the United States of America
The books in the Ohio University Research in International Studies Series
are printed on acid-free paper ♾ ™

22 21 20 19 18 17 16 15 14 13   5 4 3 2 1

An earier version of chapter 2 appeared as "Contesting Authenticities:
The Emergence of Local Video Production in Ghana" in
Critical Arts: A Journal of South-North Cultural and Media Studies 22,
no. 1 (2008): 21–48, and is available at the journal's website,
http://www.informaworld.com. Permission for reuse of this
material is courtesy of Taylor & Francis Group.

Library of Congress Cataloging-in-Publication Data

Garritano, Carmela, 1968–
African video movies and global desires : a Ghanaian history / Carmela Garritano.
    p. cm. — (Ohio University research in international studies, Africa series ; no. 91)
Includes bibliographical references and index.
ISBN 978-0-89680-286-5 (pb : alk. paper) — ISBN 978-0-89680-484-5 (electronic)
1. Video recordings—Social aspects—Ghana. 2. Video recordings—Economic aspects—
Ghana. 3. Video recordings industry—Ghana. I. Title.
PN1992.934.G48G37 2013
384'.809667—dc23
                    2012043475

Dla Mikołaja i Bartka, moich kochanych

Contents

Illustrations

Acknowledgments

Research for this project has been supported by grants from Michigan State University, FLAS, Fulbright IIE, the West Africa Research Association, and the University of St. Thomas. The professors I worked closely with at Michigan State, including David Robinson, Jyotsna Singh, and David Wiley, deserve special thanks for their help and encouragement. The support of the African Studies Center at MSU, and especially of John Metzler, was instrumental to obtaining the funding necessary to complete a significant portion of the research on which this project is built. I am grateful to Tama Hamilton-Wray, my boss at the African Media Center, who was a bright light during my time at MSU. Keyan Tomaselli, whom I had the pleasure of getting to know when he was briefly at MSU, has helped me along in various ways over the years.

I owe my deepest debt of gratitude to my advisor and dear friend Ken Harrow. His guidance and support have been my fortune. As a mentor, activist, and scholar, his is an example I hope to follow.

Since 1998, Socrate Safo has been a close friend and colleague. His gumption and creativity drew me to the industry of which he is a founding member, and he has been an unwavering source of support and encouragement. I thank him for sharing his knowledge and expertise with me these many years.

This work would not have been possible without the help of friends and colleagues in the Ghanaian film and video industries. For their generosity and patience, warm thanks to George Arcton-Tetty, Mark Colemen, Veronica Quarshie, and Bob Smith, Jnr. I am also grateful for the cooperation of Mustapha Adams, William Akuffo, Ashangbor Akwetey-Kanyi, Mohammed Al Hassan, King Ampaw, Fred Amugi, Emmanuel Apea, Nat Banini, Alex Boateng, George Bosompim, Nii Saka Brown, Munir Captan, Nanabanyin Dadson, Pascaline C. Edwards, Shirley

Frimpong-Manso, Steve Hackman, Martin Hama, Rev. Dr. Chris Hesse, H.M., Idikoko, Ramesh Jai, Alfred Kumi-Atiemo, Albert Kuvodu, Albert Mensah, Vera Mensah, Mr. Mettle, Saul Mettle, Abdul Salam Munumi, Haijia Muzongo, Samuel Nai, Samuel Nyamekye, Samuel Odoi-Mensah, Helen Omaboe, Kofi Owusu, Albert Owusu-Ansah, Regina Pornortey, Brew Riverson, William Sefa, George Williams, and Moro Yaro. I remain indebted to Godwin Kotey, a talented friend who left the world too soon.

Many thanks to my hard-working research assistants: in Ghana, Adu Vera and Joseph Koranteng; in Nigeria, Oluchi Dikeocha; and in St. Paul, Nana Yiadom. Time spent in Ghana has been enriched by Lydia Amon-Kotey, Francis Gbormittah, Elijah Mensah, and Sam Nyeha. During the Fulbright year, I was privileged to have JoAnn Brimmer as a friend and intellectual interlocutor.

I thank Ato Quayson, who was generous enough to read several chapters of the manuscript while it was very much in process. I also thank Carmen McCain, who offered helpful comments on the introduction. I am indebted to the many colleagues and friends whose provocative responses to papers I have given at various conferences, in particular at the African Literature Association and African Studies Association conferences, have helped me reconsider and sharpen my ideas. I want to thank Lindiwe Dovey and Teju Olaniyan for their expressions of support. Thanks are due to Jean-Marie Teno for the rough cut of *Sacred Places* and talking with me on several occasions. Thanks, too, to fellow video movie researchers Moradewun Adejunmobi, Africanus Aveh, Jonathan Haynes, Ono Okome, and John McCall. I look forward to all that is yet to come! Jon Haynes deserves a special expression of gratitude for publishing my first article on Nollywood and, since then, supporting my work in countless ways. I thank him especially for his incisive and generous comments on this manuscript. I also wish to express my gratitude to the anonymous reader whose discerning and detailed comments made this a better book and to Gillian Berchowitz at Ohio University Press for her patience and assistance.

Laura Dagustino deserves huge thanks for helping with childcare and more during several very long and difficult years. If not for her, I would not have been able to complete research for this book. I am also grateful to my parents for the assistance they provided in St. Paul during a summer I spent in Ghana. I have benefitted in countless ways from Padmaja Challakere's brilliant mind and caring heart.

Finally, to my beloved Bartek, unending appreciation.

Introduction

African Popular Videos as Global Cultural Forms

The emergence of popular video industries in Ghana and Nigeria represents the most important and exciting development in African cultural production in recent history. Since its inception in the 1960s, African filmmaking has been a "paradoxical activity" (Barlet 2000, 238). Born out of the historical struggle of decolonization and a commitment to represent "Africa from an African perspective" (Armes 2006, 68), the work of socially committed African filmmakers has not generated a mass audience on the continent. Under current conditions marked by the international hegemony of dominant cinema industries, the dilapidated state of cinema houses in Africa, and the prohibitive expense of producing celluloid films, African filmmakers have become locked in a relationship of dependency with funding sources and distribution networks located in the global North. As a consequence, African films remain "foreigners in their own countries" (Sama 1996, 148), more likely to be found in Europe and North America on film festival screens and in university libraries than projected in cinemas or broadcast on television in Africa.

Though the film medium has failed to take root in Africa, video has flourished. An inexpensive, widely available, and easy to use technology for the production, duplication, and distribution of movies and other media content, video has radically transformed the African cultural landscape. In perhaps its most consequential manifestation, video has allowed videomakers in Ghana and Nigeria, individuals who in most cases are detached from official cultural institutions and working outside the purview of the state, to create a tremendously popular, commercial cinema for audiences in Africa and abroad: feature "films" made on video. Freed from the requirements for cultural and economic capital imposed by the film medium, ordinary Ghanaians and Nigerians started making and exhibiting their own productions in the late 1980s. In Ghana, the tremendous success of William Akuffo's *Zinabu* (1987), a full-length feature shot with a VHS home video camera, sparked what those working in the Ghanaian video industry call "the video boom." Local audiences, who had been watching scratched and faded foreign films for years, responded to Akuffo's video movie with enormous enthusiasm. They crowded into the Globe Theatre in Accra for weeks to watch the video on the large screen. In a few years, film projectors in all of the major film theaters were replaced with video projection systems and hundreds of privately owned video centers, of various sizes and structural integrity, sprung up throughout the country to meet the growing demand for video viewing. Within ten years of the first local video production in 1987, as many as four videos in English were being released in Ghana each month, and over twenty years later, in 2009, Ghanaian movies appeared at the rate of approximately six per week, one in English and five in Akan, a Ghanaian language spoken across the country.

The Nigerian video industry, which began to take shape around the same time, soon became the economic and cultural power of the West African region. Now one of the largest movie industries in the world, the Nigerian industry releases a staggering 1,500 movies each year (Barrot 2009). Nollywood, the name popularly used to refer to Nigerian English-language movie production, speaks to the size and ambitions of the industry, but also obscures its diversity. Large numbers of Nigerian movies are also made in Yoruba. In fact, more Nigerian movies are produced in Yoruba than English, and in the city of Kano in Northern Nigeria, there is a well-established and prolific Hausa-language industry, called "Kannywood." Small numbers of Nigerian movies are also produced in Nupe and Bini (McCain 2011). Based on the models established in Ghana and Nigeria, budding industries in Kenya, Uganda, Tanzania, and Cameroon have emerged. Produced transnationally and broadcast on television, streamed over the Internet, distributed and pirated globally in multiple formats, African video movies represent, in the words of Jonathan Haynes, "one of the greatest explosions of popular culture the continent has ever seen" (2007c, 1).

The growth and expansion of African popular video has engendered a rapidly developing body of published work dispersed across three continents (Africa, Europe, and North America) and several disciplines.[1] Prominent among the numerous journal articles and book chapters on African video movies are the ongoing contributions of the pioneers in the field, Haynes and Onookome Okome, and important articles by Moradewun Adejunmobi, Akin Adesokan, John McCall, and Birgit Meyer. Noteworthy too are anthologies edited by Jonathan Haynes (2000), Foluke Ogunleye (2003), Pierre Barrot (2009), and Mahir Şaul and Ralph A. Austen (2010), as well as Brian Larkin's brilliant monograph *Signal and Noise* (2008). Important research on African video movies has featured in special editions of the journals *Postcolonial Text* (2007), *Film International* (2007), *African Literature Today* (2010), and the *Journal of African Cultural Studies* (2010). African Studies conferences regularly include panels on African video movies, and specialists in the field have organized several international conferences dedicated to the dissemination and sharing of research on this new cultural form.[2] In addition, the many documentaries on popular video in Africa indicate a solid and growing interest among nonspecialists.[3] Without question, the largest part of this scholarship has concentrated on the Nigerian industry, and in particular the English-language video industry based in Southern Nigeria.[4] Too readily ignored or merely absorbed into Nollywood's dominant narrative have been the more minor industries in Nigeria, such as the Hausa-language industry, and in the region, the historically and aesthetically distinct video industry in Ghana, which is the focus of this book.

The focus on Nollywood, moreover, has overlooked the transnational interaction between the two industries and has tended to simplify and reify "*the* local" that Nollywood is said to represent, flattening the multiplicity of transnational cultural articulations that move through regional cultural economies in Africa and often in relations of disjuncture and competition. By subsuming all West African video under the example of Nigeria, the region's dominant national power, critics have erased the movement, complexity, and *contestation* that mark the West African regional videoscape, where "the local" remains a contested signifier, not a self-evident descriptor. Faced with the relentless onslaught of Nigerian videos in Ghana, some Ghanaian videomakers have come to regard Nollywood as a far more pressing threat to their survival than Hollywood. Seen from this point of view, Nollywood looks a lot like an invader, a regional cultural power whose success has endangered local production. This study of Ghanaian video, including its points of intersection with and divergence from Nollywood, reminds us that margins, like centers, are multiple, relational, and shifting. *African Video Movies and Global Desires: A Ghanaian History* accounts for the singularity of the history of Ghanaian film and video as it has been shaped by national and transnational forces and strives to enrich our understanding of the diverse cultural ecology of West African screen media.

African Popular Video and African Film Scholars: A Brief Historical Overview

I first learned of the emergence of the local video industries in Ghana and Nigeria at the 1997 Annual Conference of the African Literature Association (ALA), the theme of which was *FESPACO* (Festival Panafricain du Cinéma et de la Télévision de Ouagadougou) *Nights in Michigan,* a decade after Akuffo screened *Zinabu* to audiences in Accra. Organized by Kenneth W. Harrow and hosted by Michigan State University, where I was a PhD student at the time, the conference was unprecedented: the first conference of the ALA dedicated to screening, discussing, and celebrating African cinema. Many African filmmakers were in attendance, and so not surprisingly, discussions and debates concerning the obstacles impeding African film production and distribution in Africa consumed a fair amount of time and energy. Looking back, it seems remarkable, given the preoccupation with funding and the limited availability of African films and functioning cinema houses in Africa, that not one paper was proposed on the thriving local, low-budget, commercial video industries in West Africa.[5] In the margins of the main event, video, mentioned by chance, came to represent little more than a notation. It was at the Women's Caucus luncheon that I initially heard about African video movies and only during the question and answer session that followed the well-received talk by Tsitsi Dangaremgba, the Zimbabwean novelist and filmmaker, who spoke on the making of her first feature film *Everyone's Child* (1996). After commending Dangaremgba for her sensitive and honest representation of AIDS and its impact on families and communities, an audience member who had recently been to West Africa spoke briefly about the booming market for locally produced videos in West Africa. Unlike *Everyone's Child,* an artistic African film animated by social justice and activism, the videos, she claimed, were brazenly amateurish and profit-driven. Influenced by Hollywood, they promoted stereotypical and extremely negative images of Africa. She reached out to the audience with a sense of urgency, as if this example of local cultural production were a harmful, invasive pestilence that needed to be eradicated. She wondered how we, the experts and intellectuals, could intervene in the local cultural scene on behalf of Africa.

I have included this anecdote because it expresses the moralistic overtones that dominated the initial responses of African film and literature scholars to popular video and that, although far less frequently, continue to color criticism of the videos. Carmen McCain's (2011) description of the position assigned to Nollywood at FESPACO 2011 attests to its ongoing marginalization. The founding figures of African cinema set the still widely held notion that popular or commercial cultural products were little more than imitations of Western forms that provided distraction in the form of cheap entertainment, and as Alexi Tcheuyap notes, these governing ideologies mandated that African cinema "was meant not for pleasure, but for (political) instruction" (2011, 7). Unabashedly commercial and melodramatic, video movies have frustrated expectations of what African film is supposed to be. Frank Ukadike has described video productions as "devoid of authenticity" (Ukadike 2003, 126), and Josef Gugler argues that these "market-driven" products promote the "political processes that engender extreme inequalities" (2003, 78). Lindiwe Dovey states that commercial videos "tend to affirm" violence, while serious and oppositional African films "[explore] restorative, nonviolent means of resolving social and political problems" (2009, 23). Most problematic is that these generalizations are stated without substantiation or reference to any of the thousands of popular movies that have been released in Ghana and Nigeria since the late 1980s. They demonstrate little awareness of the incredible range and variety of popular movies or interest in the audiences who consume and take pleasure from them. These criticisms, it seems, have functioned chiefly to produce and police a particular idea of what African screen media is or should be.

African film scholars' reluctance to engage popular video in a serious way explains why the earliest and some of the best work, with the noteworthy exceptions of writing by Haynes and Okome, has been done by anthropologists. Tcheuyap (2011) has shown that the governing ideologies of African cinema, though animated by proletarian and emancipatory desires, were instituted and have been policed by elite intellectual institutions, which I would emphasize, remain detached from African sites of cultural consumption. Like the makers of other popular products in Africa, the producers of popular videos, in most cases, are not affiliated with intellectual institutions or institutions of official culture; most have not attended film schools or university, have little formal training in video or film production, and so have not been initiated into the political and aesthetic disposition and conceptual vocabulary of African cinema.[6] As Haynes remarks, "The international dimension of their cultural horizon is formed more by American action films, Indian romances, and Mexican soap operas than by exposure to English literature" (2003a, 23). The makers of popular movies have never been principally concerned with authenticity, cultural revival, or cultural preservation, the founding motivations of elite African cinema. Addressing a popular, mass audience in Africa, the videomakers are not obliged to speak on behalf of an African minority community to an audience of outsiders and remain unencumbered by "the burden of representation" (Desai 2004, 63) that inflects the criticisms voiced by makers and scholars of serious African film.[7]

Since the 1990s, the differences between African popular video and serious African film have become less pronounced. Advances in digital video technologies have obscured the lines separating film and video, and over time, as the Ghanaian and Nigerian industries have become more formalized and videomakers have developed significant expertise and experience, the disparities between "amateur" videomakers and "professional" filmmakers have diminished. In content and form, recent big-budget, flashy African films such as Gavin Hood's sentimental drama *Tsotsi* (2005), which won an Academy Award for Best Foreign Picture, and Djo Tunda Wa Munga's gangster thriller *Viva Riva!* (2010) resonate more with Nollywood than politicized African film, further troubling simplistic binaries between the two forms of African screen media. The features of Nigerian moviemakers Tunde Kelani and Kunle Afolayan, which grow from and are marked by Nollywood aesthetics and modes of production, self-consciously invoke and revitalize Yoruba cultural antecedents and move in and out of film festival and academic circuits if not quite effortlessly, than with less and less resistance.[8]

As technologies and forms change, the divide between critics of popular video and elite African cinema has started to close, too. Several important books on African film have discussed the unparalleled significance of the local video movie phenomenon to the study and production of African film and media (Harrow 2007; Dovey 2009; Tcheuyap 2011). Tcheuyap's *Postnationalist African Cinema* (2011), referencing Nollywood, illustrates that entertainment and performance have always been features of serious African cinema, even if rarely discussed by critics more concerned with history and politics. A conference at the University of Illinois in Urbana-Champaign in 2007 provided the opportunity for comparative analyses of the two forms and cultivated dialogue between scholars of local video and African film, and two significant publications, a special edition of the *Journal of African Cultural Studies* (2010) edited by Lindiwe Dovey and *Viewing African Cinema in the Twenty-First Century* (2010), a collection of essays edited by Mahir Şaul and Ralph Austin, the conveners of the conference, grew from that meeting. Manthia Diawara's *African Film: New Forms of Aesthetics and Politics* (2010) combines analyses of film and video, treating them with equal attention and rigor. In *Postcolonial Artists and Global Aesthetics* (2011) Akin Adesokan situates African cultural production, including literature from Africa and the diaspora and the films of Sembene Ousmane and Tunde Kelani, along the transition from decolonization to globalization, reading across several genres to demonstrate the interpenetration of the material, the historical, and the aesthetic. These efforts have gone a long way toward bridging the divide between scholars writing about different forms of African screen media, provoking critical methods and theoretical questions attuned to the spirit of Kenneth Harrow's (2007) call for change. And although I agree with Dovey, who argues that the opposition between local video and elite African film has been "rendered obsolete" (2010, 2), I do think we can attend to the meaningful differences among African cultural forms without falling into binary logic. Rather than elide these differences, we should probe their sources and effects. Whether subsidized or produced commercially, African screen media circulates and has value symbolically and economically, and as in all cultural forms, these different configurations of value overlap and interact. Serious African film, African popular video, and the many hybrid forms that fit neatly into neither category are enabled and constrained by different material conditions of creation, circulation, and consumption. To my mind, the study of video movies has been crucially important to African film criticism because the videos have resisted incorporation into the field's dominant critical discourse and engendered methodologies attentive to materiality. Looking seriously at African video movies, and with critical scrutiny, has facilitated exciting new ways of defining, analyzing, and teaching many types of African screen media.

Whether adopting the theoretical language of Marxism, feminism, cultural nationalism, or psychoanalysis, critics of African film, in the main, have practiced what Julianne Burton (1997) has called an immanent criticism, a critical methodology that locates meaning within the world of the film text. Typically, in order to amplify the African film's political message, the critic positions herself beside the film text, carrying out a formalist analysis of the text or describing its explicit content. Even when the critic sets out to engage history, that history is understood to be located and made present in the film. This methodology has functioned primarily to facilitate African cinema's founding objective, which, as Harrow explains, was to be "a genuine expression answering the needs of the people through a cinema of struggle and cultural representation" (2007, 42). Yet, immanent criticism, as Burton convincing shows, abstracts and reifies the film text, sealing it off from the "dynamic historical and social forces" (1997, 167) it is intended to transform. A committed intellectual, Burton sets out to reroute politicized critical practice as it applies to oppositional filmmaking. In particular, she calls for the implementation of a more "constructive and meaningful critical relationship to the tradition of oppositional filmmaking in Latin America" (1997, 167). This relationship is based on a contextual criticism, a practice that charges the critic with "attempt[ing] to demonstrate how interacting contextual factors impact upon the film text itself and the interpretation of that text at a given point of reception" (168). Though Burton addresses her critique to politicized critics and has developed this methodology for Latin American oppositional filmmaking, her intervention inspires the method adopted in this book about African video movies. Contextual criticism attempts to account for the fluidity and complexity of context, which Burton describes as "a mutually influential dynamic between the film product, the organizational structure in which it is produced, the organizational structure in which it is consumed, and the larger social context" (Burton 1997, 170). As practiced here, contextual criticism posits a dialectical relationship between the cultural form and its many contexts and investigates how those contexts shape the text and how the text affects its context. Far from abandoning close reading, it couples that reading with the investigation of the materiality and social life of the video-text. An inherently interdisciplinary method, it recognizes that meaning is contingent and variable, constructed by the text's modes of production and consumption and the dynamic circuits it migrates along.

Whereas the critical discourse of politicized African cinema has privileged the film-text, what have yet to be fully accounted for in the scholarship on popular video movies are their formal properties and aesthetics. This is not to discount or diminish the importance of Birgit Meyer's provocative analyses of Pentecostal modernity or Brian Larkin's brilliant discussion of the aesthetics of astonishment that inflect Nigerian videos. Nor do I want to ignore Esi Sutherland-Addy's article in which she describes the affiliations shared by video movies and West African oral forms. Still, much more attention needs to be paid to the videos as texts, to the narrative conventions and generic modes they deploy, to the anxieties they seek to quell, and to the spectatorial processes they put in motion. This book brings the insights of literary and film analysis to bear on a range of video movies. Close readings of select video features highlight the ambivalent significations produced by Ghanaian movies amid profound material and ideological transformation and investigate how Ghanaian video reconstitutes, even as it is complicit with, the grand narratives of modernity and globalization.

The booming commercial video industries in Ghana and Nigeria, which produce movies meant first and foremost to entertain, have brought pleasure into visibility as a crucial dimension of analysis. Early scholarship on video movies, drawing on the explanations offered by the videomakers themselves, explained their appeal as representational. Video movies presented Ghanaian and Nigerian audiences with characters who looked and talked like them and with stories that were familiar. Meyer explains that Ghanaian popular video "was born out of people's desire to see their own culture mediated through a television or cinema screen" (1999, 98). Recent writing has associated the appeal of the movies with not only their content, but their function, as well. Adesokan offers that the lavish displays presented by Nollywood domestic dramas fulfill "a mass desire for wealth and power" (2004, 191), and Larkin (2008) has associated the appeal of Nigerian videos with their capacity to express and imaginatively contain the vulnerabilities and desires associated with everyday life in the African postcolony. Moradewun Adejunmobi (2010) has considered the transnational reach of African popular movies to audiences outside the countries where the movies are made and has theorized the specific types of identification audiences find in Nollywood movies and the various pleasures spectators across Africa and the diaspora, from a variety of places and backgrounds, derive from watching them.

Adejunmobi uses the term "phenomenological proximity" to capture this transnational appeal. She explains, "Nollywood films in English are able to generate audiences in diverse locations in Africa because they present recognizable struggles, they appeal to widespread fears and familiar aspirations" (Adejunmobi 2010, 111). Audiences identify with the hardships that drive characters to corrupt and immoral acts, and they admire the lifestyles achieved through illicit means. Both Adejunmobi (2010) and Larkin (2008) associate the appeal of videos with their adoption of melodramatic narrative and visual conventions. Melodramatic movies "provide a medium for rationalizing" the attractions of global modernity in the face of the extreme poverty and distress that signal Africa's exclusion from the status of modernity (Adejunmobi 2010, 114).

In this book, I draw from and build on this research to more closely examine the pleasures the movies offer and the ambivalence they generate. Statements about audiences' responses to video movies are grounded in extensive ethnographic research conducted over a ten-year period during numerous stints in Ghana, which included formal and informal conversations with ordinary Ghanaians, as well as with producers, distributors, marketers, and others involved in the video industry. Film reviews and commentary published in local newspapers have also contributed to my understanding of audiences' responses. In close readings of the videos, I have tried to pay attention to the televisual and cinematic codes that suture the spectator to a particular point of view or subject position. In other words, I think it is crucial to attend to the subject positions created by the video-text in our attempts to understand the responses of real audiences and to acknowledge the role of the unconscious in pleasure and identification. Although I do not draw directly on psychoanalytic film theory to elaborate on the functioning of the unconscious, this theory informs my analyses. My use of the word "desire" in the title and throughout the book is meant to signal the interpenetration of the psychic and the sociopolitical in the formations of pleasure, anxiety, and aspiration.

Addressing spectators similarly marginalized by global modernity, the videos offer a multiplicity of pleasures derived from the oscillations between mimesis and fantasy, proximity and distance, desire and revulsion. Audiences imaginatively experience the fantasy of a glamorous lifestyle far removed from their everyday experiences. They identify, too, with a character's struggles to escape poverty and suffering and *dis*identify with the immoral practices that the same character engages in to get rich. Again and again, the videos generate profound ambivalence; they issue strong moral condemnations of greed and the immoral attainment of wealth and yet position the spectator as a consumer, one who gazes on and desires the movie's extravagant commodity displays. They criticize the dehumanizing impulse of capitalism and, simultaneously, produce spectator-subjects who desire the luxuries exhibited. Daniel Jordan Smith (2007) identifies similar expressions of ambivalence in Nigerian witchcraft accusations and stories of the occult. On the one hand, they articulate discontent with the appropriation of wealth and power by a privileged few and illustrate "the continuing power of moralities that privilege people and obligations of social relationships above the naked pursuit of riches" (Smith 2007, 138). On the other hand, they "highlight the intimate connections between popular condemnation of the unequal accumulation of great wealth and the widely shared fantasies about being rich" (142). Here, I argue that a split between narrative condemnation and visual desire commonly structure the movies. Narratives denounce and punish the greedy or selfish protagonist, engaging the spectator as a moral witness, while a visual economy of pleasure that aestheticizes consumption addresses the spectator as a desiring subject. Produced and consumed under circumstances of dire shortage and scarcity, video movies narrate and domesticate the desires and anxieties engendered by Ghana's incorporation into the global cultural economy. They are fertile ground for the growth of an "imaginaire of consumption" (Mbembe 2002, 271) and of a morality that is highly critical of materialism and capitalistic values.

Ghallywood and Its Global Aspirations

About fifty miles outside of Accra on a vast track of land that sits beside the Tema-Accra highway, Ghanaian videomaker William Akuffo has been constructing a movie production complex called Ghallywood, which he hopes will become the creative center for video movie production in Ghana (see figures I.1 and I.2). When I traveled to Ghana in 2009, I drove out to Ghallywood to call on Akuffo, whom I had first met in 1999, and to tour this most ambitious project. Crossed by streets named after Ghanaian actors and filmmakers, the complex houses Akuffo's large office and editing studio, a restaurant, and a classroom building. Pushing through the tall grass were the foundations of several other structures, which, when complete, will be the housing units for actors and production crews. Akuffo's plans also include the construction of a studio, several film sets, and an outdoor movie theater.

Of particular interest to me was the name Ghallywood, which like its predecessor Nollywood, aligns this marginalized, African video movie industry with Hollywood and Bollywood. During this trip to Ghana, I was struck by how often I heard the term Ghallywood,

Figure I.1. Planet Ghallywood restaurant sign at entrance to William Akuffo's Ghallywood. (© Carmela Garritano, 2009)

Figure I.2. Portrait of William Akuffo (© Carmela Garritano, 2009)

or another variant of it (Gollywood or Ghanawood), used by movie producers to refer to the Ghanaian commercial video movie industry. The name had also appeared in numerous movie and entertainment publications and, on one particular occasion, inspired a provocative debate among members of FIPAG, the Film and Video Producers' Association of Ghana. Among those reluctant to adopt the label was Richard Quartey; he voiced the minority opinion that Ghallywood is inappropriate to Ghana's movie industry because it is imitative. "Shouldn't we tap into our unique cultural reserves to find a better name?" Quartey asked. "Maybe Sankofa?" Supporters of adopting Ghallywood as the official name of the industry argued that imitation was precisely the point. Videomaker Socrate Safo answered, "We have Hollywood, then Bollywood, now Nollywood. Why not Ghallywood, too? We can be as good as those!" This sentiment was echoed by many others. Safo's adamant support for the label Ghallywood, like Akuffo's substantial investment in the creation of a Ghanaian movie production center, demonstrates the reach and intensity of the aspirations of moviemakers in Ghana. For those who have adopted the label, Ghallywood is a call to be taken seriously in the global arena of commercial cinema. Quartey's reluctance replays a concern familiar to African cultural producers, a concern about maintaining African authenticity and originality. James Ferguson has noted that the authenticity of

African aspirations to be modern have consistently been called into question out of fear "that the [African] copy is either too different from the [Western] original or not different enough" (2006, 16). In both configurations, Africa is the shadow of the West, its distorted and empty projection. In his book called *Global Shadows: Africa in the Neoliberal World Order* (2006), Ferguson insists on a different way of reading Africa's shadowing of the West. He torques the metaphor to show that a shadow is not only a distorted double; it also "implies a bond and a relationship. A shadow, after all, is not a copy but an attached twin. . . . Likeness here implies not only resemblance but also a connection, a proximity, an equivalence, even an identity" (2006, 17). This conceptualization of shadowing glosses Safo's proclamation: "We can be as good as those," reading it not merely as an attempt to imitate or assimilate to the Western model, but as an expression of a desire for proximity, a desire to attain the status and success of global film industries and to stand beside those global media industries as equal partners. The difference is worth elaborating on. To dismiss the ambitions of Ghanaian videomakers as iterations of cultural imperialism means disregarding their efforts to overcome their marginalization and participate fully as producers of their own cultural forms in the field of global culture.

Borrowing from the conceptual vocabularies of Ferguson, Achille Mbembe, and Sarah Nuttall, this book treats African popular video as a practice through which Africans articulate "worldliness." Worldliness, as defined by Nuttall and Mbembe,

> has to do not only with the capacity to generate one's own cultural forms, institutions, and lifeways, but also with the ability to foreground, translate, fragment, and disrupt realities and imaginaries originating elsewhere, and in the process place these forms and processes in the service of one's own making. (Nuttall and Mbembe 2008, 1)

As cultural forms and commodities, popular video movies, like other forms of African popular culture, embrace foreign influences as sources of newness and singularity (Barber 1987). Their appeal is linked to their enormous capacity to recontextualize and localize forms and styles associated with global mass culture, and much as in the African urban environments in which video movies circulate, it is the meeting of the local and the global that generates the energies and uncertainties that drive their production and consumption. As modern African cultural articulations, they participate in the "world-ing" of Africa (Simone 2001) and the "indigenizing" (McCall 2002) of global technologies, styles, desires, and discourses.[9] As global vernacular forms, they trouble generalizations about an African or national identity because they emerge from, are shaped by, and reshape "a mass-mediated imaginary that frequently transcends national space" (Appadurai 1996, 6).

Despite the expressions of global membership they convey, African popular videos have gone unnoticed outside African area studies by critics and scholars of world cinema. Largely attuned to cinematic forms and flows predominant in the first world institutions of global cine-literacy—film festivals, art-house cinemas, classrooms, and libraries—the current configuration of global media and cinema studies has included scholarship on elite African cinema, but eclipsed minor and commercial cultural forms and circuits that never intersect with these institutions.[10] Produced and disseminated through decentralized, private, and nonlegal circuits that variously have been called "minor" (Lionnet and Shi 2005), "unofficial" (Adejunmobi 2007), and "parallel" (Larkin 2004), African video movies move across local landscapes as well as through global cities (Sassen 2001) and media capitals (Curtin 2003), but travel along networks located under, around, and adjacent to major commercial and academic institutions and networks of exchange. They are among the multiplicity of unmapped media flows and forms that have emerged in the wake of the many changes linked to globalization: increased privatization, a proliferation of new, small media and electronic technologies, including video, satellite TV, and the internet, and the expansion of informal markets. Centered on this new African grassroots media form, and the uncharted media migrations and publics in West Africa and the African diaspora it has created, this study deepens our understanding of globalization and its cultural ecology. It pries open the closed circuit of the academic domain of cultural production by investigating a popular and commercial visual form that circulates within the space of the African everyday.

My notion of the everyday evokes Ravi Sundaram's description of the electronic everyday of Indian technoculture (1990).[11] Sundaram describes the electronic everyday as "a space" wrought from vast inequalities of wealth "where practices of quotidian consumption, mobility, and struggle are articulated" (1990, 48). It is a space of non-legality maintained in large part outside the reach of the state, where mobility and innovation are rewarded, and much as in the Ghanaian video industry, its agents exploit new technologies to improvise creative survival strategies and practices of piracy. The fragmented and dispersed networks of production and distribution of the everyday are organized by small entrepreneurs, or the petty-commodity sector. Part of the informal economy, "the actors in this space have simply ignored the state as the regulator of everyday life" (Sundaram 1999, 64), and they take little notice of the official conventions that govern the formal economy.

In the Ghanaian video industry, the space of the everyday shares several important characteristics with Sundaram's electronic everyday. Most obviously, its networks and processes operate in a zone of nonformality, which can frustrate the researcher's attempts to gather numerical data and precise information. Transactions are conducted without documentation. If records are kept, they are often irregular and not reliable. Very little in the system is codified. Artists and crew negotiate their fees with producers, directly and privately; payments for equipment or services rendered are often made in an ad hoc manner. On the set of a movie, money is readily exchanged informally for favors, as small loans, as gifts, or to fulfill social expectations. Producers always seem to be waiting to receive their money from distributors, and the people involved in the making of a movie, at every level, always seem to be waiting for the producer to pay them an outstanding balance. The ubiquity of piracy, the expansion of opportunities for domestic viewing, and the fluidity of the multiple sites for consuming videos publicly confound attempts to figure out how many people actually see any one video movie. Neither the state nor independent producers could possibly regulate the public, informal sites of movies consumption, which include the video parlor, "tie-in spaces" (Ajibade 2007), and numerous, temporary "street corner" gatherings (Okome 2007b) that assemble unpredictably throughout the city. It is also nearly impossible to state with certainty how profitable a movie might have been. Haynes and Okome note, "All figures on sales and profits need to be treated with extreme caution, as they are frequently inflated for publicity purposes, or deflated in order to defraud partners" (2000, 69). And because money and favors are continually being exchanged, and because the financial life of one movie project runs right into the next production, producers themselves have a hard time knowing exactly how much profit they might have made from any one movie. It is perhaps for these reasons that the everyday tends to be an overlooked space, one largely absent in the critical discourse on global cinema, which, like the discourse on technological globalization, has tended to center on "elite domains of consumption and identity" (Sundaram 1999, 63) and, I would add, the artistic and politicized products that move through those domains. This book sketches the broad parameters and shifts of the everyday culture of Ghanaian video movies, while conceding that its fluidity and informality continually disrupt this aim.

Adding to the many articles that examine, and often criticize, the representation of women in Nigerian and Ghanaian movies, this book attends to the enunciation of gender difference in the videos. In other words, it analyzes not only the ways women are portrayed but uncovers the gender norms and ideologies that the movies produce. Without question, video technology has expanded opportunities for women to work as producers of media in Nigeria (Haynes and Okome 2000; Okome 2007c) and in Ghana. As I note in chapter 4, no Ghanaian women had directed or produced a documentary or feature film before the advent of video movies. Yet, today in the Ghanaian industry, the number of men who hold positions as producers, directors, editors, screenwriters, and so on is far, far larger than the number of women in the same roles. That the products of a male-dominated media industry would be misogynistic or sexist is not inevitable, of course. It is true, however, that many Ghanaian movies do tend to recycle gender stereotypes with a long history in African popular culture and naturalize a similarly deep-rooted "ideology of patriarchy" (Okome 2007c, 166). Wisdom Agorde (2007), for example, has described an ethic of masculinity reiterated in Nollywood movies. Rooted in gender difference, this ethic defines manhood through violence, wealth, and ownership of women. Newell has identified the good-time girl and "the infinitely patient wife" as two common feminine character types in Ghanaian popular literature (2000, 37), and these characters appear frequently in videos, too. Agbese Aje-Ori (2010) has added the "mother-in-law" as another female stock character, and in this book, I describe the figure of the "monstrous woman." A reimagining of the good-time girl, this frightening powerful woman unleashes evil on the men who misuse or abuse her. Highly symbolic, she dwells at the limits of morality; her punishments reinstate social norms violated by selfish men with enormous appetites for women, food, and money.

Like Stephanie Newell (1997; 2000), I conceptualize African popular culture as a gender apparatus, a technology that produces and naturalizes particular gender ideologies. Gender is not incidental or supplemental to the worlds and identities imagined in the videos, but necessary to the articulation of these identities (Garritano 2000). The work of gender theorist Judith Butler undergirds the feminist readings included here. In her writing, Butler theorizes "the performative" function of gender norms, demonstrating that through repetition across multiple sites of culture, gender ideologies sanction and naturalize ways of being and of desiring. As Butler notes, "A performative" works "to produce that which it declares" (1993, 107). Crucially, then, cultural forms do not simply reflect dominant ideologies but are productive of those ideologies. They have the capacity to reiterate norms and to question or parody them. Women videomakers such as Veronica Quarshie and Shirley Frimpong-Manso have challenged gender stereotypes common in Ghanaian movies. Like the female writers Newell describes (2000), these women moviemakers speak from within dominant narratives of gender and open possibilities for the emergence of alternative ways of being men and women.

Although mainly centered on Nollywood, the scholarship on African video does include some very promising book chapters and articles on Ghanaian video movies. Several of these studies, in their attempts to introduce readers to and generate interest in Ghanaian video, have tended to be either wide-ranging and overly general, or limited in scope, discussing common thematic or generic features of small selections of video texts. A notable exception to this preliminary scholarship on Ghanaian video is the groundbreaking work of anthropologist Birgit Meyer, whose series of articles have examined Ghanaian popular video as an articulation of Pentecostalism. For Meyer (2004), Ghanaian popular video, the emergence of which converged with a marked increase in the number of Pentecostal-charismatic churches, represents one of many "pentecostalite" expressive forms that have flourished as a result of the liberalization of the media. Video enacts a "pentecostalite style" that "recasts modernity as a Christian project" (Meyer 2004, 93), warning against the evils modernity introduces and promoting Christian discipline as the only method for warding off those evils. In Ghanaian video features Meyer finds that "pentecostal concerns merge almost naturally with melodrama as an aesthetic form" in that both assert "the need to go beyond the surface of the visible to reveal hidden reality underneath" (2004, 101). Video functions then as a technology of modern pentecostal subjectivity and vision. Meyer writes: "Moviegoers are positioned in such a way that they share the eye of God, technologically simulated by the camera. Indeed, audiences are made mimetically to share the super vision that enables God to penetrate the dark; they are addressed as viewer-believers and even as voyeurs peeping into the otherwise forbidden" (2004, 104). The appeal of video, then, involves the attainment of vision that is panoptical and voyeuristic. It is all-encompassing, secretive, and illicit.

Following the path cleared by Meyer, critics have tended to center on this one genre, variously called the occult video (Okome 2007a), the horror film (Wendl 2001, 2007) or a pentecostal expressive form (Meyer 1998, 1999, 2003, 2004). Although much of this work is compelling, its limited scope has created the false impression that Pentecostalism and its representation of occult practice figures prominently in all Ghanaian movies. Attention to the Christianity-occult binary has overshadowed the other ideological investments the videos make, the meanings they enact, and the subjectivities they produce. Certainly, Pentecostalism animates many Ghanaian movies, and even when not championed or invoked explicitly, it remains a significant discursive strand in many more. But video movies are not monolithic, nor are they controlled by one dominant way of looking or mode of narration. Unrestrained and unruly heterogeneity is a pronounced feature of videos movies. They are, in the words of James Ferguson, noisy.[12] Borrowing from Ferguson's *Expectations of Modernity: Myths and Meanings of Urban Life on the Zambian Copperbelt* (1999), this book advocates for and strives to employ an analytics of noise. Noise, Ferguson writes:

> has its social logic—a logic that makes itself visible only if one is able at some point to set aside the search for signal, and to maintain a decent respect for the social significance of the unintelligible, for the fact that signs may produce puzzlement, unease, and uncertainty (and not only for the ethnographer) just as easily as they may produce stable and unequivocal meanings. (Ferguson 1999, 210)

Ferguson's analytic seems well suited to video movies because, like the ethnographic sites and situations he interprets, videos are messy, crisscrossed by multiple flows of meaning. They grow out of and speak to an urban, African context not entirely dissimilar to that studied by Ferguson, and as urban cultural texts they are held together by "conflicting strands of meaning and style" (1999, 229). They resist ideological domestication (Ferguson 1999, 229) and instead invite multiplicity, complexity, and contradiction. Ferguson insists that to plot the noise of a particular scene is to listen for "multiple implied and imagined communities of meaning that only partially exist, only partially overlap and are geographically and socially dispersed" (Ferguson 1999, 227). By conceptualizing popular video as an expression of one master and overarching discourse, contained by a consistently deployed logic of surface and depth, or even assimilated to one dominant ideology, we risk silencing the flow of noise and closing off the multiplicity of potential meanings, looks, styles, and sensations produced by video features across time. Plotting the dynamic range and variable tempo of the noise, narratives, and silences of video movies also allows us to capture their incredible diversity and ideological implications, which have, so far, gone unheard.

In the emergent scholarship on African video movies, little attention has yet been given to historical change. *African Video Movies and Global Desires* aims to enrich our understanding of African video movies by bringing historical specificity to bear on the study of locally produced video features. Popular video is described here as a shifting and historically contingent discursive field marked by myriad ideologies, anxieties, discourses, and desires, and each chapter examines a loosely defined historical period as demarcated by significant structural changes in the industry. The chronological organization of the book outlines the changes in narrative forms and cinematic features that mark the thousands of videos produced by Ghanaian videomakers for over twenty years, and it engages the often ambivalent and contested meanings and identities produced by Ghanaian cinema at different historical moments and for different publics. It examines historical and technological change within the local, national, and transnational contexts in which video texts circulate and as it is revealed in the style and content of the video-texts.

The readings of the films and videos contained in each chapter purposefully complicate the neat and linear chronology implied by the chapter organization. Each text, much like a palimpsest, carries artifacts from that which came before, and in this way, the textual analyses present Ghana's cinematic history more like a layering than an unfolding. Traces of the pedagogical imperative that informed the colonial film productions of the Gold Coast Film Unit inflect the most recent video features, for example, while iterations of the figure of the monstrous woman, who consumes selfishly and excessively, appear in movies made during all periods of Ghana's film and video history. The close readings of visual texts are not intended to suggest a chronology of development from amateur to professional productions, from the visual pleasures of spectacle and astonishment to narrative containment, or from analog to digital technologies. Rather, in each period, we can see variations in aesthetics, narrative form, and modes of spectator engagement and in the anxieties, desires, subjectivities and styles reiterated across multiple video texts. These changing textual properties are analyzed as effects of the economic, technological, and political shifts indicated in each chapter division.

The first chapter of the book, "Mapping the Modern: The Gold Coast Film Unit and the Ghana Film Industry Corporation," describes the early years of Ghana's film history. Beginning with the earliest film screenings in the 1920s, this chapter offers an account of colonial film production in the Gold Coast and the formation of a national film company after independence. Rather than seeing the birth of a national Ghanaian cinema as a complete turning away from colonial influence, I identify the discontinuities and continuities between the feature films of the Ghana Film Industry Corporation and those of the Gold Coast Film Unit. Close readings of *The Boy Kumasenu* (1952) and *A Debut for Dede* (1992) permit us to focus on the cinematic production of modernity as articulated in the late colonial and the national film. Emerging out of institutions connected through the history of colonialism, these films share a gendered language of modernity, tradition, and nation. Both films represent modernity as a relationship between space and time; the journey from village to city functions as an allegory for the evolution from African tradition to European modernity, and both films illustrate that each narrative of modernity relies, for its production, on gender difference.

Chapter 2, "Work, Women, and Worldly Wealth: Global Video Culture and the Early Years of Local Video Production," investigates the period between roughly 1980 and 1992, when the erosion of state support for and control of filmmaking coupled with the ready availability of video technology allowed individuals situated outside of the networks of official cultural production to produce features entirely unregulated as commodities and artistic objects. The first video movies articulate the deep ambivalences generated by Ghana's encounter with global capitalism and the concomitant shift from economies of production to consumption as illustrated in three representative examples: *Zinabu* (1987), *Big Time* (1988), and *Menace* (1992). In these early video movies, it is gender that structures and distinguishes these two articulations of capitalistic value.

Chapter 3, "Professional Movies and Their Global Aspirations: The Second Wave of Video Production in Ghana," traces the shift toward more professionalized production and a more organized and regulated industry during the second phase of commercial video production in Ghana, from 1992 until around 2000. In this period, the privatization of the national film company and the emergence of several independent media outlets in Ghana parallel the privatization of cinematic space, as viewing shifts from the public cinema hall or video parlor to the privacy of watching a video or video compact disc (VCD) at home. In addition, as opportunities for employment with state institutions diminish, professionally trained film- and videomakers enter into the commercial video industry in large numbers, bringing new ideas about professionalism, art, and modernity. These dramatic changes in the economic and structural organization of film and media institutions, in no small part driven by the state's liberalization policies, correspond to the iteration of a professional style, a "performative competence" (Ferguson 1999, 99) that signaled aspiration toward an imagined global standard. This chapter focuses on the emergence of the "professional" movie, describing the historical changes linked to its appearance and then analyzing the themes taken up by and stylistics deployed in several groundbreaking professional videos.

Chapter 4, "Tourism and Trafficking: Views from Abroad in the Transnational Travel Movie," maps the transnational networks and flows that link West Africa to global cities such as Amsterdam and New York, concentrating mainly on Ghanaian video movies about travel. The analysis focuses on several examples of transnational Ghanaian popular movies, including *Wild World* (Ghana and Italy 2002), *Amsterdam Diary* (Ghana and Amsterdam 2005), *London Got Problem* (Ghana and UK 2006), and *Love in America* (Ghana and USA 2008), examining this genre of movie as a site crossed by overlapping and intersecting discourses of gender, globalization, and consumerism. It argues that Ghanaian travel movies capture the aspirations of Ghanaians to be modern and mobile global subjects and imaginatively link Ghana to the global city.

Chapter 5, "Transcultural Encounters and Local Imaginaries: Nollywood and the Ghanaian Movie Industry in the Twenty-first Century," investigates how the inundation of the commercial video movie market by Nollywood and the shift from analog to digital technologies have fragmented and realigned the Ghanaian video movie industry in the last decade. I read representative examples of two types of video movies: the transnational "glamour" movies of Shirley Frimpong-Manso and a series of local "sakawa" movies. I suggest a correspondence between these two types of movies, which at first glance seem completely dissimilar. I argue that "sakawa" and similar types of occult movies made for local audiences bring into visibility the uncanny excised from Frimpong-Manso's aesthetics of consumption.

African Video Movies and Global Desires adopts an interdisciplinary approach to the study of Ghana's commercial video movie industry, coupling contextual criticism with close readings and formalist analysis of individual video texts so as to contribute to the burgeoning scholarly conversation on African video movies. It investigates how video movies participate in the normalization and refashioning of dominant discourses of globalization, gender and sexuality, neoliberalism, and consumerism and highlights the ambivalence generated in the reproduction and repetition of those discourses across time and in the thousands of video movies that have been made since the 1980s. This ambivalence, the contradictions, and the cracks revealed through reiteration, matter a great deal because it is ambivalence that creates spaces for new imaginings of self, subject, family, and community.

A final note about terminology: In the title and throughout the book, I use of the term "video movie" instead of the more common "video film" in a minor attempt to acknowledge the singular importance of video technology to the history of African popular video, which to my mind is diminished by "video film." The technology, or medium, of the text is not incidental to its symbolic life. "Video movie" retains an emphasis on video as a medium that generates particular material conditions at the level of the artifact, and it more broadly highlights video as a form of technological mediation and commodification that is different from film. Larkin (2000; 2008) has written on both of these aspects of video, and I draw on his work at various points in this book to describe the role of video technology in the history of Ghanaian screen media. Finally, "movie" calls up very different connotations than "film." Movies are associated with the commoditized forms of screen media produced by dominant commercial industries, like Hollywood. The word "movie" best captures the aspirations and ambitions of video producers in Ghana, which might be why "movie" is widely used in the Ghanaian industry, by journalists, movie producers, and actors alike. The national industry's annual awards ceremony, The Ghana Movie Awards, most obviously speaks to the term's prevalence.

1

Mapping the Modern

The Gold Coast Film Unit and the Ghana Film Industry Corporation

In 1995, to mark the centenary of cinema, the Ghanaian Ministry of Information sponsored a one-week film festival and symposium organized around the theme of North-South cross-cultural influences in cinema. The celebration featured screenings of films made in Ghana by the national film company and the internationally recognized independent filmmakers Kwah Ansah and King Ampaw. Among the titles included in the festival program was *The Boy Kumasenu* (1952), a British colonial film created by the Gold Coast Film Unit (GCFU). The film, organized around the motif of the journey, replays the colonial opposition between tradition and modernity. Kumasenu, the protagonist, migrates from the traditional village to the city, where the film's voice-over narration explains, "Everything is new," and his journey to modernity allegorizes Ghana's evolution from primitive tradition to modern nationhood. In a series of promotional articles published in the government-owned daily newspaper, the *Mirror*, Nanabanyin Dadson described *The Boy Kumasenu* as "the first full-length feature film to be made in Ghana" (Dadson 1995c). Sean Graham, the founding director of the GCFU and the director of *The Boy Kumasenu*, was an invited speaker at the festival, and coverage of his visit was given prominence in Dadson's coverage. An article by Dan Adjokatcher, this one announcing Graham's visit, called Graham the "father of Ghanaian cinema" (Adjokatcher 1995).[1]

Aside from references to the film in books by Rouch (2003) and Diawara (1992) and brief commentary by Tom Rice (2010) intended to supplement its viewing in the online archive *Colonial Film: Moving Images of the British Empire*, *The Boy Kumasenu* has attracted little scholarly attention.[2] Yet, the rather laudatory characterization of this unabashedly colonial film in Ghanaian public discourse speaks, I think, to its significance as a nexus of several important historical, ideological, and aesthetic crosscurrents. Not surprisingly, *The Boy Kumasenu* shares affinities with colonial educational films and British imperial cinema, but it also has much in common with the documentaries of John Grierson and with Hollywood cinema of the 1930s and 1940s. Although obviously imperial in its narrative and mode of address, the aesthetics of the film mark a radical departure from the "primitive style" of many colonial film productions, a style developed by the Colonial Film Unit for the "illiterate" African who was thought to lack the capacity to read cinematic images. Graham moves far away from the conventions of narrative and spectatorial address established in colonial educational cinema, focalizing long segments of the film through the point of view of Kumasenu, an African subject, whose desires and anxieties are represented as driving much of the film's action. Although written and directed by Graham, *The Boy Kumasenu* was shot, edited, and acted by Africans. It was one of the last productions of the Gold Coast Film Unit, and many of the feature films made by the Ghana Film Industry Corporation betray its influence; its creation and narrative stand between the final period of British colonial rule and the beginning of Ghana's independence.

Likewise, the Ghana Film Industry Corporation's 1992 production *A Debut for Dede*, the second film closely examined in this chapter, bears the imprints of an important liminal moment in Ghana's film history. *A Debut for Dede*, like *The Boy Kumasenu*, narrates the protagonist's migration from her village to the capital city of Accra. The journey signifies Dede's turn from the rituals and customs practiced in her village toward a modern female subjectivity in the city. The film, too, appeared during a crucial transitional period, one shaped by technological change, when GFIC moved away from film to video production, and by structural and ideological transformation as state-funded filmmaking gave way to independent, commercial video production. The feature was the last production shot *on film* by the Ghana Film Industry Corporation. Four years after its release, as part of the IMF program to liberalize the economy, GFIC was privatized; 70 percent of the company shares were sold to TV 3 Malaysia, while the Ghanaian government retained a mere 30 percent of the corporation. In subsequent years, the restructured and renamed film company, now called the Ghana-Malaysia Film Company Limited (GAMA Film), became little more than a video production unit,

producing feature-length movies for TV3 Ghana, the first independent television station in Ghana.³

This chapter describes the early years of Ghana's film history, from
the earliest film screenings in the 1920s to the formation of a national
film company after independence and, finally, to the end of celluloid
film production in Ghana in the 1980s. Rather than seeing the birth
of a national Ghanaian cinema as a complete turning away from colonial influence, I examine points of connection and disconnection
between the feature films of the Ghana Film Industry Corporation
and those of the Gold Coast Film Unit. To this end, I look closely
at *The Boy Kumasenu* and *A Debut for Dede*, focusing on the cinematic
production of modernity as articulated in the late colonial and the
national films. Emerging out of institutions connected through the
history of colonialism, these films share a gendered language of modernity, tradition, and nation. Kumasenu, the male subject, grows into
a citizen as he moves from rural to urban space and into the conjugal,
Westernized family. The nuclear family acts as a metaphor and model
for the nation, and the film naturalizes male citizenship and imperial
patriarchy. Films made by the Ghana Film Industry Corporation after
independence articulated a new, national consciousness and imagined
an African modernity distinct from its European counterpart, and in
A Debut for Dede the female subject embodies this difference; her body
is presented as a site for the articulation and preservation of an African interiority threatened by the modern. If Kumasenu must abandon
his African past to become a modern citizen, Dede must internalize
hers. Both films represent modernity as a relationship between space
and time; the journey from village to city functions as an allegory for
the evolution from African tradition to European modernity, and each
narrative of modernity naturalizes gender difference.

Entrepreneur Exhibition and the Gold Coast Film Unit

In Ghana, cinema exhibition appears and develops within the larger
context of an emergent culture of "modern commercial entertainment" (Barber, Collins, and Ricard 1997, 5), whose artists, aesthetics,
and popular forms migrated among the coastal cities of West Africa,
a heterogeneous zone inflected by a long history of contact with Europeans. As Barber, Collins, and Ricard point out (1997), new commercial entertainment forms were made possible by the sudden and
dramatic changes that occurred throughout the colonial period and

independence. Rapid urbanization and the increased availability of education contributed to the birth and growth of a culture of commercial entertainment. The enormous expansion of new classes of paid employees, including entrepreneurs, cash-cropping farmers, low-paid civil servants, and the highly educated African elite, all of whom had money to spend on new leisure activities, furthered the cultivation of this culture. It was the entrepreneurial class, primarily composed of local businessmen and expatriates, who brought motion pictures to the Gold Coast. The British merchandise company Bartholomew and Co. erected Merry Villas cinematograph palace, the first entertainment establishment in Accra, the capital of the Gold Coast, in 1913. Here, Gold Coast audiences were exposed to the novelty of imported films (Cole 2001; Dadson 1995a). In the 1920s, Alfred John Kabu Ocansey, a successful African merchant, opened the Cinema Theatre at Azuma and Palladium, both in Accra, where he showed silent films for 3p, 6p, and one schilling.[4] The stratified admission fees allowed "a great range of Accra citizens to attend," including Africans and Europeans (Cole 2001, 72). Between 1922 and 1925, Ocansey established cinemas in several large towns: the Park Cinema in Accra, the Recardo Cinema at Nsawam, the Capitol Cinema in Koforidua, the Royal in Kumsai, and Arkhurst Hall in Sekondi. Both Bartholomew and Ocansey were linked to the burgeoning transnational distribution of Hollywood films and imported titles such as *Custer's Last Stand*, *Al Jolson in Casino de Paris*, and *The Gold Diggers of Broadway*, the first color film brought to the Gold Coast. Supported by the "incipient classes" of the Gold Coast (Cole 2001, 55), early cinema exhibitions were among a variety of commercial entertainments offered to patrons. According to Catherine Cole's *Ghana's Concert Party Theatre* (2001), the Palladium hosted some of the earliest performances of the Ghanaian concert party, a comic musical theater that fused Western and African influences to create an innovative combination of drama, music, and audience participation. Modeled on London's music hall variety theater, the Palladium featured not only cinema shows, but magic acts, variety entertainments, and dances. Ocansey hired concert party performers such as Augustus Alexander Shotang Williams to do comic sketches and sing popular songs before or after a film showing.[5]

The influence of cinema reached far beyond the urban centers of the Gold Coast. Individual, itinerant film exhibitors, who relied on portable 16mm cinema projectors, introduced film exhibition and Hollywood fare to rural audiences in the late 1920s. Dadson (1995a) reports that many of these traveling exhibitors bypassed merchant distributors such as Ocansey, obtaining their films from seaman arriving at the Takordi port, which opened in 1928. Their mobile cinema shows toured small towns and villages in the cocoa growing regions of the country. An account of the film show of one of these exhibitors, Ata Joe, who toured the Eastern region of the country, reads as follows:

> When he arrived at a village, he and one assistant would hire a courtyard of a house, set up an electricity generator and projector and show a number of films for a few days. The films were mainly American cowboy, war and Charlie Chaplin types. (Qtd. in Dadson 1995a, 11)

In subsequent years, the number of film exhibitors and commercial theaters increased substantially in the Gold Coast, and by 1942, West African Pictures Limited, Captan Cinema Company, and the Nankani Cinema Company, three privately owned distribution and exhibition companies, owned approximately twenty-five theaters (Dadson 1995a; Sakyi 1996). Munir Captan, who inherited the Captan family cinemas, explained that most of the films screened at these commercial theaters were Hollywood movies and, periodically, independent features made by the fast-growing Indian commercial film industry; feature films from Britain and South Africa were also exhibited, although infrequently (personal communication).

Colonial Interventions in Film Exhibition and Production

Prior to World War II, it was the influx of Hollywood films into the colonies by independent commercial exhibitors that brought cinema to the attention of British colonial authorities.[6] The Colonial Office Films Committee presented a report to the Conference of Colonial Governors (1930) that highlighted the crucial need to censor films exhibited in the colonies "as the display of unsuitable films is a very real danger" to "primitive communities" in Africa (qtd. in Smyth 1979, 437). Rosaleen Smyth explains that Hollywood "was seen as a threat to the British *imperium* because of the unsavory image of the white race that was being projected" (1979, 438), and, therefore, colonial governors were provided with guidelines for censoring films exhibited in the colonies and advised to be mindful of "the special character and susceptibilities of the native people" (qtd. in Smyth 439).

According to *Advance of a Technique: Information Services in the Gold Coast* (1956), a pamphlet published by the Gold Coast Information Services, the censorship panel was made up of volunteers who applied "the terms of reference of the British Board of Film Censors . . . with extra vigilance against racial discord, violence, and new methods of committing crime." The effectiveness of these increased censorship measures in the Gold Coast were negligible. Newspaper advertisements from the period indicate that commercial cinemas continued to feature a range of Hollywood films. Commercial exhibitors had little motivation for submitting their films to be censored, and the censorship panel had no power to prohibit exhibitors or distributors from making Hollywood films available to audiences.[7]

Attention shifted from censorship to the distribution of British war propaganda films to the African colonies at the start of World War II. To this end, the British Ministry of Information created the Colonial Film Unit (CFU), which established branches in East, Central, and West Africa. This was the beginning of *cinema aban*, or government cinema. In the Gold Coast, a cinema van, imported from London, toured towns and villages exhibiting films and short documentaries such as *The British Empire at War* series and *Burma: West African Troops Cross the Maturahari River.* The large majority of the CFU films were made in Britain, although the content was often adjusted to appeal to African audiences. The Raw Stock Scheme, implemented in 1942, provided 16mm cameras and film to information officers in the African colonies who would film African scenes and locations. The exposed film would be sent to Britain to be developed, edited, and spliced into CFU productions.

At the end of WWII, facing escalating anticolonial criticism, the CFU redirected its focus toward the production of films in Africa by Africans. According to Smyth, in 1947, Creech Jones, the Secretary of State for Colonies, "dramatically revised Britain's colonial policy. Suddenly decolonization was pushed to the top of the agenda. The life expectancy of the Empire was reduced from a leisurely eighty years to twenty" (1992, 164). Priya Jaikumar's book *Cinema at the End of Empire: A Politics of Transition in Britain and India* (2006) describes the context this way:

> If World War I exposed the extent to which imperial Britain was vulnerable to a changing global economy and polity, World War II revealed the moral anachronism of the British

Empire. With the visible cruelties of German and Italian Fascism and the invisible exploitation of American finance capitalism, Britain's brand of colonialism looked awkwardly similar to the former and just plain awkward compared to the latter. Symptomatic of Britain's changing imperial status in this new century, the British State became invested in earning the approbation of an emerging international community of nations by demonstrating its moral responsibility toward its colonies. (11)

Colonial officials described the formal inauguration of film units in the colonies as one of its moral responsibilities, and this is clearly demonstrated in remarks made by Jones in his opening address at the 1948 conference "Film in Colonial Development":

I think we visualize today our colonial responsibility in a manner constructive and positive, in effect the creation of nationhood, the establishment of free political institutions, the creation of colonial democracies, democracies possessed with that sense of values which we prize in Western Europe and democracies supported by our social services and good economic conditions. (4)

He continued to explain that training African filmmakers was imperative because "we are recognizing today that Empire (if we continue to use that particular word) is not an opportunity of exploitation to our material advantage, but the occasion of service" (Jones 1948, 4). At the same conference, the filmmaker John Grierson, who was at the time Films Controller at the Films Division of the Central Office of Information, emphasized that "international criticism is growing on how we use and develop our work in the colonies" (Grierson 1948, 12). He affirmed the new objective of the CFU: "It is no longer a question of people dropping into Africa to make a picture, to 'do something' for the natives as, only a generation ago, the Squire and his lady 'did something' for us. . . . It is a question of working with Africans and of creating a genuine African Unit that can work with native units in the other Colonies" (13). CFU's motives, certainly, were not entirely in the interest of "serving" Africans. Film was believed to be an essential tool in educating Africans for citizenship, in the development of a national outlook, and in creating a Commonwealth sensibility among the soon-to-be former colonies of Britain (Smyth 1992; Jaikumar 2006).

Film production began in West Africa in 1946 when a four-person production team came to the Gold Coast. Its inaugural film was *Fight TB at Home* (1946), followed by *Weaving in Togoland* (1948). In 1949, the CFU set up a film training school in Accra for West African students. Its aim "was to train students to a standard which would enable them to film local events in newsreel fashion and also to produce simple instructional films of more lasting importance" (Smyth 1992, 168). Among the first class were several Nigerians and Ghanaians, including Sam Aryeetey, who later became director of the Ghana Film Industry Corporation, R. O. Fenuku, and Bob Okanta. That same year, the Gold Coast Film Unit was organized, largely as a result of the success of the film training program. In 1949 the Unit was reorganized under the guidance of Sean Graham, and within seven years it had become one of the best-equipped film units in Africa capable of shooting films and completing postproduction editing and sound recording in its Accra facilities. The GCFU shot on 35mm film, and Africans were trained in all aspects of filmmaking. It was Graham, however, who directed most productions; even African students trained under him were rarely given the chance to create and direct their own films. This system, Manthia Diawara (1992) argues, impaired the Ghanaian national film company, leaving it at independence with an inexperienced production team and, because the unit used 35mm instead of 16mm film, reliant on the Overseas Film and Television Unit in London for film processing. Before independence, the unit's staff consisted of three Europeans and twenty Africans. All were men. A few of the African filmmakers were sent to London for advanced training (*Advance* 1956, 9), and between 1949 and 1956, the unit made forty-four films. The majority of these films were educational documentaries, although a few feature films were also produced. Titles included *Amenu's Child* (1950), *The Boy Kumasenu* (1952), *Theresa, the Story of a Nurse in Training* (1955), and *Mr. Mensah Builds a House* (1955).[8] Many of the unit's films were released commercially in Ghana while they were exported for nontheatrical release in Britain and other Commonwealth countries.[9]

African film units operating under the jurisdiction of the Colonial Film Unit (CFU) were guided by the filmmaking theories of George Pearson and William Sellers, leading figures at the CFU. Pearson and Sellers believed that films made for African audiences would be most effective if they employed a primitive film style: "a simple doctrine for gaining by cinema, and holding by cinema, the attention of an illiterate audience, while imparting knowledge that is appreciated and later applied" (Pearson 1948, 24). Informed by colonial and racist notions about the "native" African, the primitive style purged from its productions "all the conventional methods for short-circuiting time and place" (25), such as mixes, montage, and wipes. Camera movements such as panning and dollying were prohibited because "trees seemingly running along the far horizon, buildings apparently rising or sinking, static objects seeming to move of their own volition, only divert [the native's] attention from the scene message to the mystery of seeming magic" (25). Films were required to maintain "visual continuity from scene to scene" and, because "the native mind needs longer time to absorb the picture content," to adopt a slow pace. Manthia Diawara (1992) aptly points out that the CFU

> wanted to turn back film history and develop a different type of cinema for Africans because they considered the African mind too primitive to follow the sophisticated narrative techniques of mainstream cinema. Thus they thought it necessary to return to the beginning of film history—to use uncut scenes, slow down the story's pace, and make the narrative simpler by using fewer actors and adhering to just one dominant theme. (4)

Most significant to the analysis of *The Boy Kumasenu* is Pearson's effort to distinguish the primitive style from "our British Documentary" (Pearson 1948, 25), a reference to the work of Grierson and the filmmakers who worked with him in developing the British Documentary Movement of the 1930s and '40s. While acknowledging the British documentary's "power, under wise control, to do magnificent work towards colonial development," Pearson insists that its comprehension lies beyond "the illiterate field" that is Africa (25). He writes: "In that field of work Documentary technique, excellent as it is for its cinema-minded audiences, is useless for ours. It uses a pictorial idiom beyond the comprehension of the illiterate" (26).

In Close-Up: *The Boy Kumasenu*

Although firmly rooted in colonial discourses of modernity and in imperialist ideology, many of the films made in the Gold Coast are noteworthy in their deviations from the primitive aesthetics developed for colonial educational and propaganda films. Smyth notes that the Gold Coast Film Unit distinguished itself by "attempting to break new ground in the format to get around the problem of patronizing commentaries and simplistic plots of many of the CFU films" (1992, 169). Jean Rouch, too, has remarked on the "high quality, both technically and dramatically" of the unit's films (2003, 66). Rouch credits the unit's achievements to the decision, made by Graham, to "split off fairly early from the Colonial Film Unit, in favor of association with groups of independent English producers" (2003, 66). Graham recruited filmmakers such as Basil Wright, Terry Bishop, and George Noble to participate in various capacities in GCFU productions. Additionally, according to Sam Aryeetey, Graham worked collaboratively with the young African trainees involved in his productions (personal communication). He drew on their creativity and solicited from them information about local audiences.

Larkin (2008) describes two types of cinema distribution in colonial Nigeria: commercial cinema theaters, which exhibited feature films from the US and UK; and the mobile cinema vans, which screened colonial content exclusively. In *The Boy Kumasenu* Graham merges commercial and colonial forms in an entertaining and educational colonial feature film that audiences both in the colonies and in England would pay to see. *The Boy Kumasenu* incorporates the conventions of the British documentary and Hollywood narrative cinema to create a sympathetic African subject, Kumasenu, from whose point of view most of the film is focalized. In this and other ways, it also challenges the pervasive, racist representations of Africa in British and American commercial films. It featured only black African actors, recasting the great white, benevolent colonizer, embodied by Lord Sandy in Korda's *Sanders of the River* (1935), as an educated, elite Ghanaian. And unlike the entrenched stereotypes of Africans as unfeeling savages or childlike adults, many of the Africans we meet in Graham's film are individuals capable of participating in the modern nation as citizens. This difference is important because the film was the most successful film made by the Gold Coast Film Unit; according to Graham, it recovered its costs in the first few days of its screening in Gold Coast theaters and was exhibited abroad, in Britain, the Commonwealth, and America, to acclaim (Adjokatcher 1995; Dadson, 1995c). It also was screened at several international film festivals. In 1953 it earned a diploma at the Venice Film Festival and was shown at the Berlin Film Festival the same year (Rice 2010).

In her analysis of the redemptive aesthetics of British imperial cinema, Priya Jaikumar argues that British imperial film policies and aesthetics of the late colonial period were marked by "the divergent legitimacies granted to imperialism and nationalism" (2006, 11). British Empire Films attempted to rehabilitate the image of the colonial encounter and resolve the inconsistencies and contradictions inherent in Britain's dual identity as colonizer and liberal nation-state.

> Cinema, coming in the late 1890s, participated in the internal contradictions of a modernized language of empire. Liberalism's impulse toward self-governance put pressure on imperialism's essential unilateralism to define the internal form and formal contradictions of British film policy and commercial film style. (9)

Employing a redemptive rhetoric, late colonial British commercial films "rearticulat[ed] Britain's' identity as demonstrably liberal in relation to its imperium" (Jaikumar 2006, 25). Here, I want to suggest that *The Boy Kumasenu*, though the production of a state-funded colonial film unit in Africa, enacts a similar imperial redemptive aesthetics. Through the motif of the journey from the premodern to the modern, the feature works at erasing the contradictions inherent in Britain's dual identity as liberal nation and colonial power by superimposing a narrative of national modernity onto the urban and rural landscapes and, therefore, constructing the modern as a spatiotemporal relation. In this way, it naturalizes what Timothy Mitchell calls "the time-space of European modernity" (2000, 16). For Mitchell, the time-space of the modern relies on the non-West to "play the role of outside, the otherness that creates the boundary of the space of modernity" (16). The African village, rendered through an ethnographic gaze, signifies "the place of timelessness, a space without duration, in relation to which the temporal break of modernity can be marked out" (16). The coastal city of Accra, ushered into modernity by British imperialism, stands as the imminent outcome of Africa's evolution.

 The Boy Kumasenu tells the story of Kumasenu, an orphan, who lives in a quiet fishing village with his Uncle Faiwoo, his aunt, and his older cousin Agboh. Kumasenu, enchanted by Agboh and his tales of the city, begs for permission to follow his cousin to Accra. Uncle Faiwoo refuses. He tells Kumasenu that he wants him to grow up and become a leader among the people. After a poor fish harvest, however, Faiwoo concludes that Kumasenu's "restlessness" is frightening the fish and that it is best for the village if he be allowed to go and "to know what is beyond, to read and write, and find out why iron cars go as swift as the shark."

Uncle Faiwoo finds Kumasenu his first paid employment in a small store on the city's periphery. All goes well for Kumasenu, who is happy among the new people, music, manners, and languages he encounters there, until Agboh turns up, dressed like a gangster in a Hollywood movie and full of swagger. Kumasenu, desiring to please and impress Agboh, shows his cousin where the storekeeper hides his money. Agboh steals the money without Kumasenu's knowledge, suddenly sending Kumasenu off to the city with a ten pound note, remaining behind so he can frame Kumasenu for his crime.

Kumasenu, alone and dressed only in the clothes he carried from his village, finds Accra foreign and inhospitable; he is frightened by its traffic, unfriendliness, and crowds. On his first day in Accra, he wanders the streets cautiously, and when night falls he has no place to sleep. He is rescued by a beautiful woman, Adobia, who speaks to Kumasenu in Ewe and invites him to stay with her. Adobia is a successful trader, and she hires Kumasenu to be her assistant. An economically and sexually independent woman, Adobia is involved with two men: the rich and powerful lawyer, Mr. Mensah, and his driver, Yeboah. Mr. Mensah, unaware of Adobia's affair with Yeboah, is furious when he finds the two together. He assaults the couple, and, the next day, uses his position in the courts to have Adobia and Yeboah arrested for attacking him.

Kumasenu, having lost his guide and friend, finds himself alone and on the city streets again. Hungry and desperate, he attempts to steal a loaf of bread from a bread seller, but is arrested and taken to juvenile court before he can carry out the deed. The court sends him to Dr. Tamakloe for a physical examination before his trial. Moved by Kumasenu's demeanor, the doctor and his wife, Grace, decide to adopt him. Under the couple's care and support, Kumasenu is cleared of the charges against him and released into their custody. The doctor finds Kumasenu work as a member of a fishing crew that sails and maintains motorized boats, and his labor, like his subjectivity, is brought into the realm of the modern.

Historically, the film links directly to Grierson and the British documentary film movement. Basil Wright, one of Grierson's "disciples" who is perhaps best known for his acclaimed documentary *Song of Ceylon* (1934), was the coproducer of the film, and Graham, who wrote the screenplay for the film and directed it, was Grierson's student.[10] Ideologically, the feature shares with the Griersonian documentary tradition a deep faith in the British Empire and an unquestioned belief in its evolutionary development. In her analysis of British documentary film, Jamie Sexton makes an observation about *Song of Ceylon* pertinent to *The Boy Kumasenu:* It "links nature and tradition to the process of modernization, all configured as part of a natural, evolving pattern" (Sexton 2002, 54). *The Boy Kumasenu* erases economic exploitation, violence, and colonial agents from its narrative of British imperialism, which is portrayed as a force for good in Africa, bringing civilization, justice, medicine, the rule of law, education, order, and, finally, national independence. The film presents modernity as the end result of an evolutionary narrative that unfolds naturally from colonialism. The opening montage visualizes the binary on which this chronology depends. It sets in opposition the natural landscape, portrayed as if untouched by modernization and industrialization, and the bustle and productivity of the modern West African city. The first sequence, composed of a combination of multiple shots from close, medium, and long focal distances, sees African men and women dressed in formal Western clothes in a dance hall where big band music plays and couples jitterbug. This shot dissolves into a fast-paced and dynamic sequence, assembled from several shots of the wide streets of Accra, along which cars, buses, and crowds of people move. The voice-over reads as follows:

> This is the story of the old and the new where the changeless ways of uncounted centuries collide with the changing ways of our own. Here the city of Accra sprawls its growth on the west coast of equatorial Africa with no buffer between the new and the old.

The words "the old" signal a visual transition to the village. Rendered naturalistically in one static long take of a beach, bordered by a line of coconut trees and empty except for two people, a large fishing boat, and several small fishing shacks, the village landscape appears unmoving, unchanged, and unmarked by modernity.

In *Kumasenu*, the camera, in effect, works like a virtual time machine, reenacting for the spectator the movement from the primitive to the modern by positioning the spectator differently in each space. First, the spectator adopts the perspective of an outside observer, one far removed from the space and time of the village. Later, the spectator is aligned with the subject of sight in the city. Through variations in scale and spectator address, the film represents time as a spatial relation between the spectator and the world that unfolds on the screen, incorporating her into the spaces of village and city through different modes of realism. As the narrative migrates from village to city, an ethnographic mode of realism gives way to a narrative mode of realism, simulating cinematically the passage of time.[11] In the village segments, the film deploys an ethnographic mode of realism in which an ethnographic chronotope organizes time and space. Long takes and slow pans produce visual space between the viewing subject and filmed object, creating a sense of spatial and temporal distance between the modern spectator, aligned with the narrator's objectifying voice and gaze, and the traditional and exotic African village he observes. An ethnographic gaze contains the colonized and aligns the spectator with the observing eye of the camera, here a metaphor for modernity. This is perhaps best illustrated in a staged reenactment of Uncle Faiwoo and a group of fishermen casting and pulling in their nets to the accompaniment of African drums. Seen through medium and long focal lengths and shots of extended duration, the men seem far away. They resemble a moving, primitive exhibit. Kumasenu, frequently presented in a panoramic long shot as a solitary figure on the beach, seems as if he, too, were a feature of the village landscape. Reproducing several of the archetypal images of African safari and adventure films, the feature captures the boy as he frolics in the waves of the ocean, climbs a coconut tree, walks along the shore, and sits on the beach, dreaming of the city. After his uncle refuses to let him leave the village, Kumasenu, seen through an extreme long shot, walks against a vast cloudy sky (see figure 1.1). The threatening sky and Kumasenu's isolation are meant to express his unhappiness and restlessness; in this, the film translates and externalizes his interiority for the spectator, producing physical and psychological distance between the spectator and the African subject.

As Kumasenu moves from the changeless time and space of the village to the "outside world," the camera repositions the spectator, moving inward and creating the illusion of closeness. Long takes and slow pans of the village landscape give way to close-ups, mid-takes, and shot-reverse-shot sequences as ethnographic realism gives way to narrative realism. As Phil Rosen notes in his reading of Sembene's *Ceddo*, such a shift in scale signifies "movement into a scene normalized as physical closeness" (2001, 274). In presenting Kumasenu at work in the store where, the voice-over remarks, he "first met the

Figure 1.1. Kumasenu on the beach (*The Boy Kumasenu,* 1952)

twentieth century," the frame of the camera narrows considerably, replacing the expansive village landscape at which the spectator looked
from a distance, with the intimate and immediate interior of the store,
which is focalized through Kumasenu's point of view. The spectator
enters the time and space of the narrative of the film, where the act
of looking is concealed by continuity editing that simulates "real"
time and creates what Teresa de Lauretis refers to as "the achieved
coherence of a 'narrative space' which holds, binds, entertains the
spectator at the apex of the representational triangle as the subject
of vision" (de Lauretis 1984, 27). The first close-up in the film appears here, as Kumasenu discovers the joy of listening to a record on
the gramophone while the men who have come to the store to buy
beer dance (see figure 1.2). The scene recalls a similar, iconic moment
in Flaherty's *Nanook of the North* in which the primitive subject marvels at what is to him a strange and wonderful European technology.
This shot, however, expresses Kumasenu's interiority, the pleasure he
derives from listening to music. It humanizes and passes narrative
authority to him. From this moment forward, point-of-view shots
and eyeline matching position Kumasenu as a subject of sight, and
although his is not the only perspective from which the remainder of

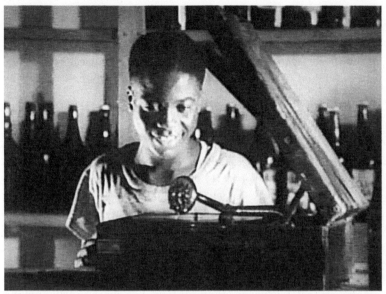

Figure 1.2. Kumasenu listens to gramophone (*The Boy Kumasenu*, 1952)

the film is focalized, his is the foremost point of view from which the spectator sees.

The film's soundtrack, a layering of extra-diegetic narration and music, ambient sounds, including music and speech, and character dialogue inflects space as rural and urban.[12] In the opening segments of the film, almost imperceptible ambient sounds are veiled by the voice-over narration, which addresses the audience in British English. The narrator and extra-diegetic music speak for and silence the sounds of the village. The audience sees the mouths of characters moving but hears only the narrator's summary and explication of their speech. This extra-diegetic interpreter addresses the spectator throughout the village sequence, translating Akan or Ewe into English, explaining customs and behaviors, and interpreting the actions and thoughts of characters. As Kumasenu moves toward the city, the soundtrack changes. The narrative voice-over yields to the voices of people speaking Akan and Pidgin English, a language the narrator describes as "a blend of the old and the new." In the city, characters speak for themselves and the narrative voice-over, although still present, is no longer dominant. Its purpose becomes primarily pedagogical, highlighting significant moments in the plot, but no longer narrating them.

The colonial teleology that structures Kumasenu's journey is underscored by the alignment of each space with a different construction of the family: the "traditional" family or kin network is located in the space/time of the village, and the modern nuclear or conjugal family is found in the modern city. In a historical context marked by conflicting discourses of marriage and family, the film asserts the primacy of the conjugal companionate model of marriage and family. A great deal of scholarship documents the dramatic shift in the meaning of marriage and family that occurred in Ghana as a result of missionary activity, colonialism, the imposition of a cash economy, the increase of private property ownership, and the expanding cocoa market.[13] Jean Allman and Victoria Tashjian, in *"I Will Not Eat Stone": A Women's History of Colonial Asante* (2000), argue convincingly that the dramatic changes initiated by British colonialism produced "nothing short of widespread gender chaos" (75), which intensified during the last decades of colonialism. In very general language, one can say that prior to the rupture brought about by colonialism, marriage among several Ghanaian ethnic groups, but most notably among the Asante, the largest ethnic group in present-day Ghana, was not understood as a static and monolithic state-of-being, but a process that varied considerably among families and kin networks and that afforded women a high degree of autonomy and independence. Marriage was "open to the interpretations of the parties involved at a particular moment in time," and it was couples and their families, not the state, that "retained the power to define the status of any known conjugal relationship" (Allman and Tashjian 2000, 57).

During the colonial period, the British and the native courts sought to rein in and control what they regarded as perplexing and unwieldy "traditional" marriage forms by enforcing legislation "aimed at clearly defining and strengthening the marital bond in opposition to the lineage bond" (Vellenga 1983, 145). Colonial discourse, in effect, transformed flexible and heterogeneous marriage forms into the static and monolithic entity of the traditional or customary marriage. The texts of cultural producers, such as writers and filmmakers, enter into this ideological and discursive contest over family, marriage, and proper gender roles. In her study of Ghanaian popular fiction, Stephanie Newell argues that during the colonial period Ghanaian writers "seem to be conscious of their status as generators of narratives that will help to stabilize and codify a 'modern' marriage ideology" (2000, 61). Likewise, colonial film production in the Gold Coast, as exemplified by *The Boy Kumasenu*, sets out to normalize the conjugal family by defining it against the more "traditional" extended family form.

The film casts the nuclear family as the foundation of the nation, and Kumasenu's journey to modernity is achieved when he enters its fold. While in the village, the narrator emphasizes that Kumasenu is "an orphan," alone, without a mother, and left under the supervision of his uncle and aunt, who are portrayed as little more than figurines in the exotic village. Uncle Faiwoo, the audience is told, clings to the "old ways" and is fearful of the anger of the ancestors, and although he speaks directly to his nephew in the diegesis, the soundtrack includes only very faint traces of the sound of his voice. The narrator's voice-over translation of Faiwoo's words effectively enacts an aural erasure of Faiwoo. It seems more like an overdub of his speech than a commentary on or translation of it. Predictably, the narrator's performance of Faiwoo's lines, originally delivered in Ewe, adopts, in English, a broken syntax and crude diction, marking Faiwoo as an unintelligent and primitive African. Faiwoo's wife, nameless and completely silent, appears only once in the film. In this scene, she visits the hut of the village fetish priest, whose counsel she seeks, the narrator derisively explains, because she, too, is worried about her nephew's restlessness.

The village uncle and aunt stand in sharp contrast to the articulate, urban, and modern man of science and his equally articulate and dutiful wife. Dr. and Mrs. Tamakloe exemplify the elite class of Ghanaians charged with running the country after the end of colonial rule and are portrayed as models of fatherhood, motherhood, and citizenship. The doctor is "a man trained to take his place in the complicated life of the city," a gentleman, educated in science and art, and charitable, the benevolent patriarch of his nuclear household. His academic prowess is emphasized as the camera pauses at the sign posted at his front door listing his numerous university degrees. This shot, which functions like an intertitle, hails an audience literate in English, whose members, like the doctor himself, are able to decipher and appreciate the university degrees that verify his modernity and civility. When the audience first encounters the doctor in his home, he is sculpting an abstract human form. His wife enters his studio, explaining that she has been doing the monthly accounts and has noted a few discrepancies. Their affectionately playful exchange seems to be modeling the companionate marriage for audiences. She embraces her husband and gently scolds him for not charging his clients more money for his services, and he responds, earnestly, "If I turned them away because of their poverty, it would be on my conscience. If they don't pay me when they can afford to, that's on their conscience."

Anne McClintock, among others, has written extensively on the gendered character of the nation-state, arguing that "nations have historically amounted to the sanctioned institutionalization of gender *difference*" (1997, 89). The conjugal family functions as the primary institution for naturalizing the historical and ideological configuration of the nation and reproducing gender difference. Significantly, it is Kumasenu, a boy who grows to be a man, whose emergent subjectivity allegorizes the emergent nationalism the film intends to produce. The film asserts this explicitly with the authority of the narrator's voice. Since taking Kumasenu into his home, Dr. Tamakloe has struggled to sculpt the boy's face. "As a sculptor, he saw in it the youth of his country, swiftly emerging from its ancient tranquility into the confusion of the present age. In Kumasenu he saw a boy on a bridge, uncertainly and unhappily making his way from one world to another." Much as Tamakloe shapes wood into human form, the film shapes Kumasenu into a citizen.

Kumasenu's journey into citizenship is defined not only by the spaces he crosses, moving from the village to the city, but by severing all ties to his extended family. Cousin Agboh signifies, most obviously, the corruption of the city, but he also represents the dangerous bonds that link Kumasenu to the village and his lineage. In every instance, Kumasenu's blind admiration for Agboh leads him to break laws and act against the interests of the nation. While Kumasenu is living happily in the Tamakloe household, Agboh suddenly appears, flanked by a group of young thugs, and he convinces Kumasenu that the police have been hunting for him because they believe that he stole the storekeeper's money. He threatens to turn Kumasenu over to the police if he does not unlock the door to the doctor's examination room, where the doctor keeps the drugs which Agboh and his friends intend to steal. Kumasenu refuses and, for this, receives a brutal beating from Agboh and his gang. On a subsequent evening, when Mrs. Tamakloe is out of town and the doctor on a house call, Agboh and the gang of boys manage to break into the doctor's surgery. The narrator solemnly proclaims, "At that moment, Kumasenu became of age. The child became a man." Kumasenu alerts the police and, after a long chase and struggle, apprehends Agboh. The narrator concludes: "Kumasenu the hunted had become Kumasenu the hunter." Within the logic of the film, the admiration of the young boy for his delinquent cousin must be displaced in order for the boy to enter manhood and become a member of the Tamakloe family. Only when he comes to know Agboh for what he is, the narrator surmises, "an enemy of all those who observe the simple laws that allow men to work and enjoy their lives without fear," can he defeat his cousin in an act of physical violence that validates his manhood and his place in modern Ghana.

The mention of work merits consideration. Agboh is described as an enemy because he is an inherently transitional figure. Transitional between the village and the city, he himself represents a type of character that is improperly assimilated. He is a "monster" precisely because he is anomalous. He cannot work as a fisherman, nor does he work in the city. And yet his anomalousness, disclosed as it is in the form of criminal impulses, also speaks to an ethical domain. What Agboh represents for Kumasenu, then, is the claim of an improperly constituted ethical dimension, since Agboh is no Robin Hood, but merely a thug and a scoundrel. Thus with this disavowal, what Kumasenu displays is the capacity to transcend this improperly constituted ethical dimension and to embrace the modern.

Within the narrative, Kumasenu's attraction to the sexualized character Adobia, whom the narrator describes as "a friend to many men but faithful to none," must also be sanctioned in order for him to become a son and citizen. Neither a mother nor a wife, she too is improperly assimilated into urban life, her independence equated with sexual promiscuity.[14] The film coordinates a comparison between the two female figures, presented as polarities of the Mother Africa trope, the good mother and the bad prostitute (Stratton 1994). Kumasenu must leave one in order to find the other. Indeed, when Kumasenu meets the doctor and his wife, the narrator comments that he "found new friends to take the place of Adobia." Grace Tamakloe epitomizes maternal affection and devotion to her husband, never appearing before the camera without the doctor, Kumasenu, or her daughter Ama at her side. Nor is she sexualized by the spectator's gaze. Upon seeing Kumasenu when he first enters her home and hearing his story, "her heart ached." She asks her husband, "If our Ama, at that boy's age, were alone and friendless, and fell among thieves, and a man came by who could help her, what would you expect of that man?" It is her heartfelt, motherly appeal that convinces the doctor to assist the boy and guide him toward manhood. In *Nationalisms and Sexualities*, the authors suggest that the fraternity of the nation enacts an "idealization of motherhood" and "the exclusion of all non-reproductively oriented sexualities from the discourse of the nation" (Parker et al. 1992, 6). The narrative treatment of Grace and Adobia verifies this conclusion. The film suggests that the stability of the new nation depends on the stability of the family unit, and the security of the family, in turn, relies on a woman who fulfills her "natural" duty as mother, producing and caring for children, instead of seeking economic independence or sexual pleasure.

The film visualizes Adobia, from her first presentation, as an object of Kumasenu's desire. Seen from Kumasenu's point of view, she is an erotic spectacle on display. Theories of film spectacle, perhaps most commonly associated with Tom Gunning's work on early cinema and its attractions (1995) and Laura Mulvey's feminist film theory (1989), activate the idea of spectacle to describe those moments in cinema when the novelty, scale, or intensity of an onscreen image momentarily disrupts the spectator's engagement with character psychology or narrative. Exhibitionist and soliciting "a highly conscious awareness of the film image engaging the spectator's attention" (Gunning 1995, 121), the cinematic spectacle offers the pleasure of plentitude, of visually consuming an unconcealed and fascinating attraction. Mulvey deploys the language of spectacle to theorize the eroticized and fetishistic portrayal of woman, which, she argues, represents the primary spectacular investment of classic Hollywood cinema. An image "displayed," the woman as erotic object functions as the focal point where "the gaze of the spectator and that of the male characters in the film are neatly combined" (Mulvey 1989, 19). It is the female form, then, that assures "the active power of the erotic look" (20). I want to suggest that in *The Boy Kumasenu*, the suturing of the film's spectator to the African male subject through the spectacle of Adobia is intended to humanize Kumasenu and demonstrate his coming into subjectivity. The film asserts his agency through the active and erotic look he casts on Adobia, so this articulation of masculine desire and subjectivity produces, as Mulvey (1989) first explained, a gendered division of labor. Adobia remains the passive object whose purpose is to demonstrate Kumasenu's agency.

The most pronounced enunciation of gendered spectacle occurs in the film's one musical number. In this segment, Kumasenu tags along when Adobia goes to a local dance club to meet Yeboah. There, Kumasenu watches Adobia and Yeboah as they slow dance and she sings a love song. Adobia's song, seemingly meant for Yeboah alone, flows beyond the confines of narrative, crossing over into extra-diegetic space. Foregrounded on the soundtrack, it silences the film's voice-over narration and directly engages the film's theatrical audience. It becomes like a musical performance, incorporating and modifying aspects of the 1930s Hollywood musical number, which loosely follows the standard arrangement of the musical attraction as described by Pierre-Emmanuel Jaques (2006):

> The camera is on the spectator's side or backstage, making the theatrical location of the singing and dancing number quite clear. Having made us aware of this special demarcation, the camera makes its way into the space of the number itself, literally breaking apart the diegetic universe. The number area is specially organized and built for the film spectators only. (282)

Filmed on location, not on a stage or in a studio, and in the midst of club patrons, *The Boy Kumasenu* alters the spatial arrangement of this format, integrating Adobia's musical number more smoothly into the space of the film's narrative. The camera's movement, furthermore, does not penetrate the closed-off world of the diegesis. Shot/reverse shot editing and eyeline matching focalize the spectator through Kumasenu's gaze, which remains fixed on Adobia. Only the soundtrack, as I described previously, and, significantly, the display of Adobia as object of desire, "break[s] apart the diegetic universe." Positioned as spectacle, her image, and the musical performance it is set within, disturb the trajectory of the narrative and invite a different engagement from the spectator. She is a thing to be looked at. Captured in close-up, Adobia's image functions as a projection of Kumasenu's desire, and it is this visualization of his desire that documents the presence of an interiority that reveals him as a subject. She is the surface on which his interiority, his subjectivity, and the "active power" of his gaze (Mulvey 1989, 20) are inscribed.

Having disavowed Agboh and Adobia and abandoned superstition and lineage ties, Kumasenu approaches the conclusion of his narrative, and the closing segment of the film returns to a pronouncement about work, emphasizing that work is as crucial to the modern nation as is absorption into the Westernized family. Kumasenu's labor, to be legitimate, must be modernized, as demonstrated in the final scenes of the film. A shot of Kumasenu, lying on his back after his last tussle with Agboh, dissolves to a panoramic view of the village coast. A slow pan across the beach lands on a long shot of Faiwoo, sitting beneath a tree and mending a fishing-net. The narrator announces that "the story" of Agboh's fate and his nephew's role in it had "traveled far up the coast." Thinking about his nephew's future as a fisherman on a new boat called the *Lydia*, the narrator says that Faiwoo, who at that moment casts his glance out toward the sea, "spoke quietly to himself, making of his words a prayer." The "prayer" is worth quoting in full:

> Oh Father of the winds and seas, if it be thy wish that these new things come to pass, then let thy hand fall lightly on [those] on whom the dangerous burden of change must fall. Let them find strong hands among their people to help and guide them. Give them strength and fortitude, for their way into the new world is set about with snares and pitfalls, which can cause great, great suffering if they stray too far from the old ways, if they stray too far, too soon.

Faiwoo's ventriloquized prayer erases the authoritative and exploitative hand of British colonialism, which is rewritten as change, inevitable and natural. An image of Kumasenu, sitting among a fishing crew on a motorized fishing boat, spools over Faiwoo's prayer. Smiling broadly, his hand on the engine, Kumasenu waves to Dr. and Mrs. Tamakloe, who watch from the pier. "Thus the past uttered its wisdom and spoke to the future," concludes the narrator, as on the image track, Kumasenu's motorboat overtakes a group of traditional fishing boats, powered by groups of rowing men. This image narrates not only the passage of the old into the new, but the assimilation of the old and what is presented as modernized and new. This work as a fisherman, unlike the job he performed miserably in the store, guarantees Kumasenu's modernity and declares that as a worker and a man, the modern city, a metonym for the liberal nation, has a place for him. The film ends by offering a paternalistic warning to the soon-to-be independent nation of Ghana and its guardians: "Sail boldly into the new, but let the wake of your craft be gentle. Let your past remain upright and proud until we build our ships of the same timber." The only trace of Kumasenu's village life allowed entry into the modern city is the work he has been assigned to do.

The Ghana Film Industry Corporation and the Challenges of Film Production in Ghana

At independence in 1957, film production was nationalized in Ghana. As Anne Mette Jørgensen notes, Kwame Nkrumah, the first president of Ghana, "was highly aware of the potential role of the mass media in Nation building" (2001, 122). Nkrumah upgraded the country's radio infrastructure, inaugurated, in 1965, the Ghana Broadcasting Corporation (GBC), a noncommercial, state-controlled television station, and erected new facilities for the national film company. The state, understood as the protector of Ghanaian values and culture, exercised a great deal of control over film production. GFIC owned the filmmaking equipment and controlled the importation of film stock. It trained and employed many of the filmmakers working in the country and played a central role in the inauguration and staffing of the National Film and Television Institute (NAFTI), a film and video training institute, founded in 1979. GFIC selected and supported those among its employees who would study at NAFTI or travel to the British Film Institute or the Film and Television Institute of India for training. It also censored all films exhibited in the country, and after purchasing West African Pictures in 1956, had significant control over film exhibition in Ghana.[15] GFIC owned and operated six cinemas in Accra: the Rex, Royal, Regal, Roxy, Plaza, and the Film Theatre, located on the grounds of the film company. It also owned the Rex at Asamankese and the Dam at Akosombo.

At its founding, the Ghana Film Industry Corporation (GFIC) was charged with using film to educate and modernize the masses, to define and celebrate traditional values, to develop a unifying national consciousness, and to counter stereotypical representations of Africa and Africans abroad.[16] GFIC was a node on a network of artistic, media, and cultural institutions founded or enhanced by Nkrumah "to meet the demands of the new state of Ghana" (Agovi 1992, 4). Among these were the Institute of African Studies and the School of Music and Drama at the University of Ghana, and the film company worked collaboratively with both academic units in its formative years. It is worth emphasizing, too, that the first generation of Ghanaian filmmakers were, like the first African writers, "products of the institutions that colonialism had introduced and developed" (Gikandi 2004, 379). Among the first filmmakers and managing directors at GFIC were many former students of the Gold Coast Film Unit, including Sam Aryeetey. Others, such as Ernest Abbeyquaye and Bernard Odjidja, received instruction in filmmaking at the British Film Institute. Sean Graham remained at GFIC as managing director until 1965, when the Ghanaian novelist, Kofi Awoonor was appointed to administer the company from 1965 to 1967. No women were included among this group of filmmakers. GFIC's output, although extremely limited and generally inconsistent, was in every instance informed by the ideologies of anticolonialism and cultural nationalism. As Chris Hesse explained, the company's aim was to educate and "boost our cultural heritage" (personal communication). Simon Gikandi's claim about "the key motivations" for the creation of a modern African literature applies with equal validity to the genesis of film production in Ghana. Its driving force was the restoration of "the moral integrity and cultural authority of the African in the age of decolonization" (Gikandi 2004, 381). Likewise, the central paradox confronted by this first generation of African writers, intellectuals, and filmmakers was that in order to oppose colonial domination and assert the rights of Africans they had to "turn to a recently discovered European language of tradition, nation, and race" (382).

Incorporating codes and conventions affiliated with West African oral traditions, the earliest features produced by GFIC represent attempts to Africanize film. The company aspired to the articulation of a distinctly Ghanaian national cinema. To again borrow a particularly apt phrase from Phil Rosen, GFIC mobilized "a culturally rooted stylization" of narrative and address in order to "collectivize" its Ghanaian audience (2001, 297). This objective is perhaps most pronounced in the first production of the newly independent company, *No Tears for Ananse* (1965). Based on the play *Ananse and the Gum Man* (1965) by Ghanaian playwright Joe de Graft, who from 1961 to 1969 served as head of the drama division of the School of Music and Drama at the University of Ghana, and written and directed by Sam Aryeetey, the film re-creates the performance of an *Anansesem*, or a tale of the trickster Ananse. It intends to celebrate the richness of Akan oral tradition and, like the first modern African literary texts, to illustrate in the famous words of Chinua Achebe that "African people did not hear of culture for the first time from Europeans" (Achebe 1975, 8).

As much as Aryeetey's film taps into a reservoir of cultural knowledge in its incorporation of oral tradition, it also exploits the narrative and theatrical capacities of cinema to produce a sense of national identity based in the articulation of a shared culture and the organization of a national space. Ravi S. Vasudevan (2001) has described the new and emergent forms of subjectivity constituted in Hindi commercial cinema during the first decade after Indian independence, suggesting that the mixed modes of address and systems of narration that structure these films outline new forms of subjectivity and national identity. *No Tears for Ananse*, like several of the Indian films Vasudevan examines, incorporates a mixed address. In this case, it combines the "character-driven codes" (Vasudevan 2001, 149) associated with Hollywood and codes and conventions affiliated with African storytelling. Most notable among these techniques is the use of audience direct address. Direct address refers to the sequences where the film overtly addresses the spectator and ruptures the closed-off world of the narrative space, or the diegesis. The first instance of direct address in *No Tears for Ananse* occurs in the film's opening as the introductory text quoted below scrolls down the screen:

> Story-telling is a form of entertainment very popular among Ghanaians. Of the many stories that one may hear, there is a particular cycle that has come to be identified with the fictitious character Ananse, the spider-man or man-spider. These are the stories known as Anansesem, the stories of Ananse. Kweku Ananse symbolizes shrewdness and cunning. In Akan mythology, he is the younger brother of Nyankopon, the great god of the sky. Unlike his brother, however, Kwaku Ananse is more earthy. His greed knows no end. A figure of fun, he seems at his best when engaged in some mischief. But like all mischief makers, he often ends up in trouble and disgrace, thus earning the laughter and scorn of mankind.

Although identifying Ananse as an important character in Akan mythology, the intertitle claims Ananse as an important national figure, suppressing other ethnic identities, languages, oral discourses, and mythologies while claiming a shared national culture and oral literature. The reference to "Ghanaians" has a double function here. It is, to borrow a phrase from Homi Bhabha (1994), pedagogical and performative, asserting an ethnographic "truth" about Ghanaians and, in that, producing "Ghanaian" as a national identity. Ghanaians are doubly inscribed; described *and* addressed, their national identity is the subject *and* product of the enunciation.

In *No Tears for Ananse* it is the direct address of a traditional storyteller, played by Ernest Abbeyquaye, that frames the Ananse story and invites the film audience into "a familiar community of meaning" (Vasudevan 2001, 149). The architecture of these opening and closing segments theatricalizes space to reenact a storytelling event for two audiences: the diegetic audience (the audience within the world of the film) seated around the storyteller and the film audience located in the film theater. Placed in a position external to the Ananse story he will tell, centered frontally, and standing among a large group of rapt listeners, the storyteller looks directly into the camera when he introduces his tale. An ensemble of traditional drummers and dancers, located behind him and to the side, punctuates his address. The camera, tilted slightly upward, places the film audience among the crowd of listeners, who appear in a brief cutaway sequence. Here the camera pans across the faces of the listeners as they laugh, nod, and smile, representing the audience as the nation, heterogeneous, including the old and young, men and women, and happily unified around this cultural performance. The film's creation of a storytelling event, a culturally familiar and culturally coded arena of meaning, opens a national space, shared by Ghanaians within and external to the film, that, significantly, affirms the idea of community found in the Ananse narrative.

The mode of spectatorial address shifts with the actual telling of the *Anansesem.* Rendered through Hollywood-style narration that uses continuity editing to invoke the grammar of realism, the narrative of the Ananse story positions the spectator fully within the story's "real" world. Set in an unspecified past, the narrative moves between the perspectives of Ananse and his son Kwaku Tsin. It chronicles the avaricious Ananse's ploy to trick his wife Okonnor, his son, and their village into believing that he is dead so that he can harvest and eat all of the food grown on the family farm. Ananse, feigning sudden sickness, asks his wife, upon what he claims is his approaching death, to grant him a last wish: "When I die, don't bury me in a grave. Lie me on a pyre on the farm and build a hut around my body." Ananse dies in Okonnor's arms, and in the following days, the entire village mourns and partakes in the funeral rites and festivities. Taken to his farm on the pyre and left to meet his ancestors, Ananse, very much among the living, sneaks out of his hut each evening to pick ripe tomatoes, ground eggs, and cassava and prepare for himself a plentiful feast. While enjoying a large bowl of soup, he remarks, "How I pity all family men who have to share their food and never get the chance to put on a bit of fat." When Okonnor and Tsin return to the farm several weeks later, they find their plants picked clean. Furious, Tsin vows to find the "scoundrel" who has been "feeding fat" on his father's farm and devises an elaborate ploy to capture the thief. Kwaku Tsin carves a human figure from a large piece of wood, paints the statue with a thick and sticky sap, and places it on the farm, where he is certain the thief will find it. The foolish Ananse sees the figure and, mistaking it for a man, attempts to slap and kick it. When he makes contact with the sappy glue, of course, he sticks. Unable to free himself from the figure, he is captured by Tsin, who returns the next morning with his mother to check the trap he has set.

After Tsin captures the thief, he immediately informs the entire village, whose members run to the farm to find Ananse caught in his own son's trap. Point-of-view editing again aligns the camera with the crowd whose members heckle Ananse, and in the final scene, when the storyteller returns to impart the story's lesson to his listeners, Ananse's exposure and his shame, and therefore the story's moral, are linked to Ananse's "suffer[ing] in the eyes of his own wife and child," and, importantly, to the disapproval and sanction of the community. The storyteller, looking into the camera, imparts the film's lesson: "Thus, Kwaku Ananse was exposed. And his greed brought upon him greater shame than any other man ever suffered in the eyes of his own wife and child. Take heed then to all who will listen." The architecture of the film aligns, in censure, the gazes of the Ananse's family, his community, the storyteller and his audience, and, significantly, the film spectators in the dark film theater. In this way, it organizes "a circuit of imaginary communication, indeed, a making of audience into imaginary community" (Vasudevan 2001, 149). The mixed modes of narration deployed in the film position the spectator "both inside and outside the story, tied at one moment to the seamless flow of a character-based narration from within, in the next attuned to a culturally familiar stance from without" (150).

The same year, the Ghana Film Industry Corporation released *Hamile the Tongo Hamlet* (1964), a Ghanaian retelling of Shakespeare's *Hamlet*. Set in the village of Tongo in northern Ghana among the Gurunsi, the film, made in English, adheres closely to the original text. Only the location and characters' names have been changed: Hamlet has become Hamile, played by Kofi Middleton-Mends; Ophelia is Habiba, played by Mary Yirenkyi, and Polonius is called Ibrahim and acted by Ernest Abbequaye. The film features performers from the University of Ghana School of Music and Drama, many of whom appeared in *No Tears for Ananse* and other GFIC releases. Its screenplay was written by Terry Bishop, an English national who was a close friend of Sean Graham's, and the film was produced by the Ghanaian writer Joe de Graft, who throughout the course of his career directed many Shakespearean plays.

Based on a stage performance premiered earlier in the year, *Hamile* was made for inclusion in the 1965 Commonwealth Arts Festival in London and was de Graft's first attempt at adapting one of Shakespeare's major plays to a Ghanaian context (Agovi 1992, 5). As explained by Kofi Ermeleh Agovi, "De Graft was attempting to extend the dimensions of the Ghanaian theater to accommodate a universal experience in a distinctly Ghanaian setting" (5). Like similar assimilations of Shakespeare produced by first generation Africa writers in many former British colonies, the Africanizing of Shakespeare by well-educated members of the African elite was meant to demonstrate Africa's civility and humanity (Johnson 1998; Gikandi 2004). It grew out of and reproduced the colonial idea that British literary culture represented a shared humanity. The re-creation of Shakespeare in Ghana, as in other parts of British colonial Africa, was bound up with the assertion of a national identity and culture. Gikandi explains: "To the extent that African nationalism justified its political claims through the invocation of the essential humanity of the colonized, the production of a literary culture was conceived as an important step in sanctioning the case for African rights and freedoms" (2004, 387). The film received a tepid response from the local press and local audiences. The *Weekly Spectator*, for example, described the film as "a bit high-browed" and criticized it for being unlike *The Boy Kumasenu*, which is reported to have "gone down well with the public" (June 4, 1966).

With little revenue, diminishing resources, and no prospect of new government investment, the beleaguered film company was unable to sustain the promise offered by these first films. It was not until 1970 that the next feature appeared, *I Told You So* (1970) directed by Egbert Adjeso. Like *No Tears for Ananse*, Adjeso's production combines the codes of narrative cinema with a Ghanaian performance tradition, in this case, the concert party. Adapted from a stage play by concert party artist Bob Cole, *I Told You So* tells the story of a poor girl whose mother pressures her to marry a rich stranger, who, in the end, is revealed to be a diamond smuggler. The film's close affiliation with the popular concert party theater and its incorporation of highlife music and performances by Bob Cole and the African Brothers Band undoubtedly accounted for its wide appeal. Music figures even more prominently in Bernard Odjidja's *Doing Their Thing* (1972). The first color film made in Ghana, *Doing Their Thing* features The El Pollos and Kwanyako Brass Bands, two popular highlife bands that performed widely in the 1970s. In 1975, Aryeetey embarked on several unsuccessful coproductions, including *Contact: The African Deal* (1973), which was directed by Giorgio Bontempi and produced with Ital Victoria, and *The Visitor* (1979), a musical tour coproduced among GFIC, the Musicians Union of Ghana, Mick Fleetwood of Fleetwood Mac, and Micky Shapiro. The films were, by every measure, unsuccessful, and Aryeetey was widely criticized for his decision to look abroad for coproducers and directors (Diawara 1992; Ukadike 1994).

The production of two family dramas, *Genesis Chapter X* (1979) and *Aya Minnow* (1987), indicated a shift in the form and content of the national film company's productions. These films rely exclusively on the conventions of Hollywood narrative cinema and move away from the incorporation of indigenous performance forms and the mixed modes of spectator engagement described previously.[17] Here the narratives are focalized through individual characters and plots driven by private, family conflicts. Each of these films constructs closed story-worlds and, through the use of continuity editing, place spectators within this "hermetic universe on-screen" (Vasudevan 2001, 151). Both explore broken or failed nuclear families and detail the negative repercussions those failures have on children. In *Genesis*, Zaria Garba, who works as a doctor in England, travels back home to Ghana to find the mother he was taken from as a child. As the plot unravels, Zaria uncovers the truth of his past, that his mother, Hawa, had an adulterous affair with her current husband, Adamu, while she was married to Garba's father. The affair lead to the murder of Zaria's father, for which Hama was put in jail, and her then very young son, Zaria, was taken away. In the second feature, the death of Aya Minnow's mother during her birth casts a long shadow on Aya's life as portrayed in *Aya Minnow*. Controlled by an overprotective father, Aya fights to find love without her father's interference, and only after he dies does she seem to have real hope for a happy life with Kobi.

In the 1980s and 90s, independent Ghanaian filmmakers Kwaw Ansah, Ato Yanney, King Ampaw, and Kofi Nartey attempted independent projects with tremendous difficulties. The award-winning feature films of Ansah, *Love Brewed in the African Pot* (1980) and *Heritage Africa* (1988) achieved international recognition and, as a consequence, have attracted the most critical attention outside of Ghana; as widely discussed as his films, however, are the financial obstacles he scaled to make them (Ansah 2000, 2002). In an interview with Frank Ukadike, Ansah (2002) discusses the hard struggle he waged to secure and repay private loans from banks to produce his films, especially without revenue generated with the assistance of an international distributor. Ato Yanney, similarly, was not able to distribute his film internationally. The film, *His Majesty's Sergeant* (1984), is set during World War II and is framed as a conversation among an African sergeant, an Indian corporal, and a British private. It explores the contradiction between Europe's fight to defeat Nazism and fascism and its maintenance and defense of its own colonies in India and Africa.

Perhaps the filmmaker who has worked most successfully from outside GFIC is King Ampaw, whose success is in part linked to long-standing relationships with German coproducers, which began in the 1980s. Both *Kukurantumi, the Road to Accra* (1983) and *Juju* (1985) were coproduced among GFIC, Reinery Film, Ampaw, and NDR Television. In a personal interview in 1999, Ampaw described the partnership as a fruitful creative adventure, but one that didn't make him rich. Finally, Kofi Nartey and Bob Johnson made *Back Home Again* (1995), the last Ghanaian film produced on film. Although Nartey submitted his film to several international film festivals, he never found a distributor interested in purchasing the exhibition and distribution rights for it. Financed from his own personal savings, the film, he told me, depleted his financial and emotional stores. Set in Ghana and Britain, the film chronicles the hard life of a Ghanaian trying to make it in London.

Despite Nkrumah's substantial investments in the film company, until the late 1980s and the arrival of independent video production, more than 95 percent of all films shown in Ghana were foreign films (Sakyi 1996, 10). GFIC produced, during the forty-eight years of its existence, over 200 documentaries and approximately 385 newsreels, but only 14 feature films. The availability of very few Ghanaian films meant that exhibitors, including GFIC, showed films from the United States, India, and China. Scarce resources were channeled to the production of state propaganda, educational films, and coverage of state visits and events by Nkrumah and successive governments. For example, Chris Hesse, one of the most accomplished cinematographers and film directors at GFIC, spent most of his time filming Kwame Nkrumah.[18] Assignments such as these generated no income for the company and, instead, drew money and expertise away from the production of feature films. The company's commercial division, responsible for the distribution and exhibition of films, was expected to earn enough income to cover its costs and channel any profits into film production, but it was unable to meet this goal largely because the exhibition and distribution of films increasingly became organized through private companies. Cinema owners, such as Salim Captan, who took over Ocansey's cinemas in 1942, obtained licenses from the state and paid taxes to import films, but their film theaters operated in direct competition with state-owned cinemas. Furthermore, film distributors and exhibitors, including GFIC's commercial division, were held down by foreign exchange rates and the bureaucratic tangle of obtaining import licensees and, as a result, could not import sufficient numbers of films for cinema screens. Between 1968 and 1980, distributors imported two hundred films into the country, although eight hundred were required to meet demand (Masters 2006). Cinemas were forced to screen the same feature films over and over again, and not surprisingly, people simply stopped patronizing the cinema halls.

Although *A Debut for Dede*, made in 1992, was the first film to be produced on video by the Ghana Film Industry Corporation, the company's film directors had been asking the managing director, Chris Hesse, to consider producing and exhibiting feature "films" on video for some time prior to its release. Ashong Katai, a NAFTI graduate who joined the film company in 1981, explained that he and his colleagues were surprised and encouraged by the success of the amateur video producers, who had been releasing video features in the country since 1987. If audiences were willing to pay to see video features made by videomakers without training, then surely, Katai reasoned, audiences would support professionally produced video movies (personal communication). However, Hesse refused to consider video production, arguing that video was a broadcast medium and an amateur production technology not suited to the creation of feature films.

A Debut for Dede's slapdash production forecast the dissolution of the national film company and of state support for filmmaking. Director Tom Ribeiro relied on old black-and-white film stock, the only stock available to him at the time, to produce *Dede*, but, in the end, the feature had to be released as a video production. As was standard practice at GFIC, Ribeiro shot the film on both celluloid and video, intending only to use the video footage to study each day's rushes prior to the next day's shoot. The black and white film was never processed, however. The GFIC labs were inoperable, and the company simply lacked the money to send the exposed film stock abroad.[19] Ribeiro stitched together *Dede* from video footage never intended for public screening. For postproduction, he relied on analog editing benches at the national film and television school, NAFTI, because GFIC did not own video editing equipment. Still, *A Debut for Dede*, the film company's first video feature, made a profit, and from this point forward, GFIC considered video as a viable option for the production of Ghanaian films.[20]

In Close-Up: *A Debut for Dede*

Filmed in Accra and the village Dome, *A Debut for Dede*, like *The Boy Kumasenu*, replays the motif of the journey, its "evolutionary trajector[y] moving in the direction of a Western modernity" (Quayson 2000, 117). In this film, the protagonist is a young woman called Dede, who finds a secretarial position in the city and flees her village without performing the Dipo puberty ritual or seeking her parents' permission and blessing. In the city, Dede finds modernity, and it threatens to corrupt and contaminate her. The film presents the African woman's body as a metaphor for Africa's authenticity, at once tempted and threatened by Western modernity. Dede's roommate Nako initiates the innocent Dede into her life of sex and alcohol. Nako, like Adobia, is the bad city-girl figure, but unlike Adobia, who practices a legitimate trade as a seller of cloth, Nako achieves economic independence through illicit labor. A prostitute, she sells her body to enjoy a modern and independent lifestyle complete with a luxury apartment, furnished with a well-stocked liquor cabinet and stereo system, a foreign car, and flashy clothes, for which Dede expresses unrestrained admiration. Nako's deviance is tied to a modernity that has come at the cost of her African values. When Dede asks Nako if she has lost her "chastity," Nako replies curtly, "Wake up and live. It's the twentieth century."

Dede works as a secretary for Dauda, who seems, at first, a perfect gentleman. When Dauda invites her for a drink one evening, Dede accepts, choosing to disregard the advice offered by one of her female colleagues, who warns Dede not to become "his next victim." Dauda gets Dede drunk, drives her home, and carries her into the bedroom and, although she seems barely conscious, has sex with her. When Dede awakes the next morning, she pledges her love and life to Dauda, who admits that he is already married. Dede is devastated and eases her pain in bouts of heavy drinking. It is only the friendship and guidance of an old widower whom Dede calls "Godfather" that rescues Dede from total debauchery. She returns to her village to ask for the community's forgiveness, and after a cleansing ceremony is performed, she returns to a new job and apartment in the city.

The feature reveals the "deeply gendered nature of a nation's imaginary" (Jaikumar 2006, 32). Dede's body functions as a contested site, drawn between village and city and fought over by the representatives of tradition and modernity. The film opens onto a naturalistic, outdoor village landscape during an initiation ceremony, where bare-breasted young women dance, guided by the village patriarch, a traditional priest, and before an assembly of community members. As the priest declares, "Our little girls will now see, face to face. Let the girls with just-flowered breasts pay heed and be accepted into the priceless role of womanhood," the camera zooms in on and pans across the breasts of the young women, whose heads have been cut off by the camera's frame. The gaze seems simultaneously ethnographic and pornographic, engaging the spectator in the act of looking at an exhibition of exotic nudity. Throughout the ceremony segment, the breasts of the initiates captivate the camera. They index the female purity the ceremony is meant to test and celebrate and embody the African traditional values and way of life threatened by the modernity Dede desires.

The opening segments set Dede's modernity, signified by her physical remove from the ceremony and her dress and makeup, against the traditions her mother defends. When a woman, who in the next scene is identified as Dede's mother, abruptly stands up and leaves the ceremony, the film cuts to an interior location and a close-up of Dede's face, reflected in a mirror, in front of which she puts on lipstick and straightens her hair. The frame widens as the woman enters and asks, "Why apply a mask? Don't you appreciate the way you are?" Dede laughs and answers: "Mother, you are so old-fashioned. This is modern." In the exchange that follows, Dede's mother expresses her wish that Dede "pass through the puberty rites" before she leaves. Dede ridicules her mother, insisting that only "uneducated girls" participate in such an "arcane custom." Furious, her mother replies: "I went through it. So did my ancestors. The virtues of this society have not changed. A maiden found not to be a virgin brings disgrace to her family." Dede storms out, and, in the next shot, we watch from behind as she walks toward a speeding train, another marker of the modern, as it cuts through the village. Her mother calls to her: "Your grandmother advised me, when I was your age, that your self-respect is all that lies within. Abuse it, you are doomed forever. You respect it, you bring honor to yourself and the family."

The village is coded as a female space. The performance of the topless initiates dominates the village sequence, interrupted only by the dramatic exchange between Dede and her parents. Within this narrative episode, Dede's mother lords over her family, while her father appears befuddled and weak. After Dede leaves home, her mother angrily blames her husband because he allowed her to go to school and in this way fueled her ambition. "Her education should have been limited to the kitchen," Dede's mother screams. Her father pleads for understanding, explaining that he "could not deny her the opportunity." This same point of view is later echoed by Nako, who tells Dede that education "has broken up the social order." But the film implies that in fact it is the education of women in the Western tradition that has disrupted the indigenous order. The education of African men is never scrutinized. Every man Dede interacts with in the city is educated—the sleazy boss, the avuncular friend, and the long-lost boyfriend—their characters and actions, whether good or bad, are not linked to their educational background or place in the urban environment. Education offers men careers as doctors and rich businessmen, while it takes women from their cultural roots and therefore puts their purity at risk.

The film marks the city as a male space. Here young unmarried women become either prostitutes, exploiting their objectification for economic gain, or heartbroken victims of predatory men. In the city, men, without restriction or reservation, gaze at, approach, and make advances toward women. In every place she travels, Dede's untouched body is threatened by men. At the office, in the home she shares with Nako, and on the street. This point is clearly communicated in a scene set shortly after Dede's arrival in the city. She goes for a walk down the street, and men continually harass her: whistling, leering, and stopping their cars to ask her if she would like a ride. At the office, Dede is among a large pool of female secretaries who work under the male boss, Dauda. The women share one room, connected to the boss's office by a door, and at his command, they enter. While out with Dauda, Dede is victimized by the male bartender, too, who colludes with her boss to get her drunk. In a brief aside, Dauda leaves Dede to order a drink for her and winks and nods at another man, who escorts an intoxicated young woman toward the door to the bar's upstairs suites. The film creates the impression that in the city, men hunt women at every turn.

If Kumasenu, the male citizen-subject, casts tradition aside to enter into modernity, Dede, the female subject, internalizes it. The film celebrates village life and tradition, and like the West African folktale about the disobedient daughter, it punishes Dede for disregarding custom and her parents' wishes in pursuit of her beautiful stranger. Exactly as her mother warned, Dede loses her self-respect to the city, and she must return to her family and community to ask for their forgiveness. In the village, the priest performs a purification ceremony for Dede where her parents promise to "appease the gods as custom demands" and then sacrifice a goat. After reconnecting to African tradition and receiving the embrace of her community, Dede, reformed and resilient, returns to Accra. She moves out of Nako's house to make a "change for the better," finds a new job, and in a rather implausible plot twist, reunites with the boyfriend who left her before she came to Accra. (We learn that the boyfriend, who is never named, was a doctor stationed in Dede's village for his national service. He left for another assignment and never returned.) Dede's redemption brings her happiness, while Dauda, the unrepentant villain, suffers. Reported by one of his female employees for inappropriate behavior, he loses his job and wanders the streets looking for employment and begging for money. When he is hit by a car and hospitalized, Dauda calls Dede for help. At the hospital, Dede meets her former boyfriend, who happens to be the doctor treating Dauda. He explains that when he had returned to Dede's village to find her, she had already left for Accra.

Dede, like Kumasenu, does not remain in the village. She returns to Accra to enter the modern order of the nation as a wife. In the last scenes of the film, Dede invites her boyfriend to join her for dinner at her "godfather's" house. In another fortuitous and farfetched turn in the plot, the two men, surprised to see the other with Dede, address each other as father and son. The last shot of the film, a freeze frame shot, captures the three people laughing and embracing. In this new family, Dede stands in for the absent mother, and her migration from village to city allegorizes the female citizen's absorption into the nation's patriarchal order. Dede veers dangerously close to being spoiled by the vices of modernity, but in the end she happily accepts her role as wife and daughter(-in-law). In effect, her journey to the city moves from one side of the Mother Africa trope (Stratton 1994) to the other, from the prostitute to the wife-mother.

Partha Chatterjee in his compelling book *The Nation and Its Fragments* (1993) offers a critique of Benedict Anderson's *Imagined Communities* (1983). He asks of Anderson: "If nationalisms in the rest of the world have to choose their imagined community from certain 'modular' forms already made available to them by Europe and the

Americas, what do they have left to imagine?" (1993, 216). Chatterjee alleges that "the most powerful as well as the most creative results of the nationalist imagination in Asia and Africa are posited not on an identity but rather on a *difference* with the 'modular' forms of the national society propagated by the modern West" (216). The attempt to produce this difference results in a split construction of nationalism, one with an inside and an outside. Chatterjee writes:

> By my reading, anti-colonial nationalism creates its own domain of sovereignty within colonial society. . . . It does this by dividing the world of social institutions and practices into two domains—the material and the spiritual. The material is the domain of the "outside," of the economy and of statecraft, of science and technology, a domain where the West had proved its superiority and the East had succumbed. . . . The spiritual, on the other hand, is an "inner" domain bearing the "essential" marks of cultural identity. (217)

The inner realm of national culture houses the "real" and authentic India, while the "outer" realm confronts and capitulates to the West. In this way, "The colonial state . . . is kept out of the 'inner' domain of national culture" (Chatterjee 1993, 217). In *A Debut for Dede*, as in many African texts—literary and cinematic—the production of postcolonial nationalism lays a gendered binary over the dichotomy between an authentic, inner cultural space and a modern, Westernized realm. As Eileen Julien has remarked in another context, "The choice between 'becoming modern nations' and 'being ourselves' can be seen as a form of politicocultural schizophrenia. . . . Women are the symbolic markers of 'true identity'" (2007, 208). The metaphor of woman as the authentic African essence resolves the conflict. *A Debut for Dede*, like its predecessor, *The Boy Kumasenu* normalizes a gendered representation of the nation and the conjugal, patriarchal family on which it stands, in this way affirming not only a colonial teleology of the modern but also its reiteration of gender difference.

2

Work, Women, and Worldly Wealth

Global Video Culture and the Early Years of Local Video Production

In 1987, when William Akuffo, a film importer and distributor, produced and screened *Zinabu*, a full-length feature shot with a VHS video
camera, film production in Ghana was at a standstill. Dilapidated cinema houses, film equipment in need of repair, and the dire state of
the economy had made the production of films financially untenable.
The Ghana Film Industry Corporation (GFIC), without a functioning laboratory or the foreign currency needed to purchase film stock,
had not released a feature film, without the assistance of foreign investors, since 1979. Independent filmmaker Kwaw Ansah had just com-
pleted shooting his award-winning film *Heritage Africa* (1988) and was
publicly contemplating the end of his filmmaking career. Ghanaians
who visited cinema houses watched scratched and faded films from the
United States, India, and China. In this market, a video feature made by
a Ghanaian and featuring Ghanaians in local settings was a smash hit;
its phenomenal success encouraged other nonprofessional video producers, men and women like Akuffo who had no prior training or experience in film, to try their hands at video production. Within five years,
over thirty local features had been released in Ghana. All of the major
theaters were equipped with video projectors, and hundreds of small
privately owned video centers were erected in urban and rural areas to
meet the growing demand for video viewing.

The early years of video production, between roughly 1987 and
1992, were characterized by radical transformation put in motion by
developments generally associated with globalization: the emergence
of new media technologies, unprecedented in their reach and rapid
progress; the liberalization, privatization, and global integration of
state economies, driven by international economic institutions such

as the World Trade Organization (WTO) and the International Monetary Fund (IMF); and the simultaneous weakening of nation-states. In Ghana in the 1980s and early '90s, the erosion of state support for and control of filmmaking coupled with the ready availability of video technology allowed individuals situated outside of the networks of official cultural production, first, to import and exhibit pirated copies of imported films and television programming, and, later, to produce their own features, which were unregulated as commodities and artistic objects. Ordinary Ghanaians living in poor urban areas, freed from the requirements for cultural and economic capital imposed by the film medium and buoyed up by new media technologies, took up video cameras and started making and exhibiting their own productions. No longer did the state control who could be given access to filmmaking technologies or whose film projects would receive support. No longer was the ability to make "films" available to members of the educated elite exclusively. Video technology and an increasingly liberalized and democratic media made possible, from this perspective, what Birgit Meyer describes as "the opening up of public space to the concerns and views of ordinary people" (2004, 93).

The recognition that the structural and technological changes that opened the media in Ghana to "ordinary people" simultaneously implemented economic policies that made life for most Ghanaians extremely difficult tempers, I think, what otherwise might be a rather too optimistic reading of the new public spaces of globalization. Video technology did allow individuals situated outside the state-controlled realm of cultural production to produce video features. The first videomakers, without access to the cultural capital needed to make films, had no chance whatsoever of being employed by GFIC, gaining entrance to the National Film and Television Institute (NAFTI), or organizing the exorbitant amount of foreign currency that would have been needed to finance a film project. Yet, it is worth emphasizing that local video production in Ghana emerges from the urban slums of Accra, where the economic realities of globalization are as disabling and dispiriting as new media technologies and a liberalized and democratic media are enabling. Undoubtedly, the history of popular video reveals a lot about the opportunities for creative expression and entrepreneurialism left behind by a restrained and weakened nation-state, but these are opportunities born out of deficiency and want, examples of barely getting by with the little that is available.

In this chapter, I examine not only the new publics and possibilities created by Ghana's commercial video industry but also describe the limitations and insecurities made manifest in Ghanaian video movies. I want to suggest that in their origins and the stories they render, the first video movies typify the deep ambivalences generated by global capitalism. Globalization created the conditions of possibility for the production of West African video movies while necessitating the amateur, low budget, and bootleg aesthetics that signals their marginalized position in relation to dominant cinema and media forms. The narratives of the first features emerge from within the "relations of disjuncture" (Appadurai 2001, 5) that characterize globalization in the time of late capitalism. In Ghana, three years before Akuffo released *Zinabu*, the Economic Recovery Package of 1984 crafted by the World Bank unleashed a torrent of imported goods and global media, the very existence of which belied the climbing rates of mass poverty and widening income disparities that ordinary Ghanaians confronted every single day. It is in this context that Ghanaian videos can most fruitfully be read. Much like the South African zombie stories studied by Jean and John Comaroff, the videos register "perplexity at the enigma of wealth, of its origin, and the capriciousness of its distribution, of the opaque, even occult, relation between means and ends embodied in it" (2002, 782). In the videos, focalized exclusively through the perspectives of the urban poor, desperate characters resort to extraordinary measures to acquire wealth and partake of global modernity, represented by the purchase of a Mercedes Benz, Italian leather shoes, and large, gated houses furnished with electronics and appliances. For these characters, wealth is everywhere visible, yet, because work guarantees little social or individual value, can be attained only by illicit means. Here, I read three representative examples of the earliest video features: *Zinabu* (1987), *Big Time* (1988), and *Menace* (1992) as ambivalent responses to globalization and its concomitant shift from economies of production to consumption. I am particularly keen to describe how gender structures and distinguishes these two articulations of capitalistic value. Women *want* while men *work*, and within this antagonism, the figure of the monstrous, beautiful woman (in her various guises as witch, greedy wife, and good-time girl) functions as a metaphor for pure consumption. She is the pleasurable and desiring body that entices and endangers the male worker.

From Video Piracy to Video Production

If film represented the optimism and promise of the Ghanaian nation, then video stands for its impossible realization in "this moment of the global" (Larkin 2000, 211). After Nkrumah's initial efforts to create a national film industry, subsequent administrations allocated no new money for film production or exhibition. The economic crisis and the political instability of the 1970s, the 1981 military coup orchestrated by Jerry John Rawlings, and, most critically, the structural adjustment policies implemented by Rawlings and the Provisional National Defence Council (PNDC) contributed to the complete erosion of the national film industry and its production infrastructure.[1] Film exhibition and distribution, also requiring substantial financial investment, were principally organized through privately owned film theaters bogged down by state-imposed licenses and import fees and other financial restrictions. As a result, theater owners were forced to rely on a small number of out-of-date imported films to satisfy the demands of audiences.[2] Taken together, these factors resulted in a stagnating cinema market dependent on battered and faded foreign films.

The denationalization and privatization of state industries set beside trade liberalization and the availability of new media technologies, such as the VHS standard and satellite television, have resulted in dramatic transformations in local media "cultural ecologies" (Sinclair, Jacka, and Cunningham 1996, 170) in the developing world. The national and local manifestations of these unprecedented global transformations in the realm of media production have been varied and many and include indigenous media projects of cultural revival (Ginsburg 1993, 1994, 1999; Turner 1991, 1992, 1995, 2002), Egyptian television melodramas (Abu-Lughod 1993, 1995, 2002), and small media revolutions in Iran (Sreberny-Mohammadi and Mohammadi 1994). Brian Larkin's work has been instructive in its careful mapping of video culture in northern Nigeria, where video technology—cassette tapes, VCRs, and video projectors—has generated "a distinctly new media arena" (2000, 219).

In Ghana, the 1980s witnessed a paradigmatic shift in the field of cinematic culture as state-financed and -managed film production, including large, expensive, and sophisticated film technologies, gave way to commercial and highly decentralized video exhibition networks that operated completely outside the purview of the state. The nodes of this fragmented and widely dispersed commercial network were strung loosely together within an unofficial and illegal media economy generated for the distribution of global media content. International programming that had been tightly controlled by the state, or available only to those who could afford satellite TV, became widely and suddenly available. VHS cassette recordings of films from Hong Kong, India, and America and of international TV programming captured from satellite broadcasts were exhibited commercially and illegally by resourceful entrepreneurs in various types of video exhibition businesses. Video centers, equipped with no more than VCRs and TV monitors, sold tickets to showings of pirated movies and sporting events, and by 1988, the Minister of Information estimated that there were more than three hundred video centers in Accra alone.[3] Most were small, dilapidated, and "wretched and poorly organized," as stated by one of several contributors to a special newspaper forum called "Commercial Video Operators: What People Say," published in the *Mirror* (1987). Video clubs such as ESN (Education, Entertainment, Sports and News) offered their members videos of CNN News, American movies, and sports events, and video libraries rented programming to those who could not afford to buy cassettes. Churches arranged for Christian Video Ministries, special exhibitions of American evangelical programming such as the *Battle of Armageddon* or *All of Satan's Apples Have Worms*.[4] Religious showings of similar types also occurred widely in Nigeria in the 1980s, linking Anglophone West Africa to another transnational network, "the nascent global Christian Movement" (Ukah 2003, 211). These venues for video viewing familiarized many with the new technology and probably created high demand for it at a time when most could not afford a TV and VCR.[5]

Another significant development in video exhibition occurred with the introduction of video projectors in Ghana. Nii Atua claims to be the first person to project video onto a large screen in a theater-like setting (personal communication). He was running a small restaurant in Accra in 1979 when an American friend gave him a video projector, which he had carried into Ghana, to cover an unpaid loan. He converted his restaurant into Coconut Grove Video Centre, which screened movies and boxing matches, recorded on video cassette from satellite TV broadcasts. Very shortly thereafter, privately owned cinema theaters replaced film projectors with video projectors. Munir Captan, who owned a string of cinemas in Ghana, installed video projection equipment in his theaters around 1980, which revived his ailing cinema business by allowing him to replace outdated and over-used films with new and more current releases (personal communication).[6] All of this content was copied and distributed in violation of international copyright laws and national censorship regulations.

The pirated exhibition of global content on video spread rapidly, making Hollywood and Hindi films and other world media available at an unprecedented speed and volume, altering the cinema landscape dramatically. The public outcry against video pirates, as seen in newspaper articles and letters to editors, reveals something of the anxieties generated by this transformation. In a news article called "Film in a Revolution," Rex Quartey proposes the creation of "a centralized body to RIGIDLY CENSOR and regulate the importation and distribution of foreign films which invade our screens" (1982). Another contributor to the "Commercial Video Operation" forum asked "what contributions these video centers make towards rebuilding the nation," and another suggested that the government should hold the film policy of the colonial governor of the Gold Coast as an example of an effective measure implemented to protect Ghanaians from the "anti-social effect" of imported films (*Mirror*, 1987).

These comments, too, call attention to the unofficial status of the video entrepreneurs, who operated completely outside of state regulation as part of a "shadow (second, marginal, informal, black) economy existing in varying degrees beyond the law" (Larkin 2004, 297). The income earned was not taxed. The centers were not registered as businesses, and the videos screened were duplicated, and shown, in violation of copyright and censorship laws.[7] Any structure could be converted into a video center, and any person with a television and video cassette recorder could charge Ghanaians to watch any films he happened to have on video. The author of a news article titled "Who's Kidding with Video Centres," explained that since the "video boom," when "more and more people were bringing in video sets and cassettes," the government and the police were "overtaken by the speed and sheer numbers of video operators" and had "lost control" (*Mirror*, 1988). The first law passed by Rawlings's government prohibited center owners from showing films during school hours because it was thought that children were skipping school to attend video screenings, and in October 1988, in an effort to rein in video exhibition, the Ministry of Information revoked all the licenses of video center owners in the country. As most operators had no licenses and the state lacked the resources to enforce the action, it had little effect.[8]

While providing nearly unrestricted access to global media flows, video technology and the pirate infrastructure it supported also created unprecedented possibilities for local cinema production and consumption. In Ghana, the first videomakers, those who took up video cameras and began producing features, were associated with commercial video reproduction and illegal exhibition. Easily and cheaply produced, unlike older forms of expensive and sophisticated mass media, video opened the making of cinema features to individuals, all of whom were men, working within commercial networks and moving their videos as commodities through those networks, which were far removed from the official, regulated, and restricted sectors of cultural production occupied by media professionals, those individuals who possessed in various forms the symbolic capital of school culture (Guillory 1995). The videomakers had no expertise in film or television production, no ties to the national film company, or to the national film school. Most had very little formal education beyond primary school. Their motives were not exclusively or even primarily artistic or educational, in part because they had not been initiated into the artistic and pedagogical discourses of Pan-Africanism or cultural nationalism. They were entrepreneurs interested in making a living by producing a commodity audiences with little disposable income would find money to buy.

The origins of commercial video production in Ghana are unlike those of Nigeria, where the production of video movies began at about the same time. In Nigeria, video production was initiated by Yoruba traveling theater artists as "the culmination of a process of adopting progressively cheaper media as the economy deteriorated" (Haynes and Okome 2000, 55). The taping of Yoruba theater performances on video was the end result of a gradual technological progression from film to video by producers with experience in performance and film production. In Ghana, the first videomakers leaped from working in exhibition or distribution to making movies on video. William Akuffo explained that he ran a video theater that exhibited illegally copied programming from aboard before he made his first feature. Prior to that, he was an importer and exhibitor of celluloid films, an experience he claims convinced him to attempt to make and exhibit a feature on video. He was confident that Ghanaians would pay to see images distorted by video projection because they had been conditioned to the low-quality images projected from scratched and faded 35mm films exhibited repeatedly, for years, when new films were no longer being brought into the country (personal communication). Socrate Safo claims to have produced the second Ghanaian video feature, *Unconditional Love*, in 1989, after he had left vocational school and had become an assistant at Sam Bea's Video Centre, the third video center to open in Accra, where owner Sam Ankrah showed pirated video-tapes of Hong Kong and Hollywood movies (personal communication). Safo said that his first "lesson" in video production occurred when he was eighteen years old. Ankrah had hired a camera operator to videotape the naming ceremony he hosted for his twins, and then he later showed the "actuality" video at his center. People who lived in his neighborhood and had attended the ceremony paid to see themselves on videotape. The following year, Safo wrote a story outline, organized a few friends, rented a VHS camera, and shot his video feature. Ankrah made his own feature called *Deliverance from the Powers of Darkness* (1990) soon after the release of Safo's video.[9]

These examples illustrate, too, that video technology, and more particularly the VHS standard, allowed for a high degree of fluidity between video reproduction and production, between legal and illegal exhibition, and between local and global media flows. Entrepreneurs established a wide array of video outlets that specialized in video taping, video duplication, and the exhibition of pirated foreign films and local video productions. At Merryland video, located near Labadi beach in Accra, for example, customers could hire a video camera or a video camera operator to record funerals, weddings, or other important events. For a small fee, they also might view a pirated copy of *Pretty Woman* (1990) or watch a legally exhibited local production at a small video theater at the back of the store. In the early years of local video feature production, in fact, the pirate and legitimate video economies operated side by side. The first Ghanaian videomakers were dependent on the pirate exhibition infrastructure that had been built for showing pirated imports on videotape to exhibit their productions. Indeed, it was access to the pirate exhibition network, not training or expertise, that was crucial to a videomakers' success. Before Akuffo made *Zinabu*, Allen Gyimah, who ran Video City Limited, produced a movie called *Abyssinia* (1985). At Video City, Gyimah employed technicians from the Ghana Broadcasting Corporation (GBC), the state-owned television station, to videotape social events, and through his contacts with GBC, he formed a partnership with Nana Bosompra, a well-known television actor and writer and a member of the Osofo Dadze concert party group. Gyimah hired members of the well-established group, which performed on television on Sunday evenings, to be in his video, assuming that the group's popularity and professionalism guaranteed the success of his movie. Unlike Akuffo, who used contacts he had established as a film distributor to premiere *Zinabu* at the Globe Cinema and then exhibit it widely at other video centers and theaters, Gyimah was not able to circulate his video outside his own video center.[10] Without entry into the pirate exhibition network, Gyimah's video, even though made by professionals, received little notice, and his place in the history of Ghanaian cinema as the first producer of a video movie has been eclipsed by the immediate popularity of Akuffo's video movie.

Some of the very qualities that made video a viable alternative for local cinema production—its mobility and flexibility—complicate the task of reconstructing the public lives of the first video movies. Obtaining copies of or information about the first video productions is enormously difficult, and the "fadeout points" (Spivak 1999, 239) of the archive unquestionably trouble the historical narrative I attempt to sketch here. Video is an ephemeral and fragile medium, and many of the first videos have degraded irrecoverably, been copied over, tossed out inadvertently, misplaced, or destroyed. At the time of their production, no one thought to preserve copies of the earliest video productions; Socrate Safo told me that he taped over his master copies in order to reuse the VHS cassettes.[11] In the first five years of local video production, well before the development of a legitimate system for the duplication and individual sale of locally produced videos, a videomaker might make no more than two copies of his production in an effort to conserve the little capital he had and protect himself from video piracy. He, or a trusted associate, delivered the video to the screening venue, where he remained until the end of the showing to collect his percentage of the gate proceeds. If the videomaker misplaced or reused his video master or one of his few copies, the video was lost. It is likely that there are video features, shown, perhaps, for short periods at a few video centers, that leave no traces of their existence behind.[12]

Gauging just how many people saw the first features is also enormously difficult. Small video centers sometimes opened and closed abruptly, and neither video centers nor film theaters maintained records of ticket sales or of revenues collected. Despite this, no doubt troubles the assertion that the first videos were hugely popular. Their commercial success and the rapid growth of the industry testify to the veracity of this claim. The demand to see *Zinabu* was so great that the Globe Cinema ran showings of it three times a day for weeks, and the video continued to play at local theaters and video centers months after its release. In 1989, Akuffo, who by this time had established his own production company, World Wide Motion Pictures, released two more successful video features, *Mobor* and the *Cult of Alata*, and Socrate Safo made *Unconditional Love I* and *II.* Seven more features were produced in 1991 and approximately fifty-two in 1993. When asked to explain the enthusiastic response to their productions, the videomakers answer simply that they provided a large market with an affordable and irresistible commodity. They appealed to audiences who looked a lot like them and the characters of their films: those who were not among the elite, but who lived in the poor urban areas where video centers were located, who didn't own television sets, and who had been hit extremely hard by a decade of economic decline. Ankrah explained that his business and the Ghanaian videos he projected there were for the "fisher folks," the fishermen and their families who lived in Bukom, one of the most economically depressed areas of the city (personal communication). William Akuffo offered that, for the first time, ordinary Ghanaians found stories about their own lives and neighborhoods at the cinema, and these audiences flocked to video centers to see videos created for them (personal communication).

Dirty Money and Wicked Women

International loaning agencies have held Ghana up as an exemplar of economic recovery, but if macroeconomic indicators substantiate the effectiveness of structural adjustment policies (SAPs), then local video productions narrate what those statistics have missed. Indeed, one explanation for the tremendous popularity of the first video features is that at a time of great social disruption and widening income disparities, the videos put forth narratives that addressed the material uncertainties many Ghanaians faced. The worldwide economic recession of the 1970s set off a terrible downturn in Ghana. Scarcities of foreign exchange, fuel, and spare parts meant that Ghanaians faced an endemic shortage of consumer goods and foodstuffs, and, between 1974 and 1980, cuts of more than two-thirds in the average wage (Nugent 1995). Development spending was drastically reduced, and as Maxwell Owusu notes, "The considerable negative impact of 'hunger' on morality, morale, and economic productivity was evident everywhere" (1996, 310).

Paul Nugent (1995) has argued that the surreal disjuncture between the severity of the economic crisis that plagued Ghana throughout the 1970s and 1980s and the unfathomable and ostentatious wealth of the Ghanaian elite provoked an ideological shift in popular consciousness. The writings of Ivor Wilks (1975) and T. C. McCaskie (1983, 1986) have documented the precolonial foundations of still powerful ideologies about wealth and the role of the state in Ghana. Private accumulation in precolonial Asante was regarded as a social act. Those who accumulated wealth earned praise and respect and were rewarded by the Asante state, whose role it was to be the guardian and promoter of collective benefits by assuring the redistribution of wealth. When faced with the severity of the economic crises of the late 1970s and early 1980s and the ever widening gap between how most Ghanaians lived and the conspicuous consumption enjoyed by the wealthy elite, people who, for centuries, had rewarded personal accumulation and trusted in the state to guarantee its dispersal for the collective good, came to view the accumulation of wealth as highly suspicious if not sinister. In this context, the brazenly brandished affluence of a small, elite segment of the population, the "big men," whose numbers included senior military officers and elite politicians, seemed wholly implausible if not otherworldly to the vast majority of Ghanaians living in abject poverty. Nugent (1995) suggests that the coupling of economic hardship and ostentatious corruption helps explain the broad-based support of the 1981 December 31st Revolution, the military coup through which Flight Lieutenant Jerry John Rawlings became head of State. J. J. Rawlings, known as "Junior Jesus," was seen as the savior who would resurrect the nation-state and bring an end to decades of national corruption and government negligence and return power to the people.

Despite the revolution's promise to improve the economy, the trends of economic hardship and income polarization continued. Confronted with the fallout of the global economic crisis of the 1970s, the Rawlings administration abandoned the socialist principles of the revolution and, under pressure from international loaning agencies, adopted a series of liberal economic reforms, or structural adjustment policies, between 1983 and 1992. This sudden move toward liberalization and privatization indicated a radical shift in policy by a government that came to power espousing socialism and People's Power. Comaroff and Comaroff have described and brilliantly theorized similar "abrupt conversion[s] to laissez-faire capitalism from tightly controlled material and moral economies" (2002, 781) as a feature of millennial capitalism common to many postcolonial countries in Africa, "where evocative calls for entrepreneurialism confront the realities of marginalization in the planetary distribution of resources; where totalizing ideologies have suddenly given way to a spirit of deregulation, with its taunting mix of desire and disappointment, liberation and limitation" (Comaroff and Comaroff 2002, 785). In Ghana, the period saw real wages drop by 80 percent, the cost of utilities and user fees increase exponentially, the Ghanaian cedi depreciate, and unemployment escalate (Boafo-Arthur 1999; Clark 2001). SAPs simultaneously unleashed a flood of foreign commodities and, as discussed earlier, images into the Ghanaian market, creating new desires for new, global things. The presence of these goods and images from abroad belied the ongoing experience of economic hardship and widening income disparities that structural adjustment, in theory, was meant to ease.

From a historical perspective, what is immediately striking about the first features is the overt and ambient presence of poverty, which was nowhere made visible in the film features produced by the Ghana Film Industry Corporation, or, for that matter, in Kwah Ansah's independently produced and contemporaneous *Heritage Africa*. The video movies also diverge dramatically from the film productions of the professionals in that they adopt the point of view of those struggling to escape urban deprivation and to partake, by any means available, of the prosperity and pleasure that seem always to reside elsewhere. In each case, money palaver generates the conflicts that drive the narratives. Characters with no money do whatever it takes to get it and once they have it, behave badly.[13] Affluence entices, but as Nugent (1995) has noted, its acquisition is thought to involve or provoke immoral action.

For characters in the videos, the occult presents one means of crossing the vast divide between poverty and wealth. As many local commentators and more recently media scholars have noted, fetish priests, juju, and witchcraft play significant parts in many Ghanaian video features, often associated with the immoral accumulation of capital and power (Meyer 1998, 1999, 2003, 2004; Wendl 2001, 2007). Although I find much of this work compelling, I fear that its limited scope has created the false impression that the occult figures prominently in all Ghanaian movies, and in regard to the first video features, that attention to the occult has overshadowed, on the one hand, the economic disparity that inflects the videos at all levels and, on the other, the significance of work, poverty, and gender to the semiotics of the amateur productions. Here, I discuss three video movies made between 1987 and 1992, *Zinabu, Big Time,* and *Menace.* These movies are typical of the first wave of video movies in that they register anxiety about the changing nature of capitalistic value made manifest in the shift from economies of production to consumption. Building on the work of Jean and John Comaroff, I emphasize that the narratives of these first features emerge from within, and speak to, a historical setting "where images of desire are as pervasive as they are inaccessible" (Comaroff and Comaroff 2002, 786) and where the connection between work and wealth has been severed clean.

Zinabu is one of few early video movies that does portray the workings of the occult in the lives of its characters.[14] In this instance, the occult transforms Kofi, a poor auto mechanic, into a rich, global consumer. He enters into an evil bargain with Zinabu, a wealthy and beautiful witch, who promises to make him "master of [her] house and of [her]," on the condition that he swears, with his life, to abstain from all sexual relations, with her or any other woman. She warns him that the last man who accepted her terms "disobeyed and paid dearly. People shouldn't break the rules without impunity." Kofi disregards the warnings of his friends who tell him that "not all that glitters is gold" and advise him to deal with Zinabu carefully because "who knows where she got her money." He accepts Zinabu's proposal and leaves his life of stark poverty to share in the pleasures provided by her immense wealth. Zinabu buys him a new car, invites him to live in her mansion with its modern conveniences, and presents him with a closet full of Western-style clothes. Made over in polished shoes, gold chain, and leopard-print shirt, Kofi proudly displays his new-found wealth, and women begin to pursue him relentlessly. Continually approached by beautiful women who want to sleep with him, he finds the promise he made to Zinabu impossible to keep. After a night of heavy drinking at a posh hotel bar, Kofi allows himself to be seduced, and just as she promised, Zinabu makes Kofi pay dearly for his deceit. In the final segment of the video Kofi is killed. The montage cuts back and forth frantically between the perspectives of Zinabu and Kofi. Zinabu, transformed from beautiful wife to horrifying witch, slices the throat of a live chicken. Shot from a low angle, with bulging eyes and a face smeared with black make-up, she is gruesome as she performs the ritual that conjures up Kofi's equally gruesome death. Trapped in his car and engulfed by a mysterious fog, he beats desperately on the windows, but is unable to escape and dies from what appears to be asphyxiation.

At one level, the movie presents a straightforward account of a man who behaves immorally, ignoring the warnings of those around him, and so suffers the consequences of his actions. Even before he accepts Zinabu's terms, Kofi devises a scheme to free himself from his promise. He considers how he can get her money, but not live the rest of his life without sex (a prospect that horrifies him). He assures himself, and the eavesdropping audience, that when the promise proves too hard to keep, he will take his money and go abroad. When Kofi succumbs to his sexual desires, breaks his pledge to Zinabu, and is killed, he gets what he deserves. As Esi Sutherland-Addy has written "the outward veneer of wealth is depicted as both spawning and masking other evils, including sexual promiscuity and criminal activity" (2000, 270). Kofi is doubly duplicitous. Not only does he earn wealth immorally by entering into a partnership with a witch, but he breaks his vow to her because he is unable to quell his appetite for sex.

The visualization of consumption and the desires it expresses, however, challenge the certainty intended by this didactic narrative. *Zinabu* produces a profound ambivalence about wealth, at once warning against the evils it provokes and fantasizing about the pleasures it makes possible. Meyer's discussion of the video *Nkrabea* (1992) makes a similar point. She explains that while the feature associates money and power with immorality, money also "is represented as the source of prestige and esteem" (1998, 18). Put slightly differently, I would emphasize that while the thematic trajectory of the first features is didactic, the attractions and pleasures offered by the camera's exhibitionist gaze engage the spectator's curiosity about and desire for commodities and pleasurable consumption. Within the videos' narratives, those who cheat and scheme to get rich, or behave selfishly or immorally when they become rich, suffer, but in gazing upon the enormous mansions, new cars, and flashy clothes money buys, the camera simultaneously desires the commodities conspicuously consumed before it, undercutting the videos' explicit message that wealth is a corrupting force in modern life. In other words, the positioning of the spectator in relation to what is seen contradicts the pedagogical intent of the videos.

This tension organizes the narrative of Kofi's leap from poverty to affluence. Kofi's transformation becomes an occasion for the spectator to embark on a tour of the pleasures of consumption. Donning new clothes and driving his imported car, Kofi treats his old friends to shoes and suits and takes them on excursions to the hot spots of the city. Focalized through Kofi's point of view, the camera follows the escapades of Kofi and his friends, who dance at nightclubs, get massages on the beach, and feast on plates heaped with food. It celebrates as it participates in their conspicuous spending and offers its audience the pleasure of imaginatively experiencing places and recreation made possible by Kofi's newfound wealth. Through these displays of pleasure, the audience virtually consumes what it sees. Excruciatingly slow, rarely edited, these urban adventure segments seem strangely out of place. Such moments of aesthetic failure, however, might be read as expository and spectacular moments that fragment the unfolding of narrative time. Tom Gunning's (2004) term "aesthetic of astonishment," which he uses to describe the attractions of early film, aptly captures the identification elicited and pleasures on offer.

> Rather than being an involvement with narrative action or empathy with character psychology, the cinema of attractions solicits a highly conscious awareness of the film image engaging the viewer's curiosity. The spectator does not get lost in a fictional world and its dramas, but remains aware of the act of looking, the excitement of curiosity and its fulfillment. (869)

Another common spectacular sequence found in many video features assembles long takes and slow pans of the landscaped lawns and lavishly furnished homes of the rich. In *Zinabu*, the first time Kofi enters Zinabu's home, the camera moves from room to room and wall to wall, inventorying the electronics, furniture, and kitchen appliances. (A variation on this occurs in *Big Time*, when the camera scans the body of a new Hyundai, from front fender to trunk, inside and out.) The camera pans leisurely over the commodities Zinabu's dirty money has enabled her to acquire. This gaze, initially, is loosely linked with Kofi's astonished look; we see what he sees and what amazes him when he first enters her home. But the montage violates the illusion of subjective perspective, reaching well beyond Kofi's range of sight and opening out to the video's audience. The display no longer imitates Kofi's gaze, but directly engages the spectator, playing upon the viewer's desire to consume goods and pleasures she/he cannot afford.

This way of looking seems to me unlike the Christian and voyeuristic gaze Birgit Meyer (2004) has described as a feature of many Ghanaian video movies. For Meyer, the camera simulates God's omniscient sight. Viewers, like God, peer into the realm of the occult: "They are addressed as viewer-believers and even voyeurs peeping into the otherwise forbidden" (Meyer 2004, 104). When applied to certain moments in the Pentecostal occult videos Meyer examines, this description is persuasive. But video movies are not monolithic, nor are they controlled by one dominant way of looking or mode of narration. They are a hodgepodge of looks, conventions, modes, and genres. Heterogeneity is an especially pronounced feature of the first videos, whose creators, in most cases, simply lacked the technical skills to achieve seamless coherence or even the aesthetic sensibilities to value univocality and consistency. This close reading of a few of the first video movies illustrates that many video movies, including occult videos like *Zinabu*, also address their viewers as consumers who take pleasure in looking at and imaginatively consuming goods put on display. If the Pentecostal video camera plays God, then this camera of attractions advertises luxurious lifestyles and produces the desire to have things.

The materiality of the first videos compromises the shine of the consumer surfaces displayed there. Low quality analog images washed out by generational loss and poorly produced and distorted soundtracks— the residue left behind by low budget VHS production and reproduction—frustrate the videomaker's attempt to create a convincing spectacle of consumption and accumulation, and, instead, express the poverty and deprivation that characterize the video's making. Brian Larkin (2004) has described an "aesthetic of piracy" that similarly inflects Nigerian video movies. Local videos reproduced, distributed, and exhibited legitimately, but through the pirate infrastructure, share certain features with pirated media. Much like Lucas Hilderbrand's "bootleg aesthetics" (2004), Larkin's pirate aesthetics describes "a set of formal qualities that generates a particular sensorial experience of media marked by poor transmission, interference, and noise" (2004, 291). Larkin and Hilderbrand elaborate on the distinct quality of analog video reproduction and consumption, characterized by resolution loss, degradation, and deterioration, which becomes a kind of "technological veil" (Larkin 2004, 308) through which the spectator experiences the diegetic world of the video text. When what the viewer is meant to see is a magnificent representation of wealth's luxuries, this technological screen, in effect, challenges the images and themes standing behind it. It continuously calls attention to Ghana's marginalized position on the periphery of global media and new technologies.

I also want to add, building on Larkin, that analog reproduction is but one dimension of the aesthetic of the first Ghanaian video features. Their very low budget and amateur production values create another, complementary, layer. The cheaply and rather haphazardly made video features reenact and render immediate the dire economic situations of their creators and patrons, erasing the distance between the audience and the video narrative. The first video productions were shot with rented VHS cameras as quickly and inexpensively as possible. Videomakers had no money or outside financial support to sponsor their productions. They rarely hired professional actors or crews, and instead relied on the assistance of friends and family. To cut down on rental charges, artist fees, and production expenses, production crews were small: perhaps one person to hold one boom microphone, and another to operate the camera, although many directors also doubled as camera operators. The result was a video overlaid by what Stephen Heath and Gillian Skirrow (1977) have described as the impression of reality. The camera was rarely steady and shots often arbitrarily or badly composed. Working without sets or studios, videomakers shot their features in real locations, which often would be the home of a friend or relative, a local restaurant, or local business. A spectator watched a story enacted in an actual setting in the midst of people who often gave themselves away by looking into the camera. Even if entirely fictional and often fantastic, the first videos seemed strangely real and alive, more like home movies than feature films. Other qualities typically associated with home video productions inflect the earliest Ghanaian movies: abrupt shifts in time and location, rapid camera movements, jump cuts, and illogical shifts in perspective and point of view. These material artifacts of production interfere with the videomaker's attempt to produce a sleek, centrally focalized, Hollywood-style narrative. Yet they simultaneously signify the poverty that the characters within the diegesis long to evade, producing a shared reality of hardship between those characters and the Ghanaian audience.

Like all of the first video productions, *Zinabu* clearly delineates the disparities between the poor and the rich. Dress, speech, and eating habits signify poverty or wealth as bodies act out their economic status. The opening scene of the video stages a confrontation between an extravagantly dressed rich man, who remains unnamed, and the video's protagonist, Kofi, who we first see wearing an oil-stained and ripped uniform. The two men exchange insults on the street because Kofi inadvertently steps in front of the well-dressed "Big Man." As the man roughly shoves Kofi aside, climbs into his new car, and drives away, Kofi

Figure 2.1. Mechanics at work (*Zinabu*, 1999)

spies the lovely Zinabu, sitting beside her rich companion. He instantly falls in love. The next scene, set in the yard of an auto mechanic's shop, finds three mechanics, Kofi, with his co-workers Joe and Mark, discussing Kofi's encounter with Zinabu and debating the possibility of love between a rich woman and a poor man. The men talk while they work under the hood of an old car. Joe and Mark insist that Kofi is foolishly wasting his time on this beautiful stranger because a rich woman would never love him, a poor mechanic. "Can you eat love?" Joe demands. "Small monkey play with small monkey, and big monkey with big monkey." The three mechanics not only dress shabbily, but speak a blend of English and Ga. Zinabu, on the other hand, wears clothes that are immaculate, flashy, and stylish, and she speaks only English, which operates as a linguistic signifier of wealth.[15]

The first videos elicit humor when poor characters cannot read the codes of affluence. In *Zinabu*, a long and comical segment of the video observes Kofi alone in his room in Zinabu's mansion. He marvels at the large bed, peers excitedly into a closet full of clothes, and, in the bath, mistakes the shower head for a telephone, receiving a spray of water in his ear when he turns on the tap. Similarly, when Kofi treats his friends to a dinner of spaghetti, the video invites the audience to laugh as they struggle with the long, slippery noodles, fumbling and slurping while the other diners stare and snicker. A similar use of humor appears in *Menace*, when Kwaku and Esi arrive in Accra from the village, wearing their poverty. Mismatched patches mottle Kwaku's pants, and Esi carries a large bunch of plantains awkwardly on her head. When the couple arrives at Kwaku's wealthy cousin's compound, Doris, Kwaku's niece, answers the door and tells her mother, disparagingly, that the "villagers" have arrived. The cousins share a meal with their city relatives, and the villagers struggle with the knives and forks laid at the table for them. Their "bush" antics mark them as poor and invite the ridicule of Doris and her mother and the laughter of the audience.

In fact, food—what one eats and how one eats it—functions as a particularly pronounced marker of the economic in *Zinabu* and many Ghanaian video features. Videos sometimes seem preoccupied with eating and often include shots and even scenes, completely extraneous to their narratives, of food being consumed. We watch Kofi, Joe, and Mark eat kenkey and pepper with their hands, but Zinabu serves Kofi a large plate of rice and chicken, shown in close-up, in her extravagant home, and she eats with a knife and fork, inviting him to do the same. In a subsequent scene, Kofi, remade and rich, returns to his old neighborhood to pick up his friends. He finds them sharing a ball of kenkey and kicks over the table. The camera pauses to take in the spilled and spoiled remains of their meal. He tells them they will not have to eat such food again, and as they turn their backs on kenkey, they walk away from their lives of depravity.

The antagonism between poverty and affluence aligns with an opposition between work and consumption. The opening segments of *Zinabu* emphasize that Kofi is a worker, and his poverty is directly associated with the work he does, work that has little value because it does not allow him to buy the most basic of provisions. This point is underlined through a series of flashbacks Kofi experiences before agreeing to Zinabu's terms. He recounts the humiliation and rejection meted out by women who were repulsed by his shabby clothes and dingy room, which lacks running water and electricity. (One woman, offended by Kofi's appearance, spits on him.) These reminders of his deprivation and low status convince Kofi to accept Zinabu's offer, and in doing so, he abandons the realm of labor and production and lurches into an identity as a global consumer. Consumption not only operates independent of production in *Zinabu*, but opposes it. Kofi is a laborer until he encounters Zinabu, who correlates with immoral and excessive consumption.

More a metaphor than a historical subject, Zinabu stands in for consumption divorced from production, and her figure invokes the idioms of witchcraft narratives so prevalent in West African popular culture (Bastian 1993, 2001; Parish 1999, 2000). Zinabu is an improper accumulator who preys upon those with whom she is intimate, interfering with their social and sexual reproduction. More specific to Ghanaian history, her figure recasts the stereotype of the greedy and corrupt antirevolutionary woman, an image dominant during the years surrounding the Thirty-First December Revolution. In rhetoric sponsored by proponents of the revolution, in popular fiction, the news media, and letters published in Ghanaian newspapers, wealthy women, known as "good-time girls" and "Makola queens" (market women), signified illicit accumulation and corruption. Emmanuel Akyeampong has argued that the worsening economy of the 1970s and '80s pushed women into the workforce and marketplace suddenly and in large numbers. Market women especially became visible symbols of the illicit acquisition of wealth, and "urban workers who could neither attack the corrupt Ghanaian government nor their protected mistresses, blamed ordinary market women for the high cost of living and all Ghana's social ills" (Akyeampong 1996, 152). Garcia Clark remarks that "official media condemned wealthy traders because they were insubordinate women insisting on earning as much as men" (1994, 419). Wealthy traders were "signaled out as 'enemies of the people'" (Manuh 1995, 116), and their very physicality as women used to justify the violence and harassment perpetuated against them by soldiers and militiamen in defense of the revolution. The rhetoric culminated in periods of intense violence against women. In 1979, the Makola Number One Market, the center of trading activity in Accra, was looted and demolished (blown up with dynamite) by soldiers, and female traders accused of price control offenses "were officially beaten, caned, and flogged naked" (Clark 1994, 383). In 1982, after the Rawlings Revolution, another eruption of violence occurred. The pages of the *Ghanaian Daily Graphic* during this period recount incident after incident of the "disciplining" of market women. Like the greedy Makola queen, Zinabu is a powerful and economically independent woman. The film makes this point emphatically when, as she and Kofi arrive at her beautiful mansion, and he asks her why she does not have a houseboy, watchman, or maid, she replies that she is alone, without a husband, and is "capable" of taking care of "my own home." But her independence is abnormal and frightening; her affluence has no source, nor does she, as a wife or mother, produce or reproduce. As a beautiful and monstrous witch, she is ambivalent. She at once signifies the negative connotations attributed to wealth mysteriously obtained and the allure of affluence. She empowers and disables; the economic power Zinabu gives Kofi depends on a kind of self-imposed castration, a physical and figurative lack.

In *Big Time* and *Menace*, gender difference similarly structures the divide between production and consumption. In Ramesh Jai's *Big Time* (1989), Nana and Yaw, a married couple, represent two articulations of capitalism: Nana defines herself through consumption while Yaw defends the moral value of labor. Nana, born into a rich family but now married to a "common working man," a bank teller, covets the cosmopolitan lifestyles of her friends, whose husbands travel abroad regularly, returning with dresses from London and New York. With the help of her drunken and greedy con-artist brother Lumo, Nana finds work as a drug runner and prostitute, receiving large bundles of cash for the drugs and sex she delivers. She gets the riches she desires, but only by prostituting herself and getting entangled with dangerous criminals. When Yaw learns how his wife has been earning money, he turns her in to the police. In the end, she, like Kofi, pays for her immorally acquired wealth.

Jai, unlike many of the first videomakers, had some professional training in video production. He made his feature when he was a student at the National Film and Television Institute (NAFTI), and his two years of instruction do distinguish his video from the movies made by untrained Ghanaian producers. Jai is aware of the technical limitations of VHS video, and instead of attempting to produce a Hollywood film with a video camera, he shoots his video more modestly, more like a soap opera that an imperfectly executed feature film. Jai, seemingly aware of video's extreme depth of field and limited dynamic range, favors interior settings and tightly composed scenes, and unlike *Zinabu*, which adopts Kofi's perspective throughout, *Big Time*, like a soap opera, moves among various points of view, principally moving between Yaw's and Nana's perspectives. Nonetheless, Jai's movie, shot with one camera instead of three, as is typical in soap opera production, does not quite achieve the effect it intends. The montage, pieced together from multiple retakes of scenes, appears fractured and in flux. A second take of a scene cannot replicate the first, and slight disruptions created by shifts in actors' positions or in the placement of lights or the camera continually disturb the illusion of a stable time and space. The sound quality is extremely poor, and the narrative, implausible and didactic, is compromised by the performance of its nonprofessional actors. In these ways, *Big Time* exhibits the analog and amateur aesthetics common among the first Ghanaian videos.

Jai's video tells a story about "money palaver," the phrase used by Yaw to describe the ongoing battle between him and his wife over money. Nana wants a lot of money and is willing to do whatever it takes to get it. When her brother offers to help her find a job that will bring her quick and easy riches, she assures him that she does not care "if this job is a kalabule one. All I want is the money."[16] Yaw, on the other hand, believes that reward comes only through hard and honest work. As far as Yaw is concerned, consumption means little. "Times are changing, Nana, and you don't know what the future holds for us. I am saving for the future."

The video includes several references to luck, a force that operates in the gap between production and consumption and guarantees "abundance without effort" (Comaroff and Comaroff 2002, 781). Lumo laughs when his sister seeks his counsel and assistance in finding a job that will allow her to have all she desires. He points to a neighbor with "two Benz cars" and assures her that his money did not come from "any hard work of his." Work cannot guarantee wealth, but luck does. Nana calls herself a "lucky lady" when Lumo introduces her to the head of the drug ring and she is hired as a courier. The video cuts between an ongoing debate between Yaw and a male colleague (who is not named) about luck and Nana's encounters with the drug pushers of the underworld. Yaw's co-worker tells Yaw about a man who "one day was driving a very rickety old car, and the next, a brand new Benz." The man, he says, found "luck." Yaw, however, insists that luck does not exist and only hard work brings real rewards. His colleague assures him that "the day opportunity knocks on my door, I will open it wide." And, indeed, he does. Like the protagonist of his story, Yaw's friend appears one day with a brand new car. When Yaw asks him how it got it, he tells Yaw he made sure that a very important man got the loan he wanted. The corrupt male banker's luck brings him what he desires. Nana, the greedy wife, is not so fortunate.

Nana might be described as a secularized version of Zinabu. She, too, is an improper accumulator and not a mother, nor a proper wife.

She refuses to sleep with her husband, and when Yaw insists that it is time for them to start a family, Nana puts him off. She assures him that she will become a mother once she has all the money she needs. The video makes no reference to the occult, but like Zinabu, Nana accumulates money immorally and without working or producing anything of value. (At various points, Nana expresses satisfaction that she earns loads of money without doing any work.) She embodies the unrestrained desire to consume and through consumption articulates her new, cosmopolitan identity. She tells Yaw, "I want to travel, dress in fine clothes" and wear "jewelry." She asks her husband "When other people are leading the good life you want me to live like a beggar?" The good life, for Nana, means having the ability to be a global consumer, to buy imported foods and alcohol, to travel overseas, and to drive an imported car. Nana and the circle of friends with whom she meets regularly interrogate one another about their husbands' overseas travel plans, whether or not a new dress comes from New York or Amsterdam, and how much it cost. The video posits a direct correspondence between a commodity's place in the global market and its value. All good things come from abroad.

The consuming and desiring female body becomes a diseased body in Richard Quartey's *Menace* (1992). Kwaku and Esi escape from their lives of poverty in the village and come to the city where Kwaku works hard to find success, moving rapidly up the economic ladder to become the manager of a furniture store. For Kwaku, hard work pays off, but once he has money, he misuses his wealth, assuming the airs of a "big man" and betraying his loyal wife, Esi, by taking the beautiful Sophia as a mistress. On the very day he announces to his wife that he has "made it," he sees Sophia on the street and offers her a ride home in his new car. Unbeknownst to Kwaku, Sophia isn't what she appears to be. A good-time girl who likes money and earns it by deceiving and seducing men, Sophia has AIDS and infects Kwaku, who infects his wife. In the end, Kwaku's treachery and greed, born of his new acquired and selfishly consumed wealth, destroys his household.

In the opening segment of the video, before the credits run, the audience watches a deranged woman escape from a hospital and, after being chased by her two assailants, invite the men to rape her. She stabs one of the men in the back while he violates her, and announces to the other after he has finished, "You now have HIV." When Kwaku meets Sophia on the street, the audience recognizes Sophia as the mad woman with HIV featured in the opening. The narrational strategy of the video, then, builds around and emphasizes Kwaku's downfall. He is the honest worker seduced, first by wealth and then by treacherous and beautiful Sophia.

Sophia, like her predecessors, Zinabu and Nana, is a voracious consumer. She, figuratively, eats men, exchanging sex for their lives. Sophia escorts men in and out of her small apartment, taking a fistful of money from each as he departs. But it is not until Kwaku has left his wife, Esi, and proposed to Sophie that he learns of her promiscuity. He unexpectedly arrives at her home and finds her with another man. He calls off the marriage and begs Esi to take him back, apologizing for his terrible mistake and selfishness. The loyal and true wife, Esi, a rather obvious foil to Sophia, forgives Kwaku and soon becomes pregnant. Meanwhile, Sophia visits a hospital where she is told that she has AIDS. The unfolding of Kwaku and Esi's renewed love is disrupted by the onset of Sophia's illness. Long, unedited scenes show her vomiting and writhing in agony. Her body transforms, before the camera, into pure abjection and suffering. Clearly, by featuring Sophia as a body in pain, the video aims to warn audiences of the dangers of unprotected sex and HIV, and this lesson is linked to its critique of excessive consumption. It unambiguously reiterates gender difference. AIDS is a disease of consumption spread by a consuming female body; Sophia's body takes and takes, and what it produces is death. When Esi and Kwaku's baby is born with HIV, the couple learns that, they too, are infected.

Through the figure of the monstrous and beautiful woman, the features discussed here reject the drift toward global consumption and consumerism and away from honest and moral work, and they document and speak out against the dire economics of their creation. The consuming female figure, represented by Zinabu, Nana, and Sophia, embodies the anxieties and ambivalence generated by new forms of consumerism and economic individualism, and in this, she is similar to the monstrous feminine theorized by Barbara Creed (1993) in that she is a "site of conflicting desires" (11). From the point of view of the male protagonist and the perspective of the spectator, she repels and attracts, much as do the commodities she greedily consumes.

Amateurs and Artists: Critical Reception as Symbolic Struggle

The untrained videomakers established new circuits of cinema production and consumption completely outside of the state-controlled,

professional cinema industry. They entered cinema production as viewers and commercial exhibitors, not as trained producers of movies,
and they had not been initiated into the cultural-nationalist, artistic,
or pedagogical discourses that defined and maintained the work of
trained filmmakers in Ghana. It is probably not surprising, then, that
professional filmmakers in Ghana, without exception, greeted local
video production with utter derision. In a scathing column entitled
"To Be or Not to Be a Filmmaker" (1988), filmmaker Ato Yanney
called for government regulation of film production because "auto
mechanics, circumcisers, [and] lotto receivers" have "started to make
crowd-pleasing motion pictures in Ghana" and have created the "mis-
leading impression . . . that one does not have to go to film school
to be in a position to make films" (*Mirror,* August 22, 1988). Quoting extensively from *The Work of the Film Director* (Reynertson 1970),
Yanney contended that because video producers lack formal training,
their movie-making efforts should be prohibited. In Ghana, he complained, "filmmaking, unlike medicine and other professions which
are strictly out of bounds to the unqualified, has no restrictive rules
because it is an art."

Singled out for especially virulent criticism were the videos
that incorporated, in any way, the occult, those supernatural forces
lodged safely away in the remote village in films by the Gold Coast
Film Unit and denied or ignored in films by the national film company. As this discussion has made a point to show, not all of the first
videos, however, were about juju, witchcraft, or fetish priests. But
for the professional filmmakers, popular video was synonymous with
narratives about the occult, which stood in for all that was deemed
inauthentic and offensive. Chris Hesse, former director of GFIC,
described the videos of the "amateurs" as "all juju" and completely
out-of-line with Kwame Nkrumah's vision of the pedagogical and
political roles of cinema in modern Africa. He compared the videomakers to members of "the colonial regime" who were "telling us
blacks what we were supposed to be" (personal communication). He
explained, "The early videomakers were trying to follow the same
pattern by shooting films on juju, nakedness, hunger, pain, suffering, what the whites were thinking that we were" in order to make
money.[17] In an interview with Kofi Anyidoho, Kwaw Ansah characterized local video productions as following "a very dangerous trend"
(2000, 312). He elaborates on the urgent need for every production
screened in Ghana to pass through a rigorous censorship process "to

ensure that it does not insult black people's integrity" (313). In an interview with me, Ansah argued that many Ghanaian video movies recycled and reaffirmed colonial stereotypes about Africa and Africans, sometimes setting African traditions against foreign ideologies and Christianity (personal communication).

This contemptuous dismissal of local video features and outright misrepresentation of their content, when seen in the context of the major technological and structural transformations of the 1980s, signifies the uncertainty and anxiety experienced by professional filmmakers and their agents in the absence of state support for their film projects or state regulation of new global and local media forms. This anxiety is clearly expressed in several film-related news articles that appeared in Nanabanyin Dadson's Arts and Entertainment column, perhaps the most comprehensive news source for film and video in the country at the time. In a column titled "Filmmaking Pangs," filmmaker Asamoah-Okae asked the government "to consider seriously the building of a colour laboratory as this will boost filmmaking by cutting down drastically the amount of foreign currency a producer requires to produce a film" (1987). Dadson's article, "Diary from Ouagadougou: Part One" (1987a), described 1987 as a pivotal year for film and video production, but not because it was the year Akuffo produced the first widely watched and locally produced video feature in Ghana, in effect, bringing Ghanaian cinema to the screens of Ghana. Dadson drew his reader's attention to 1987 as the first year since the founding of the Pan-African Film Festival of Ouagadougou (FESPACO) that "Ghanaian entries . . . could not win a prize—a fact that must violently jerk the government and all persons concerned with the fortunes of filmmaking in this country to sit up and show more concern." In "Diary from Ouagadougou: Part Two" (1987b), Dadson argued that only with government support and regulation of the film industry "shall we be able to benefit as a nation from the enlightenment that films are bringing daily to other countries." The widely publicized struggle of Kwaw Ansah to finance his award-winning film *Heritage Africa* received substantial coverage and commentary. One noteworthy article, "Kwaw Ansah: To Film and Back" (1987c), described Ansah's preparations to leave Accra for London to complete postproduction work on the film. Dadson reported that Ansah "has dropped a hint that he might quit filmmaking" because he "has had enough problems making others, especially funding institutions, see the importance of film in a developing country like Ghana."[18]

The wide availability of video technology and pirated global media, the birth of a thriving local and commercial video market, and most crucially the inability of the state to regulate or support cinema, generated a fierce symbolic struggle within the field of cultural production, one similar to that theorized by Pierre Bourdieu in "The Market of Symbolic Goods" (1985). Bourdieu describes transformations in the field of cultural production in Europe brought about by the dissolution of "aristocratic and ecclesiastical tutelage" (14) that began near the end of the Renaissance and accelerated during the industrial revolution. He explains that mass production and the expansion of primary education made possible "an ever growing, ever more diversified corps of producers and purveyors of symbolic goods" that effectively replaced centralized sources of legitimacy (the aristocracy and the church) and created the conditions for "a competition for cultural legitimacy" (14). This process of diversification, differentiation, and competition was accompanied by the development of two interrelated spheres of cultural production: the field of restricted production, "a system producing cultural goods objectively designed for a public of producers of cultural goods" and the field of large-scale cultural production, "specifically organized with a view to the production of cultural goods destined for non-producers of cultural goods, 'the public at large'" (17). According to Bourdieu, the divide between restricted or artistic production and large-scale or mass production, which surfaces after the breakdown of centralized and external legitimating sources, prepares the way for the emergence of an autonomous artistic field and "a pure theory of art" (16). Within the context of struggle, then, artists and their agents produce a critical discourse that functions to "affirm the irreducibility of the work of art to the status of a simple article of merchandise and, at the same time, the singularity of the intellectual and artistic condition" (16) in order that they distinguish the work of art from mass-produced, commercial products.

Key differences distinguish Bourdieu's European example from the Ghanaian case. Ghanaian video is not a mass-produced cultural commodity. As described in earlier sections of this book, its processes of production and consumption in the industry's first years were artisanal and decentralized. It was, however, a commodity produced and circulated within a market-oriented sphere that ran parallel to, but did not intersect with, the state-controlled network of official cultural production, and its development, although made possible by new video technologies, was, at least in part, assisted by the dissolution of state structures of regulation. The breakdown of the state as a centralized source of the production and legitimization of cultural goods created a crisis of legitimacy for professional Ghanaian filmmakers who, in response, attempted to disassociate "art-as-commodity from art-as-pure symbolism" (Bourdieu 1985, 16). At the time of *Zinabu's* release, GFIC refused to allow its filmmakers to produce features on video. Hesse, the managing director of GFIC, regarded video as a broadcast medium and a tool for amateurs (personal communication). Video, according to Akuffo, was thought to be a "kid's affair." When Akuffo approached GFIC with the idea for his video feature, the film company, in Akuffo's words, "wanted nothing to do with video" (personal communication). Akuffo subsequently organized his own production, and when it came time to exhibit his video, he again approached GFIC because it owned and operated the majority of film theaters in the country, and, again, GFIC refused him.[19]

Artistic criticism and commentary, in Bourdieu's example, function to define and maintain the border between the two spheres of cultural production. In Ghana, critical discourse about film and video, published primarily in newspapers, served a similar purpose. In the absence of effectual state controls to define and maintain official cultural production, journalistic writing about film took on this policing function. Film reviews, informative pieces about film, and letters to the editor demarcated a field of restricted, artistic production through its absolute difference from commercial production. Within this discourse, "authenticity" represented professional-produced, cultural-nationalist films as purely symbolic products that tapped into and preserved "traditional" African values. Although the videomakers produced "crowd-pleasing" features solely to make money, the professionals' art films embraced a higher aim: to fulfill the objectives on which the national industry was founded in celebrating authentic African culture and refuting colonial stereotypes. Film reviews and news articles published in the *Mirror* highlighted and reviewed only films produced by professionally trained filmmakers, films that "aim[ed] at preserving and promoting Ghana's cultural heritage" (January 23, 1988) and that drew from "an inexhaustible store of traditions and folklore" (May 14, 1988).

In 1988 and 1989, Nanabanyin Dadson's Arts and Entertainment section enthusiastically campaigned for the independently produced *Heritage Africa*. Dadson devoted extensive coverage to Ansah and his film, including weekly production updates and announcements about the international acclaim the film was receiving. *Heritage Africa*, in addition to winning the Grand Prix at FESPACO, received the Organization for African Unity's Best Film Award and the Outstanding Film Award at the 1989 London Film Festival. Local box office returns for the film, nonetheless, were very low, exacerbating Ansah's financial difficulties and leading to his much-publicized exit from filmmaking. Nevertheless, Ansah's film was called "a savior" to "the film industry in Ghana" (*Mirror*, May 6, 1988), while Akuffo's video *Zinabu*, appearing to packed theaters and video centers throughout the country, was virtually expunged from the historical archive. Dadson stated in a personal interview that he regarded video as an unfortunate trend and hoped that if he ignored it long enough, it would disappear. *The Mirror* ran only one story announcing *Zinabu's* release and reviewing it. In the article titled *"Zinabu:* A Pioneering Film" (1987d), Dadson, in fact, refused to refer to *Zinabu* as film, or video. He described it as "a *project* born out of enthusiasm, determination and dogged effort" and commended the "idea behind the *project*," proclaiming that "Akuffo's *aim* is a laudable one" that could "revolutionize the film industry in Ghana as regards the great number of films that could be turned out" (italics mine). The review commented on the cinematic qualities of *Zinabu* in one line: "The story is hardly plausible and the technicalities are not perfect."

The beginning of video feature production marks a radical shift in African cinematic practice. Video technology allowed individuals situated outside of a dying national film industry, and therefore without professional training or expertise, to produce and exhibit video features unregulated as commodities and artistic objects. Produced during a historical moment when most Ghanaians faced tremendous financial uncertainty, the humor and suspense, the very pleasure of the first Ghanaian videos derived from a shared understanding between spectator and protagonist of the ubiquity of poverty and corruption. In 1992, the year that I consider to signal the end of the truly amateur early period of video feature production in Ghana, Socrate Safo made *Ghost Tears*, the highest grossing video feature in the industry's short history. The success of *Ghost Tears* brought many new videomakers into the industry, including many recent graduates from the National Film and Television Institute and employees of the national film company. Among the new videomakers were many of the most vociferous critics of "amateur" and inauthentic popular video, and their work as actors, directors, editors, and production crew members changed the industry drastically. Instead of seeing through the eyes of ordinary Ghanaians and looking suspiciously upon extreme wealth, the videos' vision normalized the fantasy of middle-class comfort. As the following chapter explains, the economic hardships of the urban poor fade into a fuzzy background, while the domestic disputes and familial conflicts of elite Ghanaians come into sharp focus.

3

Professional Movies and Their Global Aspirations

The Second Wave of Video Production in Ghana

Across Africa, the 1990s brought unprecedented transformation into local media ecologies (Teer-Tomaselli, de Beer, and Wasserman 2007). In Ghana these changes were ushered in with the country's first democratic elections in 1992. Now president, Rawlings continued to direct the country toward economic liberalization. Throughout the 1990s, the deregulation of the state-controlled media environment, a central component of liberalization, opened the country to a multiplicity of global media flows and made available an extraordinary array of local, national, and transnational sources of news, information, and entertainment. Deregulation also made possible the further proliferation of private FM radio stations (Gifford 2004) and independent newspapers (Hasty 2005), as well as enabling the establishment of two free-to-air, private television stations, TV3 and Metro TV. New media transmission and distribution technologies, including direct broadcast satellite, cable television, and VCRs, further diversified the media landscape in Ghana and significantly broadened access to it (Dal Yong Jin 2007; Teer-Tomaselli, de Beer, and Wasserman 2007). Multichoice Africa, a subsidiary of MNet, South Africa's first private television station, began providing satellite transmission to Ghana in 1993, while the number of Ghanaians owning television sets multiplied.[1] As is the case with Nigeria (Ugor 2009), Ghana also experienced an influx of inexpensive and portable media technologies from China, Japan, and Singapore, which expanded the range and reach of global media content in the country and increased the speed at which it became available. And at a time when theater patronage throughout the country decreased, these new technologies, including video CDs (VCDs), DVDs, and compatible players in the late 1990s, contributed to the ongoing privatization of movies and other media.

These dramatic changes in the economic and structural organization of film and media institutions and the opening of the media landscape to new global media flows corresponded to the development of a more organized and regulated commercial video industry and the introduction of more professionalized video productions in Ghana between 1992 until around 2000. In this period, the divestiture of the Ghana Film Industry Corporation (GFIC) diminished opportunities for employment with state institutions, and many trained film and videomakers entered commercial video production, bringing into the nascent industry movies that represented deliberate attempts to professionalize a cultural field overcrowded with what were deemed substandard products. Among the most popular examples of the professional movies were the GAMA Films release *Jennifer* (1998) and Veronica Quarshie's *Stab in the Dark* series (1999–2003). Citing Hollywood as their model, these producers and directors claimed to be trying to upgrade and improve the poor quality of movies prevalent in the field, offering Ghanaian audiences video productions that were more "professional" than the videos produced during the industry's earliest years.

Part of the professionalism of these new videomakers was their absolute refusal to take on topics in any way affiliated with witchcraft, the occult, or blood money. Videomakers who trained at NAFTI or GFIC or who were graduates of the School of Performing Arts at Legon, in particular, aspired to a more global or cosmopolitan style. They wanted to make movies that did not represent Ghana negatively to a global audience and more than that, movies that were not tethered to the local context, like a witchcraft video or a movie produced in the Akan language would be. They aimed to achieve what they described as a global product that could be compared to a Hollywood film. The movies signal their cosmopolitan, professional aspirations in three registers. First, professional videos adopt themes and modes of narration that distance their story-worlds from the poverty and economic decline that were central to the first video movies.[2] Unlike the earliest productions, professional movies made during the second wave of video production in Ghana close off the social. Centered on the domestic realm and animated by characters' personal, moral choices, they turn inward in their representation of subjectivity and space. Second, professional movies also deploy the trope of consumerism to gesture toward global fantasy vistas that transcend the local. Made visible in patches, the cityscape appears as a site of global consumerism, and characters in these movies express their cosmopolitanism by purchasing luxury goods from elsewhere. Finally, several movies perform a professional style by engaging women's issue and gender discourses; *Jennifer* and the *Stab in the Dark* series, the examples discussed here, actively enter discussions about gender and women's rights. Through gender talk, characters in these movies assert themselves as active participants in global gender debates and gesture toward political affiliations that link the local to the global.[3]

Merging Modes of Production, Exhibition, and Distribution

Between 1992 and 2000 the embryonic video industry described in the previous chapter experienced vigorous growth, driven largely by the commercial success of *Ghost Tears* (1992), at the time the highest grossing feature in the industry. While the private video industry expanded, the national film company contracted. Under pressure from the IMF to divest state-owned corporations, the Rawlings government sold 51 percent of its shares in the Ghana Film Industry Corporation (GFIC) to a Malaysian consortium in 1996. The terms of the sale indicated that the Malaysian company would establish the first independent TV station in Ghana, TV3, as well as oversee the operation of the film company, now renamed GAMA Film Company Limited. The divestiture devastated national film production: money, resources, and expertise were channeled into TV3; state-owned theaters were closed or sold; and film equipment fell into disrepair. Confronting the lack of state resources available to them as a result of economic liberalization and witnessing the achievements of independent video producers, significant numbers of recent graduates of the state film school, the National Film and Television Institute (NAFTI), and employees of GAMA Film joined the growing commercial video industry.

The divestiture of GFIC and the migration of trained film- and videomakers affiliated with official cultural institutions into the burgeoning commercial video industry muddied the lines that in the industry's earliest years distinguished professional from amateur productions, filmmakers from videomakers, and state-sponsored from commercial movies. The distinctions between entrepreneurial amateurs, who were said to produce escapist rubbish for profit, and committed professionals, whose cultural-nationalist films were regarded as authentic African art made for the good of the nation, became difficult to maintain. Although it is true that the first productions of William Akuffo and Socrate Safo, *Zinabu* and *Unconditional Love*, respectively, were shot on home video cameras and edited by the two producers on VCRs and that neither had received professional training in video production or editing, GFIC employees worked as camera operators and editors in their subsequent productions, including Akuffo's next feature, *Zinabu II*.[4] In the mid-1990s, commercial video operators also began to rent cameras from and edit their features at the state film company, GFIC, which became the GAMA Film Company. GAMA Film was the largest supplier of analog video equipment to independent producers. It had a fully equipped sound studio and an analog video editing suite, which it rented to private producers at reasonable rates. Even after it was divested and downsized, the state film company continued to function as a central location for video production, where film company employees and independent producers discussed their projects, shared ideas and critiques, and negotiated arrangements for future productions.[5] This interaction facilitated a high degree of convergence and interaction among all videomakers.

What can be said about the first commercial video producers and directors is that they were not employees of GFIC or graduates of NAFTI and so did not share with those who were linked to or trained by these institutions certain ideas about the function of film and television in the modern African nation. They did not understand film and media as primarily a means for the creation of national consciousness or for the development of the country. They viewed their audiences as consumers not compatriots, and they were not interpolated into the dominant narrative of these state-owned cultural institutions. Tracing this narrative to the political philosophies of Dr. Kwame Nkrumah, the first president of Ghana, Anne Mette Jørgensen (2001) calls it "the narration of underdevelopment of Africa" (129). She summarizes it as follows:

> Africa has been colonized and enslaved, dominated and exploited by Europeans. Independence has formally been gained but in reality much economic and cultural power is still in the hands of Europe and USA. Because of this Africa is deprived. To prosper in the future, a pan-African consciousness must be mobilized, and reviving the rich, cultural heritage of the past does this. (129–30)

In a similar vein, Birgit Meyer has written on the different motivations that drive the creation and appreciation of films such as Kwah Ansah's *Heritage Africa* (1988) and popular video movies. She concludes that each visual form is intended to appeal to a different audience. Ansah made a film for "the educated elites" to "foster pride in the 'past,'" whereas videos were made to appeal to "ordinary people" who "are not much concerned with their 'African heritage'" (Meyer 1999, 103). Another way to distinguish the two cultural products would be to emphasize that their *producers* occupied very different discursive locations. In the 1980s, Ansah, like the filmmakers at GFIC, worked within the limited sphere of official cultural production, and he made a film that would fulfill the expectations of that discursive formation. The first independent videomakers, in contrast, occupied an alternative discursive space, a commercial space located outside state-sanctioned official culture and its normative discourses.

Yet, even the difference between official and commercial realms of cultural production fades in the 1990s as GAMA Film begins to operate like a private business, producing videos regularly in order to generate revenue for future productions and exhibiting and reproducing their movies through commercial networks. Making movies to revive cultural heritage or promote national unity was no longer feasible. Movie production within all cultural spheres had become a profit-driven endeavor as "a logic of privatization" (Larkin 2008, 240) extended further into arenas once controlled by the state. During this period, recent NAFTI graduates and younger filmmakers from GAMA, second and third generation producers of official culture, joined the commercial video industry. These formally trained film and videomakers were born well after national independence and so were ideologically removed from the political philosophies of Nkrumah. They had been exposed to a wide variety of global films and media through television and video and were familiar with the "global popular," a term used by Simon During to define those media products that are "distributed and apparently enjoyed everywhere, at any rate wherever electricity is on line or generators and batteries can be transported and where they are not successfully banned" (1997, 808). As media producers and consumers, they saw themselves as cosmopolitans. They brought into the field their knowledge and skills (cultural capital gained through higher education) and, like their self-taught counterparts in the commercial industry, their belief that movie making was an entertainment business.

When the first independent videos appeared in the late 1980s, GFIC struggled to maintain a distinction between professionally produced films and amateur videos by refusing to allow independent "amateur" videomakers to show their features in state-owned cinema halls, but as video projection in private theaters became more widespread and lucrative, GFIC changed course and began screening video movies.[6] Over time and as video projectors replaced film projectors in most cinema halls, all forms of screen media—film and video, privately produced movies and movies released by GAMA Films, bootlegged and legal videos, foreign and local movies—circulated through the same dual exhibition networks that structured the public screening of movies on video in Ghana in the 1990s.

Large movie theaters owned independently and by the state made up the first exhibition infrastructure, and the other informal and un-organized network was assembled from small, makeshift, and independently owned video parlors or centers. The first video movies, despite the limitations of the video medium, were made with the idea that like a film print they would be projected and screened in public venues on large screens. Following the film print model of duplication, the video producer created one master copy of his video movie and from this made one or two exhibition copies of the master videotape, which he intended to distribute to large movie theaters for projection. In the early years, it was often the producer himself or a close associate who carried a copy of his feature to and from film theaters. Though it demanded enormous quantities of the producer's time and energy, he had little choice because his commercial video product had no way into the distribution system used by state-controlled and privately owned cinemas.[7]

Located in major cities such as Accra, Tema, and Kumasi, large cinema halls, most of which dated back to the colonial era, converted from film to video projection in the late 1980s and early 1990s. Private cinemas in Ghana were owned and operated by the Captan and Nankani families and included the Opera, Orion, Oxford, Osu, Paladium, and the Casino cinema. Munir Captan explained in an interview with me that his family's cinemas had been hit hard in the 1980s by currency devaluation, import restrictions, a severely depressed economy, and, after the second Rawlings coup, nighttime curfews, and he welcomed video because it infused the system with new movies and media and, initially, reinvigorated exhibition (personal communication). Recent films from all over the world were suddenly available on

video cassette and could be shown, illegally and without fear of per-
secution, for only the cost of a videotape. Ghanaian video movies, released throughout the decade in ever increasing numbers, circulated
through the same private cinema halls as did the pirated films, the two
competing for time slots and viewers. High demand for local productions, in the first years of local movie production, offset the added
cost of sharing exhibition revenue with the Ghanaian movie's producer. But as time went on and Ghanaian movies became more widely
available, fewer local movies were screened in private theaters.

Unlike private theaters, GAMA Film theaters, which included the
Executive Theatre, Regal, Royal, Plaza, Rex, and Roxy, adopted a policy of strict adherence to international copyright laws and screened
movies only with proper permissions. Because they refused to screen
pirated materials and instead recycled the old films they had been
showing for years, GFIC/GAMA theaters were at an extreme disadvantage against privately owned cinemas. The decision to allow local
producers to project their videos at GFIC theaters, taken only after
GFIC had seen how profitable local video had been for private theaters, gave GFIC a much-needed revenue boost. Over time, the Executive Theatre, a large, air-conditioned, and comfortable indoor cinema
located on the grounds of TV3 and GAMA Film, became the top
venue for exhibiting Ghanaian movies. A new, local movie, anticipation for which was created by the gripping advertisements that ran
weeks before its premiere on TV3, which at the time was the most
popular station in the country, opened at the Executive Theatre every
two weeks, and from there, made its way through the network of state
theaters. At the outset, exhibition in GAMA theaters provided a reliable source of income for producers by way of its organized distribution circuit and television advertising.[8] But as more and more
producers entered the industry, including GAMA Film Company itself, theaters became overrun with video features. Hundreds of movies
lined up for their Executive Theatre opening, and they were always
placed behind GAMA Film's in-house productions. In the later 1990s,
producers could wait as long as one year to get their movies screened.
Still, most could not afford to bypass GAMA theater exhibition and
the television advertisements and other publicity that came with it.

An unstable, fragmented, and unofficial assemblage of privately
owned video centers, where video movies were usually shown on a
television connected to a VCR, made up the other exhibition circuit
in Ghana. As explained in the previous chapter, the nodes of this

disorganized and widely dispersed commercial network were strung loosely together within an illegal media economy generated for the bootleg distribution of global media content. VHS cassette recordings of films from Hong Kong, India, and America and of international TV programming captured from satellite broadcasts were exhibited commercially and illegally by resourceful entrepreneurs. By 1988, the Minister of Information estimated that there were more than three hundred video centers in Accra alone.[9] These small centers, scattered throughout the urban landscape, were similar to the nickelodeon theaters that were popular in American cities in the early twentieth century in that they catered to people living in poor urban neighborhoods where the centers were located. In Ghana, the admission fee to a video center was much less than the cost of a ticket to a large cinema hall, and most patrons were able to walk to their local video parlor, avoiding the cost of transport to a theater located elsewhere. Most centers operated outside the reach of the state, and because there were so many centers and they tended to be found in small structures or open courtyards and might appear or disappear suddenly, they could not be policed without enormous expense. The state simply did not possess adequate resources to hunt down and arrest center owners who were showing pirated material, so producers were left with few options. The most ambitious producers hired agents to carry copies of their movies to video centers and oversee the movies' legal screenings. Agents would also be asked to patrol designated neighborhoods, looking for centers showing videos illegally, and to confiscate the pirated video cassettes and demand compensation. Because such endeavors required money and time, many producers simply ignored the centers altogether and relied on revenues generated from legitimate exhibitions and, later, cassette sales.

Although at its emergence, commercial video production was highly fragmented and individualized, over time and as it expanded, the industry stabilized. New networks of commercial affiliations and the establishment of several professional associations, founded in part to provide protections and benefits no longer secured by the state, contributed to a gradual process of formalization. The 1990s saw the creation of FIPAG, the Film (and Video) Producers Association of Ghana, a professional organization intended to support film- and videomaking and promote cooperation in areas of collective interest, such as censorship and copyright. Video marketers also formed an association to protect their interests, and the Actors Guild, established in 1989, underwent radical transformation, electing a new president, Fred Amugi, in 1996, under whose guidance a shared governance structure was created, and the guild became more actively involved in lobbying for higher salaries for actors. At this time it also forged transnational links, affiliating formerly with the International Federation of Actors (IFA).

In the 1990s, another key structural development was the emergence of an organized commercial network for the reproduction and distribution of individual Ghanaian movies on VHS cassette tapes. As with exhibition, the local video reproduction and distribution infrastructure cultivated the further entanglement of state-supported and private producers and of legitimate and pirate reproduction and distribution, and in Ghana, as in other parts of the world, video contributed to a gradual decline in the public exhibition of cinema and an increase in private forms of media consumption.[10] It was the businessman Steve George Hackman, founder of Hacky Films, who initiated the duplication of locally produced movies on VHS cassettes for individual sale and home viewing. In 1993 he released *Ghost Tears* (1992), a movie he coproduced with Socrate Safo on video cassette after its very successful theater run.[11] Under the shadow of Hacky Films, pockets of distribution appeared and disappeared throughout Accra; these usually were shops opened by nascent movie producers, but over time, these small outlets were quickly surpassed by Alexiboat Films. Established by Alex Boateng in 1991, Alexiboat became the dominant video reproduction business in Ghana and the main network for the legitimate reproduction and distribution of video features made by GAMA Film Company and private Ghanaian producers, as well as for the bootleg sale of movies from Nigeria, the US, China, and India. Like many of the individuals involved in the industry, Boateng's interest in movies was entirely entrepreneurial. Capitalizing on knowledge gained and connections forged when he worked as an electrical parts dealer, he opened, in less than ten years, four video distribution outlets in Ghana, two in Accra and two in Kumasi.[12] At its height, Boateng's Kumasi dubbing factory contained over four hundred video decks that could duplicate as many as three thousand videos per day.

The dubbing and distribution system formalized by Boateng was similar to the systems in Southern and Northern Nigeria, as it has been described by Haynes (2000) and Larkin (2008). Upon the movie's completion of its theater run, the producer would design and print video jackets for his new release and supply Boateng with his original cassette and his video jackets. Boateng, in turn, dubbed the master tape, placed the copied video cassettes in their sleeves, and distributed the cassettes to marketers, some of whom were employed by Boateng and others who worked independently. Marketers would then sell the tapes to individual video vendors, who carried and peddled the cassettes along busy city streets or stocked them in their kiosks where videos would be sold or rented. Some vendors bought directly from Boateng. Video producers were responsible for all expenses incurred to produce, edit, and promote their videos, and producers received from Boateng, whose only investment was the cost of dubbing and shelving the cassettes, a mere one third of the movie's total sales. (Sales were tallied by counting the number of jackets and cassettes remaining in Boateng's inventory and subtracting that number from the total number of jackets printed by the producer. This was a highly unreliable and messy system that further put producers at a disadvantage, and many producers alleged that Boateng cheated them.)

Video producers received the introduction of large-scale video re-production very reluctantly. They feared that once their cassettes were released into the market, there would be no way to stop the rampant piracy of their movies by the owners of video centers, video rental businesses, and by private individuals; of course, piracy did increase exponentially, and producers' problems were compounded by an overwhelming influx of bootleg Nigerian movies in the local market. The broadcasting of Ghanaian and Nigerian movies on television further eroded the public exhibition and viewing of local movies and added to the financial stress of Ghanaian producers. *Price of Love* (1993) and *Step Dad* (1993) were the first Ghanaian video movies to be broadcast on the state-owned station, GBC, the only TV station in Ghana at this time.[13] In 1995 an already congested market for video movies got even more crowded when TV3 followed the lead of the state-owned GTV and began to buy the broadcast rights for Ghanaian movies that had already been exhibited in theaters. But unlike GTV, who showed movies on Sunday afternoons, TV3 broadcast Ghanaian movies on television in the evenings, when people were most likely to go to the theater.[14] Producers protested, but to no avail, and over time attendance at the theaters dropped precipitously.

In 1993, the arrival in Ghana of a pay-per-view digital station, Multichoice TV, and in 1997, a new free-to-air television station, Metro TV, made a dire situation critical. Nollywood movies, most of which were pirated and so obtained for free, flooded the airwaves and came to dominate the national television market, undercutting the efforts of Ghanaian producers to make and sell their movies. By the end of the decade, many producers were no longer releasing their features in theaters at all, relying exclusively on individual sales. As television sets and VHS or video CD players became less expensive, many more Ghanaians than previously could watch movies at home or with friends or family, and, connected to this, the number of video parlors in Accra decreased markedly. Squeezing into a small, overcrowded market stocked full of less expensive, bootleg Nigerian titles and competing with a flood of new television programming, Ghanaian producers struggled to survive, and most did not. By 2004, as the next chapter will explain, the production of video features in Ghana had slowed to an almost complete halt.

In Close-Up: Performing Professional

As has been described, shared and increasingly formalized structures and networks of production, exhibition, and distribution engendered greater levels of overlap and interaction among independent and GAMA Film producers and professional and nonprofessional videomakers during the 1990s. Distinctions between amateur and professional productions and private and state-funded projects began to diminish, and these convergences were coincident with increasingly fierce competition among ever larger numbers of local producers for consumers to buy their products through legitimate channels. It is within this context of competition and formalization that self-proclaimed "professional" video moviemakers begin to articulate and display their difference from other movies.

One of the mechanisms through which this difference was produced and made official was the Ghana Film Awards. Established in 1999 by GAMA Film, the awards set out to shore up the position of GAMA Film and to create distinction within an overcrowded cultural field in which limited structural differentiation occurred. Many private producers criticized the awards as an attempt to close them out of competition and promote GAMA Film's productions. Ashong Katai, at the time a movie director at GAMA Film who had been integral in organizing the awards, explained that the program, modeled on Hollywood's Academy Awards, was meant to encourage "excellence" and to promote the production of quality movies. Excellent movies, he continued, were quite different from "box office" films, those movies that had "mass appeal" although they did not achieve the same standard of quality as award-winning, professional movies (personal communication). Quality for Katai, and for the other professional videomakers I spoke with, was synonymous with Hollywood. Again and again in response to questions about which filmmakers had inspired them or which filmmakers they admired, professional videomakers cited Hollywood films and directors as their models. Khairuddin Othman, who at the time of my interview was the CEO of TV3 and GAMA Film, told me that his mission as CEO of the company was to promote better quality movies.[15] He dismissed what he referred to as witchcraft and ghost movies because they did not meet the global, Hollywood standards the company sought to maintain. He said that his TV station broadcast such movies rarely and reluctantly and pointed out that not one of the movies produced by GAMA was about witchcraft.[16] A "professional" movie, it seemed, was defined through difference and aspiration. It was never a movie about witchcraft, and in all cases, the professional movie was one that seemed more suitable to a global audience, one that was thought to be more like a Hollywood film, in part, because it transcended its local context.

Borrowing from James Ferguson (1999), I want to suggest that within this context professionalism, like a cultural style, functioned as a mode of signification. A "performative competence" (99), professionalism at once drew from and signaled a particular kind of expertise. Most obviously, the producer of the professional movie had the capital—economic and cultural—to produce a movie with higher production values than most locally produced movies. Yet, not every high quality movie could be described as professional, nor was every movie made by a trained videomaker considered professional. The professional movie was one that also aspired to a global standard, and it signaled that aspiration by attempting to transcend the materiality of its local context. Though not synonymous with Ferguson's cosmopolitan cultural style, the style referred to as "professional" did, like cosmopolitanism, gesture toward "'the world out there,' the place where hit songs and action films come from, where 'things are happening'" (Ferguson 1999, 215). Even if videomakers such as Quarshie had no intention of distributing their movies "outside"; they still aimed to make video movies that achieved a clean, generic global look and feel by concealing the gritty reality of the historical present and so making visible an African landscape and African characters similar to those found in any global media form. This extroverted style brought local forms of popular culture, including character types and narrative tropes current in the Ghanaian concert party theater and oral and popular literatures, into contact with globally popular cultural forms. But it principally drew from and reimaged aspects of Hollywood and the global popular (During 1997). Professional movies, in various ways and with "sliding degrees of competence" (Ferguson 1999, 95), borrowed and quoted from, remixed and reimagined the tropes, types, and techniques dominant in the global films and television programming that Ghanaians had been watching for many years.

In creating a cosmopolitan style, Ghanaian videomakers made an effort to follow the formula associated with the classical cinema of Hollywood and to move away from producing movies whose dominant modes were the melodramatic or spectacular. Miriam Hansen describes the classical cinema model as "the interweaving of multiple strands of action toward resolution and closure, a web of thorough motivation centering on the psychology of individual characters, and the concomitant effect of an autonomous fictional world offered to the spectator from an ideal vantage point" (1991, 141). The vantage point standardized by classical narrative cinema was the effect of the development of standardized narrative and stylistic conventions, such as linear narration, parallel and continuity editing, compositional unity, and closer framing. These advances in filmmaking transformed the "logic of display" (34) dominant in early cinema. Early cinema, which has been called a cinema of attractions, offered pleasure through a diversity of competing spectacles and attractions. It solicited its viewer directly, like a vaudeville act or theater production, addressing that viewer as a member of a social class and within a defined historical context. The classical mode of narrative, in contrast, made possible the absorption, or suturing, of "the spectator into the illusionist space on screen" (44). It engendered what Hansen calls a "self-explanatory and self-contained" mode of narration that was capable of producing films that could "be understood by a mass audience regardless of individual cultural and ethnic background and of site and mode of exhibition" (138). No longer was the viewer hailed by the film within a social context but was created within the film text itself as "an invisible, private consumer" (34).

Professional videomakers aspired to a similarly standardized product and spectator, and to achieve this self-contained mode of representation, they sought to contain the melodramatic excess predominant in Ghanaian and Nigerian movies. The professional movie's narrative

was linear and structured by cause-and-effect logic, unlike more melodramatic movies that favored melodramatic narrative mechanics, which
Ben Singer (2001) explains are built around "outrageous coincidence,
implausibility, convoluted plotting, deus ex machina resolutions, and
episodic strings of action that stuff too many events together" (46).
The professional movie's use of music and ambient sound was ap-
propriate to the diegetic space of the film; in other words, sound supported the movie's narrative. Again, this is unlike a more melodramatic and less realist use of music, in which dramatic music would
heighten the viewer's emotional response and call attention to itself.
The professional movie was generally averse to an overreliance on
sensationalism and spectacle, which included the incorporation of
special effects to visualize the occult or other supernatural occur-
rences. Instead, it often centered on a main character whose complexity and interiority it attempted to represent.

This is not to suggest that all so-called professional movies were
devoid of melodramatic excess. The "professional" style might be more
accurately described as an emergent structure of feeling or sensibility
that was registered in different movies in particular ways and to varying
degrees. It is crucial to acknowledge, too, that professional moviemakers working in Ghana had to adapt, and compromise with, the classical
Hollywood formula to suit video technology and the economic impera-
tives of limited resources. These modifications created an aesthetic
similar to what Jennifer Hayward has called a "soap opera, televisual
aesthetic," which she defines as a "distillation of Hollywood conventions pushed to their hermeneutic limit" (1997, 155). In this televisual
mode, Hayward emphasizes, aesthetic choices are largely determined
by the economic constraints of production and the narrow parameters of video technology. Hayward points out, for example, that scenes
center on only two or three characters "because intimate conversation
is infinitely cheaper to tape than group or action scenes" (155). Since
television dramas must communicate meaning cheaply, "camera work
is highly coded, delivering well-established cues to viewers trained to
read them" (156). Variations of this style are often associated with television dramas and soap operas; the style is predominant in American
soap operas, South American telenovelas, and the Malaysian serials that
were, and continue to be, broadcast on Ghanaian television.[17] Professionals in Ghana drew from this archive of global media, which also
included a deluge of films and media available on VHS tapes, in diverse
ways in their production of a global, professional style.

Ghost Tears

The Hacky Films and Movie Africa Productions movie *Ghost Tears* (1992) marks an important shift in the thematic focus and aesthetics of local video productions; it is among the earliest movies to register an emergent sensibility of professionalism, even if it does not quite achieve a professional style. It was a huge hit in Ghana, becoming the highest grossing feature in the industry's short history and initiating significant changes in the culture of video production. Its popularity and commercial success furthered the migration of professionally trained film and videomakers into commercial videomaking and set off a sharp and sudden increase in the number of producers, both professional and untrained, entering the industry and in the number of videos made.[18] Videomakers attribute *Ghost Tears*'s success to its coherent and engaging narrative, relatively high production values, and incorporation of special effects, which were enthusiastically received at a time when most videos were shot by a person with no training in video production.[19]

Ghost Tears was the first of seven movies coproduced by Socrate Safo's Movie Africa Productions and Steve George Hackman's Hacky Films.[20] Like many of the so-called professional movies that appeared in later years, *Ghost Tears* centers on a middle-class Ghanaian family torn apart by infidelity and selfishness. Kwesi Ampofo's affair with his housegirl Esi, who also happens to be the niece of his wife Dee, sets off the marital conflicts and domestic violence that structure the narrative. In the first thirty minutes of the movie, Dee learns of Kwesi's indiscretions and threatens to send him and Esi back to the village. Esi, however, has crafted her own plan. When alone with Kwesi in a hotel room, she tells him that she is pregnant and asks him to move her to her own apartment. Afraid that his rich wife will turn him out, Kwesi refuses and tells Esi that she must have *another* abortion. The next night, Esi brutally murders her rival and aunt, Dee, drowning her in her own home in her own bathtub. Soon after the funeral, Esi tells Kwesi that she lost his baby. (The movie never reveals if she was really pregnant in the first place.) She easily convinces him to put an end to his mourning, even though the traditional mourning period has not ended, and to marry her so they can start a new life. Emboldened by her position as madam of the house, Esi begins to act like Dee, mistreating Yaakwa, Kwesi, and Dee's daughter, in the same manner that Dee mistreated her. Esi abuses her stepdaughter, calling her lazy and

Figure 3.1. *Ghost Tears* promotional photograph (*Ghost Tears*, 1992)

stupid, and she forces the young girl to toil over housework for long hours. A weak and indecisive figure throughout, Kwesi watches what is happening with dismay, but does nothing to protect Yaakwa.

Yaakwa's dead mother, in contrast, possesses frighteningly excessive power. She returns from the dead to avenge her murder and her daughter's abuse. In a clear attempt at creating an appealing spectacle, the movie visualizes her specter through a simple superimposition in which a transparent, partially dissolved image of Dee is laid over scenes of Esi abusing Yaakwa. The effect implies that Dee is watching over her daughter. A few scenes latter, Dee materializes in person and approaches Yaakwa in the market, asking her to inform her "mother" that Dee will visit her "one of these days." Because she was only a baby when Dee was murdered, Yaakwa doesn't recognize her mother. She returns home to tell her father about the strange encounter, and he immediately knows that Dee's ghost has returned. Troubled by memories of good times with Dee and nightmares in which Dee appears, Kwesi eventually decides to come clean, and at home one evening, after knocking down a bottle of gin, he tells Yaakwa that Esi is not her real mother, but her stepmother, and that it was she who killed Dee. Unknown to Kwesi or Yaakwa, Esi overhears Kwesi's confession to his daughter. Horrified that her crime has been revealed, she hits Kwesi over the head with the gin bottle and kills him as Yaakwa watches, seemingly too shocked to intervene. In the midst of this violence, the spectral Dee appears, her figure superimposed over Yaakwa's body so as to represent her possession of her daughter. Yaakwa/Dee, suddenly emboldened, grabs the cord of a lamp and strangles Esi, killing her. Dee's image then pulls away from Yaakwa and disappears. The movie ends on an extreme close-up of Yaakwa, who wails loudly over the two dead bodies.

From a historical perspective, what is remarkable about *Ghost Tears* and other "professional" movies from this period is their deliberate obscuring and sanitizing of the social. These videos intentionally mask the privation that was the defining feature of their context. The urban landscape, when made visible at all, is largely devoid of signs of hardship, poverty, or breakdown. Instead, the city is made to resemble a display window, a framed and carefully orchestrated presentation of consumerism and consumption. The movie captures, in tightly composed shots, characters visiting fancy shops that stock imported goods and taking drinks at fashionable restaurants. An observation made by Haynes (2007a) about the representation of Lagos in Nollywood movies applies here: "Wealth in the most tangible, desired forms is fundamental to the lure of Lagos" as imaged again and again in Nollywood (140). I would add that in the Ghanaian movies, this narrowing of the urban landscape through the aestheticized shopping experience also attempts to create the illusion that Accra is a globally homogenized, world city.

This projection of the city indicates a striking deviation from the first local videos where the landscape of urban poverty was a constitutive part of the world the movies presented. The mise-en-scène of the first Ghanaian videos encoded poverty as a feature of urban life. Haynes refers to this as the "low-budget realism that springs from just going somewhere and filming" (2007a, 144). The camera moved through Accra's poor neighborhoods and entered the modest living spaces of ordinary Ghanaians, and in the narratives of these movies, deprivation was the social given that motivated characters' choices. For example, Kofi, the main character in the 1987 movie *Zinabu*, makes an unethical choice and accepts money from Zinabu, who is a witch, even though he knows this money was derived from her dealings in the occult. But he does this only because he is poor. The movie devotes extensive time to demonstrating his poverty and contextualizing his choice. His desire for wealth is clearly located in the context of scarcity and want.

In the representation of space and subjectivity, *Ghost Tears* turns inward, closing out the materiality of the historical context and the breakdown and disrepair of the urban African landscape. Most of the movie takes place in interior locations—rooms in Kwesi and Dee's lavish home, hotel rooms where Kwesi and Esi meet, high-class restaurants, and hotel bars. The urban landscape, when made visible at all, is largely devoid of signs of poverty. The surface presentations of poverty and urban collapse that were so pronounced in movies from the 1980s—open gutters, ramshackle buildings, potholes, junky cars, and trash—have been expunged. A similar interiorization demarcates the subjectivity and central conflicts of the movie. In *Ghost Tears*, it is individual, immoral actions seemingly taken independently of the social that unleash conflict and deadly violence unlike the narratives of the earliest videos, where deprivation was the social given, the structural reality, that motivated characters' choices. Kwesi's choice to have an affair with Esi is understood as a moral choice. The world that he occupies, in other words, does not force or influence him. Nor is social context or economic status presented to ameliorate our judgment of him. Although Kwesi's economic status is an important aspect of his character, the work he does is not at all significant and, in fact, is never named or represented.

According to the moral economy of *Ghost Tears*, it is unrestrained self-interest that destroys familial and social ties, and it is gender that organizes this morality. Kwesi is weak and indecisive, while his wives are violent, brutal, and controlling. The women function as grotesque figurations of a capitalist morality that transforms family relationships into economic transactions. Dee regards her marriage and obligations to her niece, Esi, as forms of monetary exchange determined by the logic of payment and profit. She belittles and abuses Esi, treating her like an employee instead of a family member. In the movie's opening scene, Esi inadvertently leaves a hot iron on one of Dee's dresses while pressing it. When Dee finds that her dress has been damaged, she goes mad. She hits Esi and screams at her: "Do you think I brought you from the village to come and ruin my things. Are you a witch or something? Stupid girl." Esi complains to Kwesi that her aunt treats her like "a maidservant, simply because she has money." When Dee realizes that Kwesi is having an affair with Esi, Dee screams at her husband, too: "I have raised you up to this person you see in the mirror. . . . You have reduced yourself. YOU are going out with the HOUSEGIRL. . . . You've forgotten where you came from. . . . I put money in your pocket" and now "you have lowered me." Later, Kwesi tells Esi, who begs him to remove her from Dee's charge and rent an apartment for her, that he cannot leave his wife because Dee "owns everything; the house, the factories, the car. Look she owns me." After she marries Kwesi, Esi subjects Yaakwa, now her daughter, to abuse and exploits her labor. In scene after scene, the young girl scrubs laundry, washes floors on her hands and knees, and irons, late into the night.

Though Safo and Hackman invested more money in the feature than had many other producers working at the time, *Ghost Tears* was still a low-budget project, shot with one VHS camera and one boom microphone. The economic constraints of the movie's production, in large part, determined its modes of representation and address and constrained its adherence to the classical narrative formula. Scenes in *Ghost Tears* tend to be of long duration and center on one or two people, captured from a mid-shot distance and from a frontal view. Close-ups, reaction shots, and shot-reverse-shot sequences—classical Hollywood conventions that bring the spectator into the narrative and focalize her/him through character point of view appear rarely. To achieve such effects with the one camera setup used in the movie's production would have required multiple takes of the same scene, lengthening significantly the time on location and the cost of production.

It is clear, nonetheless, that an emergent sensibility of professionalism inflects *Ghost Tears*. The final close-up of Yaakwa's face, extended for almost one minute and remaining as the credits run over it, certainly is meant to emphasize the depth of her anguish and the severity of the crimes her parents have committed against her. It also invites the audience to contemplate her future. Still a child, she has been subjected to, witnessed, and participated in excessive violence. The agony expressed in her face suggests that she has been damaged and that her past will continue to haunt her life. This extreme close-up is an attempt to visualize her interiority and give her a degree of psychological depth. It indicates attention to a cinematic discourse of individual psychology and interiority that later movies, and in particular professional movies, develop.

Jennifer

The first movie to win the best picture award at the Ghana Film Awards was *Jennifer: So Lovely, So Deadly* (1998), a GAMA Film production directed by Nick Narh Teye. A family drama, *Jennifer*, like *Ghost Tears*, also focuses narrowly on individuals and the moral choices they make, and the representation of space in the film reproduces the private, family themes taken up in the narrative. The camera in *Jennifer*, much like Hayward describes the camera in a soap opera, "literally pulls us into each scene, positions us at eye level with the actors, situates us inside living rooms, kitchens, and bedrooms, enables us to share with certain characters knowledge unavailable to others" (1997, 157).

Scenes generally center on one or two characters in domestic or interior settings, and the frequent use of a tighter frame, the close-up, and shot-reverse-shot sequencing works to create the impression of intimacy between the viewer and the four main characters. More melodramatic than many professional movies, the feature recycles the figure of the good-time girl whose pursuit of personal pleasure brings about her ruin. This is a character type found in West African oral tales, in Ghanaian popular literatures, and concert parties as well as in many video movies, a few of which have already been discussed in this book. In this movie, Jennifer's appetite for money, clothes, cars, and unrestricted personal freedom is insatiable. She ends her marriage to Dr. Frank Addo, a hard-working, honest, and loving husband, to marry Ben, an affluent businessman who seduces Jennifer with promises of jewelry and cars. The romantic intrigues of Ben and Jennifer are set against the slowly developing affection that develops between Frank, after Jennifer has left him, and his neighbor Ewura Ama, who is a widow living alone with her mother. Ben and Ewura Ama marry and start a new life together, while Ben and Jennifer's relationship, a superficial one fueled by materialism, implodes. Soon after Ben marries Jennifer, he enters into an affair with her best friend, Lorna, who becomes pregnant. When Jennifer, who wants to have Ben's child but cannot get pregnant, learns of his deceit, she comes to his office with a loaded pistol and shoots him before killing herself.

Jennifer is noteworthy in that it deploys classical narrative and melodramatic modes strategically to express the movie's moral economy. In other words, *Jennifer* works between these two narrative registers to emphasize that each relationship enacts very different moral values. Ben and Jennifer are primarily represented through the melodramatic mode; the movie employs what Brian Larkin (2008) has described as an "aesthetic of outrage" in its portrayal of Ben and Jennifer so as to dramatize their "intense transgression" of the moral norms of their society. They are all surface, flat figurations of a capitalistic morality that transforms human relations into economic transactions. Frank and Ewura Ama, in contrast, are presented more realistically. They have depth; the movie provides each with a personal history and allows the viewer access to their interiorities. It also represents them within the everyday, performing banal tasks such as seeing patients, preparing food, or driving in the car. Jennifer and Ben, however, are removed from the everyday and instead tend to provoke intense moments of narrative crisis or melodramatic affect. Made visible through realism, then, the relationship between Ewura Ama and Frank is normalized, whereas melodramatic excess characterizes and condemns Jennifer and Ben.

Jennifer's character exhibits little that is new or nuanced. What is striking is the intensity of Jennifer's greed and her complete and unapologetic disregard for others, including her husband and stepdaughter. She brings to mind Sandra, Thelma, and Doris, the female protagonists in the Nigerian best-selling movie *Glamour Girls* (1994). Like those characters, Jennifer represents "a world in which relations are not based on love or attraction but on financial gain" (Larkin 2008, 188). The feature opens at a restaurant where Jennifer, her friend Lorna, and Ben have lunch. Lorna has just introduced Ben to Jennifer, who is well dressed and well coiffured. Jennifer's dress and mannerisms immediately bring to mind the good-time girl figure, described by Esi Dogbe (2003) as "the stereotypical unattached 'wicked,' 'parasitic,' and 'wayward,' modern woman in post-colonial

Africa," who is recognized by "her beauty, sophisticated urban dress, sassiness, dexterity with modern gadgets, and high-society lifestyle" (104). Here, however, Jennifer *is* attached, which Ben notices immediately. He comments on Jennifer's gold wedding ring, telling her that her beauty "deserves diamonds and fancy cars." When she explains that she cannot afford diamonds, he insists that "someone else has to do the buying. Simple as that." At their cars after their lunch, Ben hands Jennifer a stack of cash, which she takes. This transaction signals the beginning of their love affair. Indeed, Jennifer is utterly reprehensible because unlike the women in *Glamour Girls* and in other Ghanaian movies, she is married and perhaps more significantly is not poor. Neither need nor hardship drives her into Ben's arms. Frank has bought her a gold ring and a car so she can travel around freely. She owns and operates her own small shop, carries a slim cell phone, and shares a lovely home with her husband. She has a great deal and wants more.

Like Jennifer, Ben is all surface; unattached and alone, he is a slick and deceitful player, the "mobile-phone-wielding globalized man" (Dogbe 2003, 104), whose international business negotiations frequently take him out of the country. Filthy rich, he entices Jennifer with money, clothes, cars, and his large swimming pool. He marries her, but when Lorna seduces him, he willingly takes her as a lover. He is Frank's foil, the affluent, philandering masculine subject critiqued and condemned in the movie. For Ben, love is little more than a contractual relation and a way to assert his power. His wealth buys Jennifer, whom he displays like a flashy accessory.

Ewura Ama, modest, shy, and devoted to Frank's daughter, Priscilla, represents the "normative female roles of wife, mother, sister, or daughter" (Dogbe 2003, 104), and in her dress, speech, mannerisms, and lifestyle, she is Jennifer's opposite. Ewura Ama dresses conservatively and wears little makeup, and when Frank invites her to dinner, she must go out and buy a new dress because she owns so few stylish or flashy outfits. Unlike Jennifer, she is not single by choice, but lost her husband tragically while he was in Liberia, and while Jennifer is completely autonomous, without true friends or extended family, Ewura Ama is embedded in social relationships. She lives with her mother, whom she regularly consults for help and counsel. Their private conversations about Ewura Ama's feelings and fears give her a depth and interiority that Jennifer lacks. Ewura Ama, before falling in love with Frank, is also a good friend to Jennifer and to Frank. When

Frank is called away on a medical emergency, she volunteers to keep his daughter. Returning after dark, he finds his daughter curled up on Ewura Ama's lap, listening to Ewura Ama sing her a lullaby. Later in the movie, after his divorce is final, he asks Ewura Ama if she might know of someone who could watch Priscilla after school. Ewura Ama suggests that her mother might be able to help him, and when Frank offers to pay her mother, Ewura Ama tells him that her mother will not take payment because "money is not everything." Money motivates every choice Jennifer makes, but Ewura Ama refuses to commodify her relations with friends.

Though Jennifer's character would have been familiar to Ghanaian audiences, Frank Addo, in many ways, represents an alternative masculine subjectivity, which appears in many professional movies of this period, including the very successful *The Police Officer* series (1995 and 2002), as well as *Dark Sands* (1999), *Aboa Bone* (2000), *Scent of Danger* (2000), and *Thorns in My Home* (2000). In these movies, this figure is held up as a model of masculine behavior and is often juxtaposed to the more common masculine type, the deceitful and sexist husband or lover, who, if he is a father, is dictatorial and controlling, sometimes even resorting to violence to control his wife and children. Stephanie Newell (2005) has found this alternative masculine subject in popular Christian pamphlets published in Ghana. This "ideal husband," according to Newell, is "a kind of romantic hero" (315). Loving and affectionate, he treats his wife not as a subordinate, but as a partner. He doesn't dominate the domestic space, but shares it with her. In his research on love and marriage among the Igbo in Nigeria, Daniel Jordan Smith (2009) has documented an affiliated gender ideal, what he calls an "egalitarian gender dynamic," that articulates with discourses about romantic love and modern identities. This egalitarian ideal contrasts with and bumps up against, sometimes in the same relationships, a firmly established "patriarchal gender dynamic." In *Jennifer*, these two dynamics are set in opposition.

Frank Addo clearly enacts the romantic, egalitarian ideal. He is a devoted and patient father and a loving and gentle man. In the movie, he picks up his daughter, Priscilla, from school and buys her a pineapple juice box at the kiosk where they know him by name because he treats Priscilla regularly. We see him prepare meals for his daughter, play games at the kitchen table with her, and wait patiently in the school yard when she asks to play with her school friends for a few minutes more before he takes her home. He is most angry with

Jennifer not for abandoning him, but for failing to love his daughter, who lost her biological mother at birth. He pleads with his soon to be ex-wife: "Can't you make [Priscilla] your own?" Ewura Ama advises Jennifer not to leave Frank for Ben: "He is a good husband. So caring, intelligent, loving. Everything a woman would want." The movie gives Frank, like Ewura Ama, a history and an interior life. In a private conversation with his nurse, Linda, he reveals that Jennifer has hurt and disappointed him. He tells Linda that he lost his first wife when she gave birth to his daughter and that he had hoped Jennifer would make his family complete again. Employing the standard shot/counter-shot technique, the movie focalizes the personal conversation through Frank's point of view and produces, for the viewer, a sense of closeness to Frank. The scene also captures each character in an extended close-up shot that is intended to register emotion, specifically Linda's empathy for Frank and Frank's disappointment and pain. Viewers eavesdropping on this intimate conversation seem to peek into Frank's interiority and so are drawn closer to him.

Though Ben and Jennifer behave immorally and so, within the movie's logic, deserve what they get, their characters act as conduits for flows of desire directed from and toward the audience. With their figures, the narrative invites the viewer to imaginatively consume luxurious lifestyles. Ben seduces Jennifer by buying her things, and she displays her attraction to him by consuming what he buys her—drinks, food, and clothes, and though the movie condemns this model of love, which finds expression in consumption activities, it plays on its audience's desire to wear, taste, and feel goods that remain unavailable, and perhaps even fantastic, to them. Entire segments of the movie serve as spectacular displays of consumption. In a particularly apt example, Ben visits a Masai car dealership, looks around, and takes a new car on a test drive. He tells the salesperson that he wishes "to buy a perfect gift for the perfect lady." She shows him a sales pamphlet, advising him to choose carefully because "each car matches a different personality." The segment, on one level, works as an advertisement for the dealership, which likely agreed to be included in the movie on the condition that its name and product (Masai) appeared prominently. On another level, it represents consumption as a mode of self-styling, as a way to express personality and affection. In another scene, Ben invites Jennifer to his home, where he offers to "conduct" her around the house. As she marvels at its extravagance and "superfluousness" (Mbembe 2004), he informs her that he bought it for "a mere forty-five million." The camera, mobile and detached from the perspectives of both characters, adopts a presentational mode of address as it tours each room of the house and surveys its plush accessories and shiny surfaces. Crossing the boundaries of the diegetic space, the camera breaks free from the narrative. Detached from character perspective or story, it moves through space as a disembodied gaze of desire.

Stab in the Dark

In the 1990s, the proliferating and accelerated global flows of commodities, capital, people, and media contributed to an intensification of gender activism in Ghana and other parts of Africa and furthered public awareness of gender as a political concept (Ampofo 2008; Manuh 2007; Cole and Thomas 2009; Tsikata 2009). Throughout the 1980s in Ghana, the PNDC government under Rawlings, according to Manuh (2007), "projected a commitment to gender issues and gender equality and a redefined place and role for women," but these efforts were belied by "two decades of authoritarian, masculinist military rule generally unfriendly to women" (130). Manuh argues that democratization in the 1990s changed this situation quite dramatically, unmooring gender activism and scholarship from the state and infusing it with new energy, resources, and information. As a result, she explains, "Gender has become a highly invested and evocative concept and has developed a prominence in public discourse and action" (131).

At the same time, the opening of the Ghanaian media environment to a broad variety of global media forms offered audiences a sudden proliferation of foreign narratives and discourses about gender, romance, marriage, and family. Video movies of this period, much like popular literatures (Newell 1997, 2000), circulate within and so are marked by this gendered discursive space. They are active and fluid sites of contestation and reiteration, at once offering viewers life lessons and, perhaps less consciously, providing viewers with scripts for performing modern gender identities. Many "professional" movies from this decade, produced by men and women, stage intertextual dialogues with global feminist discourses; indeed, citing or engaging topics associated with gender seems to function as a mode through which these movies perform professionalism. Addressing matters related to gender becomes a way for the movie to demonstrate its extroversion (Julien 2006) and familiarity with global issues, and to assert a position on or a response to debates about gender and women's issues in local, public arenas. It displays the movie's cosmopolitanism and inserts Ghanaian voices into worldwide discussions about gender.

Jennifer clearly and rather forcefully articulates an antifeminist position through the characters of Jennifer and Lorna, who describe their unfettered greed and selfishness as assertions of their rights as women. For instance, when Ben asks Jennifer to divorce Frank and marry him, Jennifer's friend Lorna advises her not to worry about what others might think and to leave her husband for Ben. Lorna says, "If you think about what people will say, you will never progress." Here, Jennifer's "progress" as an individual is deemed more important than social norms and connections, and her progress as a woman is assured because Ben is "very rich with a chain of businesses." When Ewura Ama visits Jennifer in her shop to advise her to reconcile with Frank, Jennifer responds curtly: "This is the twentieth century, and women are presently very enlightened. Women are now taking control of their lives. If you find a better man, you go for him." The references to women's progress, enlightenment, and autonomy code Jennifer's and Lorna's behavior as expressions of feminism or gender activism, equating it with a capitalistic morality that places individual desires for wealth before obligations to family or friends. Much like Zinabu before them, Jennifer, and Dee and Esi (from *Ghost Tears*) function as figurations of excessive and dangerous power and seem to address cultural anxiety about changing gender roles, globalization, and new cultures of consumption. The movies of Veronica Quarshie, which we turn to next, are remarkable not only because they are of better quality than many professional video movies produced contemporaneously, but because they rewrite this female type. Quarshie's *Stab in the Dark* series gives this figure a history and sociology, transforming her from a one-dimensional figure into a historical subject.

During the 1990s, the availability of video technology expanded opportunities for African women to become cultural producers and to write, direct, and produce screen media on video, redirecting a historical narrative from which women had been largely marginalized or excluded. During the colonial period, no women worked or trained to be film producers under the Gold Coast Film Unit, and at GFIC, women were primarily employed as librarians, office assistants, and actors. Until the mid 1990s, few women worked as directors, camera operators, or editors at the national film company or GAMA Film, even after higher numbers of women enrolled at NAFTI. As actors, women, of course, exerted significant influence, especially in video movies where collaboration between directors and actors was common. But it was women who worked as private producers and directors, women such as Veronica Cudjoe, Haijia Meizongo, and, in particular, Veronica Quarshie, who opened the cultural arena to women and, in the case of Quarshie, purposefully responded to the representation of women dominant in video movies of the period. In an interview with me, Quarshie explained that she was deeply concerned about "the negativity against women" that had become commonplace in Ghanaian movies. She said that in her own scripts, she sought "a fair balance" in the representations of men and women (personal communication).

In 1992, five years after the first Ghanaian videomakers had started producing local movies, Veronica Quarshie graduated from NAFTI, where she had studied film directing. She released her first movie *Twin Lovers* in 1994, and then averaged about one movie each year, until 1999, when she produced the first two installments of her very successful, five-part series: *Stab in the Dark I* (1999), *Stab in the Dark II* (1999), *Shadows from the Past I: Ripples* (2000) and *Shadows from the Past II: Ripples II* (2000), and finally *Rage: Ripples III* (2003). Quarshie's movies and this series in particular maintained higher production values than most features released during this period. She and her crew invested at least twice as much time as the average producer, setting aside three months for writing and revising her scripts, and approximately twenty days to shoot her features. Quarshie and Sam Nai, her editor and husband, took at least one month to edit their movies. She employed trained and experienced cast and crew and used the highest quality video technology available; Quarshie was one of the first directors to replace a VHS video camera with a Betacam. When necessary, she would use a two-camera setup during production, which was very expensive and thus rarely used by producers. Unlike video producers who minimized production costs to maximize profits, Quarshie was committed to producing high quality video movies of "professional" quality.

One of the defining features of Veronica Quarshie's movies is dialogue. Actors in Quarshie's features do not improvise, as was often the case in the earliest video movies, but deliver their lines as scripted and in well-rehearsed performances that sometimes seem stilted, as if the lines have been overpracticed. Witty remarks, truisms, quotes from works of English literature, biblical allusions, and references to world events and international personalities pervade her characters' speech, and the dialogue, carefully crafted and often adopting elaborate and elevated diction, calls attention to itself. Indeed, I would suggest that Quarshie's dialogue enacts and demonstrates her "professionalism." It seems designed to demonstrate the movie's artistry. Quarshie creates characters who speak in language styles and registers similar to, though not identical with, those used by local Ghanaian writers (Newell 2000). Unlike those writers, however, Quarshie seems less concerned with demonstrating her authorial legitimacy than calling attention to the "writtenness" (16) of her narratives. Her writing expresses what might be called a "will to style" (Jameson 1981), a particularly apt phrase used by Fredric Jameson to describe the writing of Joseph Conrad: Quarshie's scripts demonstrate an effort to create a deliberately and self-consciously aesthetic language that, in this case, distinguishes her work from the less stylized, less artistic, cultural products of the local cultural economy. The highly stylized and ornate speech of her characters marks her movies as elevated and artistic endeavors, the products of an educated videomaker. Below, a few examples illustrate the point.

In *Stab in the Dark*, Kate learns that her brother Dan has been making passes at her friend, and the family's house guest, Effe. Kate is furious with her brother, and confronting him in the kitchen one morning, she demands that he stop hitting on her friend: "You are just a little boy, learning to walk and talk properly. Effe is way, way above your station, and even if you were in her class, I don't want any scandal in this house." Dan responds as follows:

> Kate, I thank you very much for re-defining and re-classifying my position and my station in life. Now I know I have been fighting a losing battle after condoning and conniving with you and your nocturnal activities. I deprived myself of valuable sleep, nights, forcing myself to stay awake so I can let the two of you in when you return from your nightly exploits. Is this my reward for so much self-sacrifice?

Another instance of Quarshie's stylized writing can be found in an exchange between Mrs. Ansah and her friend Mary, who frequently comes to visit. Mary is horrified to discover that Mrs. Ansah is allowing Kate's sexy friend Effe to stay at the house and work for her husband, Victor Ansah. She advises Mrs. Ansah:

> I wouldn't play such a dangerous game in this day and age, when one could hardly trust any of these men. Even the ones

who call themselves Christians. To dangle such a tantalizing and succulent piece of meat in front of the carnivorous mouth is asking for big trouble. . . . As for my Johnny, even if he convinces me that he has become a monk, I would still not do him this disservice of tempting him in this manner. Remember, great storms often announce themselves in gentle breezes.

Moradewun Adejunmobi (2002) has persuasively argued that English-language video movies from Nigeria deploy English to linguistically signify affluence. She explains that the use of English in these movies "signals affluence as surely do the many cars, the extravagantly furnished houses, the rich meals, and the abundant jewelry" (96). Unlike movies produced in Yoruba or Hausa, the English language distances the English-language movie from ethnicity, Adejunmobi alleges, and so enables the production of "a sodality of social aspiration" (85) not linked to ethnic values.

In Quarshie's movies, the adoption of highly stylized English works similarly. It too performs a distancing function, removing the movie from its local setting by stripping the dialogue of references to its immediate context and signaling a desire to reach outside that context and toward a global spectatorship. At the time Quarshie made *Stab in the Dark*, almost all Ghanaian movies were produced in English. The few Akan videos that had been released had not been as successful as English-language movies, but more than that, producers explained that English was, quite simply, the language of movies.[21] If one wanted to make a real movie, one used English.

Veronica Quarshie's very successful *Stab in the Dark* series is a chronicle of self-transformation. Each movie in the five-part sequence narrates Effe Thompson's re-making into a new body and a new self. In the first feature, Effe Thompson, the only child of her unmarried mother (to whom she is a constant worry because she dates men "old enough to be [her] father") is invited by her friend Kate Ansah to stay with the Ansah family while her mother goes to the village for a funeral. Mr. Ansah, a successful business man who rules over his family with a strong arm, reluctantly allows Effe to stay, but when his secretary must go on maternity leave and he discovers that Effe has taken a computer course, he hires her as his temporary assistant. Encouraged by his sleazy friend and business associate Boakye, Victor initiates an affair with Effe, and Effe sheds her schoolgirl persona to become the mistress of her best friend's father and her boss. Donning a short-skirted business suit and a wig of bobbed, straight hair, Effe

Figure 3.2. Effe, the sexy secretary (*Stab in the Dark*, 1999)

spends long days at the office and her evenings with Victor, annoying Kate who complains that Effe has no time for fun anymore. When Victor's secretary Hilda returns from her leave, Victor promotes Effe and asks Hilda to be her assistant. Furious, Hilda vows revenge, and when she discovers that Effe and Victor are having an affair, she informs Kate. Kate confronts Effe, accusing her of stabbing her family "in the back, in the dark" and demands that she leave the house. Victor rents a place for Effe, and eventually, Kate tells her mother Ivy, who is devastated. Furious with Kate for being insubordinate to him, Victor tells Kate she must leave his house, and when Ivy defends her daughter, he wants her to leave, too. At the end of the film, Kate has moved into her pastor's house and Ivy has gone to the village to stay with her parents. Dan, Kate's younger brother, remains in the family home with his father.

In *Stab in the Dark Part II*, Effe again takes on a new self. She is now noticeably fatter, and her hair has been cut very short and dyed blond; she lives unapologetically and openly as Victor's mistress in the nicely furnished apartment that he has rented for her. Kate, too, has changed. The fun-loving party girl is now engaged to her boyfriend, Bob, who has recently returned to Ghana from Canada, and she is determined

Figure 3.3. Effe as rich man's mistress (*Stab in the Dark II*, 1999)

to make Effe pay for destroying her family. Concealed behind dark sunglasses and an American baseball cap, Kate performs the bad-girl figure. She, Bob, and her brother, Dan, hatch an elaborate plan to end Effe and Victor's relationship. They arrange for Bob and Effe to meet at the gym where Effe works out and for Bob to seduce Effe. Bob, posing as a lawyer called Kwame Grant, tells Effe when he meets her that he has recently returned to Ghana after completing law school in Canada. He drives Effe home from the gym and invites her out, and slowly, she falls for him, breaking it off with Victor, who suffers what appears to be a mild heart attack. Kwame proposes to Effe, and she promptly packs her bags and shows up at Kwame's house only to find Kate there, waiting to spring the trap. At the end of the film, Effe wanders the streets, homeless. (Her mother has disowned her for her immoral behavior.) And Ivy and Victor, under the guidance of Ivy's parents, have reunited.

Shadows from the Past I: Ripples chronicles Effe's attempts to get even with Kate and her family. Effe hooks up with Lola, an old school friend, and Lola's friend Adjoa, who offer to help Effe get her share of "the Ansah millions." Lola, who has been used and abused by men, becomes Effe's mentor. She tells her, "This life is a jungle. You've got

Figure 3.4. Effe as avenging woman (*Shadows from the Past I: Ripples*, 2000)

to have the survivor instinct," and when it comes to men that instinct tells you that "you rip them off, or they rip you off." Under Lola's tutelage, Effe refashions herself again, adopting the dress and mannerisms of her tough friends. Now with short black hair, wearing black jeans, black boots, and sleeveless T-shirts and riding a motorbike, Effe becomes an "avenging woman," a character type popularized in Hindi films of the 1990s. She adopts the rough and rude language of her new friends, and the three generally create havoc wherever they go. Their language is vulgar and aggressive; they engage in criminal activity and acts of violence. The three women assault Kate and break up her wedding ceremony, holding her hostage until Victor hands over ten thousand dollars. Once they have the money, the women turn against each other. Effe refuses to divide the money in equal shares; she packs the money in a suitcase and tries to sneak out of Lola's apartment. But Lola and Adjoa catch her, beat her, and steal the money. Injured and hospitalized, Effe hears a news bulletin announcing that Lola and Adjoa have been arrested for money laundering.

When *Ripples II*, the next installment in the series, begins, Effe is being released from the hospital. She tells her mother, with whom she has reunited, that she wants to "reorganize" her life. The last two

Figure 3.5. Effe redeemed (*Shadows from the Past II: Ripples II*, 2000)

movies of the series, *Ripples II* (2000) and *Rage: Ripples III* (2003), narrate Effe's redemption and her reunion with Kate. After being released from the hospital, Effe, who again finds herself without a place to stay, is taken in by her mother's sister Fafa and Fafa's husband Kofi. Fafa and Kofi are very wealthy; their home is enormous and outfitted with expensive electronics; they drive a Mercedes Benz and dress in expensive and stylish clothes. Effe takes a room in their servant's quarters and finds a job right away because she tells her friend and co-worker Anita that she is determined to work very hard and to keep away from men and all the trouble they could bring her. Despite her intentions, Effe soon finds herself fighting off the advances of her aunt's husband, her step-uncle Kofi and of Anita's boyfriend Patrick. A friend tells Fafa about Effe's troubles with the Ansah family, and Fafa becomes suspicious of her niece. When she sees Kofi flirting with Effe, she assumes immediately that Effe has seduced him and kicks her out of the house. Though Effe has come to regret her past transgressions, those errors seem to follow her; as another character remarks, trouble "goes on and on," like ripples. The series implies that individual, immoral behavior produces unforeseeable effects that create problems for the individual and others into the future.

The last movie in the *Stab in the Dark* serial, *Rage: Ripples III,* brings Effe and Kate back together again. Effe rents a room from yet another lecherous man, Joshua, and discovers that her neighbor Afi, another aggressive and sexy tough girl, is having an affair with Bob, Kate's husband. Effe must decide whether or not to keep what she knows to herself and avoid inviting further complications into her already complicated life, or to do the right thing and tell Kate what she knows about her husband. Afi begins to suspect that Effe and Bob are involved because when they meet they act suspiciously, though both claim not to know the other. Afi threatens Effe and chases after Bob, who is trying to break it off with her because he suspects that Kate knows about the affair. The more Effe learns about Afi and her involvement with politicians, blackmail, and gangsters, the more convinced she is that she must tell Kate about Bob. Effe eventually contacts Kate, apologizing for what happened in the past. She tells Kate that she has changed and shares with her former friend what she knows about Bob and Afi. Kate confronts Bob, who admits to the affair; with Kate and Effe's help, he eventually breaks it off with Afi, who has threatened to harm him and Kate. Although at the end of the film the future of Kate and Bob's marriage is uncertain, the embrace between Kate and Effe, captured in the final scene, celebrates friendship between women.

The last two installments of the series—the redemption movies— lack the energy and creativity of the earlier movies. It seems as if Quarshie cannot clearly articulate a narrative about Effe outside of the patriarchal economy she critiques. In the first three movies, Effe migrates through the most common stereotypical representations of women in video movies: the good-time girl and the powerful, avenging woman. Quarshie complicates these representations of women; she clearly shows that Effe, Kate, and Lola become avenging women in response to the horrible treatment they have received from the men they love and trust, and their acts of revenge can be read as oppositional. They fight back against a system that has exploited them. However, when Quarshie tries to craft a different subjectivity for Effe in *Ripples II* and *III,* the movies reintroduce the stereotypes she has abandoned. Kate now becomes the good wife, replacing her mother, who took on that role in the first three movies, and Afi acts out a conflation of the good-time girl who is also tough and powerful. The constraints imposed by commercialization, perhaps, limit Quarshie's ability to imagine a feminist future for Effe, which is merely suggested by her reunion with Kate at the series' conclusion.

These critical comments should in no way diminish Quarshie's accomplishments. This series shifts attention away from male characters and toward female characters who confront, assimilate to, exploit, or fight patriarchal ideologies and the double standards these ideologies normalize. It is the patriarchal moral economy, here individualized and represented by authoritative and immoral male characters, that drives the rather radical transformations that Effe and other women undergo in the series. Men are powerful, deceitful, dishonest, and corrupt. Unlike *Jennifer* and other movies from the period, the series includes no examples of an "egalitarian gender dynamic" (D. J. Smith 2009) and no male characters who are ideal, romantic husbands. Victor Ansah cheats on his wife, treats his children like serfs, and engages in illicit business deals. Bob, his son-in-law, finds marriage boring and moves from mistress to mistress. He breaks it off with Afi only because he is concerned that Kate's father, Victor Ansah, who is also his boss, will remove him from the most lucrative business accounts if Kate is unhappy. For women, marriage brings only unhappiness. It is highly significant that the series ends with a reunion between Kate and Effe, two women friends, and not as is typically the case in domestic dramas, with a romantic reunion between a man and a woman. Effe chooses to remain single and to make a life for herself that does not include a male partner or husband, and the *Stab in the Dark* series is among the first in Ghana to show a positive representation of female solidarity and to affirm a woman's decision to remain single. In this, it goes much further than the "uprising" women writers Newell analyzes, who tend to rely on "the rhetoric of love" between a man and a woman to "criticize the society in which wifely submission is promoted" (Newell 2000, 145). Quarshie suggests that the language of romantic love is complicit in women's objectification and exploitation, and she gestures toward the possibility of women finding fulfillment outside heterosexual romance and marriage.

The very theatrical, if not hyperbolic, performances by women of the roles of mistress and tough girl in the series suggest that gender roles are compulsory and performative, as theorized by Judith Butler (1990; 1993). Effe, in particular, takes on and abandons various gender roles; her performances reveal that gender is a sign, which "is not the same as the body that it figures" (Butler 1993, 237). Gender identity is fluid and in process in these movies. As with any act of mimicry or "citation" (Butler 1993, 232), however, Effe's gender performances invoke the gender norms they recast. In fighting back against their mistreatment by men, the avenging women, in particular, take on some of the patriarchal qualities they challenge. These tough women go too far; their excessively vulgar and violent language and actions show them to be deviant women, and the narratives resolve when such deviance is contained: Effe repents and is finally redeemed while Lola, Adjoa, and Afie end up in jail. The avenging-women type serves to interrogate and police the boundaries of acceptable forms of gender activism and women's resistance. The movies seem to say that women do not have to be violent physically or verbally, behavior commonly likened to being masculine, to challenge dominant ideologies that define gender norms.

Like other professional moviemakers of the period, Quarshie deliberately inserts her movies into global debates about gender and women's rights. In a fast-paced and lively exchange from *Ripples II*, Fafa, Effe's aunt, who has been working long hours to open a new hotel in Ghana, returns home after dark to find Kofi, her husband, relaxing on the couch with a bottle of beer. What Fafa does not know is that moments before her arrival, Kofi had been outside flirting very aggressively with Effe. Kofi has just dashed into the living room with his beer when his wife returns. He greets her with a warm embrace and proceeds to serenade her with a romantic overture intended to conceal his questionable behavior toward Effe. He calls her "my darling" as he brings his glass to her mouth and when she greets his exuberance with skepticism, he responds that he is only doing what "comes natural" when one is "overwhelmed by love." He seems a parody of the ideal husband, as represented by Frank Addo in *Jennifer*. Because Kofi has already been revealed to the audience as an adulterer who uses women for his own monetary and sexual desires, viewers understand Fafa's response that "most of you men are just actors" as perfectly accurate. Kofi and Fafa discuss the significance of the landmark United Nation's Fourth World Conference on Women, which took place in Beijing, China in 1995.[22] Among the delegates at the Beijing conference was First Lady Rawlings, whose appearance there attracted a lot of media attention in Ghana. Kofi's sarcastic reference to Beijing parallels a derisive remark he makes later, calling his wife "Margaret Thatcher" when she warns him not to bring scandal to their house by seducing her niece. These references, of course, reveal a lot about Kofi's character. They indicate that he is made uneasy by women's rights and power, including his own wife's financial independence. More significantly, the mention of "Beijing" and "Margaret Thatcher" functions to signal the movie's participation in global debates about gender.

Of the professional movies discussed in this chapter, the *Stab in the Dark* series comes closest to achieving what Hansen, in her description of the classical Hollywood style, calls "a self-explanatory and self-contained" mode of narration (1991, 138). Quarshie's series effectively contains the spectacles of consumption and consumerism that in *Ghost Tears* and *Jennifer* interrupt and suspend the unfolding of the narrative. One reason the movies are described as being more professional is because consumption is seamlessly embedded into their narratives. When Effe, Lola, and Adjoa meet Kate at a small grocery store that sells expensive, imported goods, the camera remains loyal to character point of view and the shop seems merely a setting in which the women meet, not a place to be looked at and admired for its own sake. Similarly, the gym where Effe works out and the upscale homes where her family and friends live serve only as elements of the movie's mise-en-scène. Compare this to a scene in *Jennifer* where Ewura Ama visits Jennifer's boutique to talk with Jennifer about Frank. The camera, much as it does in the home-tour scene discussed previously, breaks free of character perspective and becomes a disembodied gaze of desire. A shot of a pair of high-heeled shoes mounted on the wall next to a matching purse cuts to a shot of a fancy hat perched on the head of a mannequin, then to a pair of hats. Adopting a presentational mode of address, the camera transforms the screen into a display window, and the goods in the store become the attractions put on offer for the spectator who admires them from afar. As discussed earlier, this presentational mode addresses viewers as members of a public space and a social class. It locates its spectator within a context. A similar argument could be made about *Jennifer*. These moments of spectacle and excess situate the viewer, by visualizing her/his desire, within the social. The flows of desire projected here locate the viewer in a situation of lack, where fancy handbags and shoes are extravagant luxuries. Much as in *Zinabu*, *Ghost Tears*, and other movies, these currents of spectacle push against the movie's realist narrative and professional style and so trouble its aspirations to be global or cosmopolitan, locating the movie in its postcolonial, African context. Quarshie's movies, in contrast, effectively close off the social, representing the good life that very few actually enjoy in Ghana as if it were the everyday experienced by most.

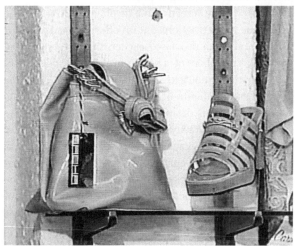

Figures 3.6–3.8. Camera as display window (*Jennifer*, 1999)

4

Tourism and Trafficking

Views from Abroad in the Transnational Travel Movie

In "Globalization and the Claims of Postcoloniality" (2001), Simon Gikandi describes the convergence of postcolonial and globalization theories, which he refers to as "the cultural turn in global studies" (634), a turn taken by scholars of globalization in search of a vocabulary to describe the transnational cultural flows and formations that have appeared in the last fifty years. Postcolonial theory, according to Gikandi, has provided a theoretical language for describing cultural transactions that have exceeded the geographical boundaries of the nation and rendered obsolete the modernization narrative, which envisioned the postcolonial nation-state as the engine driving social change. and progress in the Third World. The confluence of globalization studies and postcolonial theory has resulted in the privileging of literary texts as narratives of globalization and, even more problematic, in the occlusion of local narratives rooted in the material realities of the postcolony.[1] These are discourses that do not neatly align with the field's dominant theoretical framework. To underscore this point, Gikandi quotes, in its entirety, a letter found in the cargo hold of an airplane in Brussels in 1998 alongside the bodies of two young Guinean stowaways, who died seeking passage to a better life in Europe.[2] Gikandi's inclusion of the letter emphasizes the limits of postcolonial theory in accounting for and narrating globalization. Invoking "the very logic of the Enlightenment that postcolonial theory was supposed to deconstruct" (Gikandi 2001, 630), the letter reveals "a powerful disjuncture between the global narratives and images that attract postcolonial critics and another set of narratives and images which do not exactly fit into a theoretical apparatus that seems bent on difference and hybridity" (639). As a consequence, what we know about globalization and the multiplicity of cultural articulations it has generated has been limited by what Gikandi calls the restrictive "postcolonial scene of interpretation" (640). Critics reliant on postcolonial theory have ignored cultural articulations that germinate from Third World settings, or that speak in ways that are alien to the dominant paradigm.

Gikandi's critique, although not directed at the field of film and video studies in particular, is nonetheless instructive. Postcolonial film, like postcolonial literature, has been understood as an exemplar of globalization, and yet, the postcolonial film-texts held to represent and speak on behalf of the Third World are those that have been produced for and circulate within Western centers of knowledge production and consumption. Their creators, by and large, are the Third World intellectuals and artists who have been "transformed" into the "émigré native informants" of the postcolonial university (Gikandi 2001, 646). Located in the same institutional spaces, the scholars of transnational film, for the most part, have been attuned to the cinematic forms attached to academic and artistic global networks.[3] These are cinematic texts such as Ousmane Sembene's early film *La Noire de* . . . (1966) and Jean-Marie Teno's more recent *Clando* (1996), which take up Third Cinema or other oppositional discourses. They tend to reiterate what Achille Mbembe, in another context, refers to as "nativist and Afro-radical narratives" (2002, 635), narratives that normalize the idea that the "encounter between Africa and the West resulted in a deep wound: a wound that cannot heal until the ex-colonized rediscover their own being and their own past" (635). Such narratives adopt what Françoise Lionnet and Shu-mei Shih call the "binary model of above-and-below" (2005, 7), representing Africa's relationship with the West as principally antagonistic.

Among the multiplicity of new cultural forms rendered invisible to postcolonial and transnational cinema studies have been commercial, transnational African video movies. Like the letter from the stowaways discussed by Gikandi, popular African travel movies are incompatible with the postcolonial paradigm. They deal with some of the same issues that animate literatures and cinema of migration and displacement (Dawson 2010), but in language, tone, and aesthetics, the movies are awkwardly unfamiliar and inconsistent. In the movies, the tourist gaze disrupts any attempts at political critique or even didacticism, and melodramatic excess and improbability distort the stark realities about which the movies aim to raise awareness. Constrained by low budgets and the expense of producing a movie at home and abroad, and under intense pressure to make a return on their personal investments, videomakers are pulled between demands to satisfy audiences' expectations for entertainment and for instruction. Negotiating these constraints becomes especially tricky when the condition that enables the movies is the economic and geographic disjuncture that divides Africa and the West. Narratives swing between trafficking and tourism; their messy and contradictory plots express the gap between the postcolonial subject's global imaginary and the structural conditions that at once produce and impede it. In conditions of extreme scarcity, the fantasy of Western modernity mobilizes intense desires to gain access to the West (Mbembe 2002). In actuality, these are desires that ordinary citizens of the postcolony can never fulfill. Nonetheless, individuals embark on dangerous journeys overseas in search of better lives for themselves and their families. Once arrived, however, the displaced subject must manage a perilous and underground existence, which precludes all opportunities to partake of the status of modernity. Video movies offer a virtual exploration of these contradictions.

Articles by Haynes (2003a) and Adejunmobi (2010), both Nollywood specialists, are the only published analyses on African popular narratives of globalization. The travel videos analyzed here have been produced, cheaply and quickly, in Ghana and in one of the large European or North American cities that hosts a large African community. The travel videos are products of the mass displacement (Dawson 2010), turbulent migration (Papastergiadis 2007), and fortified borders (Bauman 2004) that characterize our global age. The United Nations Population Division estimates that there are about two hundred million people living outside their countries of birth (qtd. in Dawson 2010, 181), and according to recent calculations, among this huge number are approximately five hundred thousand Ghanaians now resident in Europe or North America (Twum-Baah 2005). Like most Ghanaian living abroad, the movies' protagonists are economic migrants (Kosher 2003), individuals who flee Africa because their economic prospects are severely limited. Characters cross national borders illegally and so struggle to maintain tenuous livelihoods in a European or North American city without the protections granted legal immigrants or citizens.

Made mainly for audiences in Africa, the earliest travel movies offered pleasures derived from imaginary travel to New York, London, or Amsterdam and tourist views of the cities' sites and spectacles.

Focalized through the perspective of the African migrant, the spectator in Africa could virtually experience global mobility and imaginatively consume the tourist experience by watching a narrative about the first-time Ghanaian traveler who leaves Africa in search of the promise of modernity embodied in the global city. But this is a promise continually deferred for the protagonist of these first travel movies, who fails to overcome the unexpected hardships he or she encounters abroad and eventually returns to Africa. In more recently produced travel movies, the perspective shifts quite dramatically. No longer does the audience adopt the point of view of the naive traveler. Instead, these movies focalize spectators through the eyes of characters well established in the diaspora, for whom Africa signifies an ongoing source of complications and obligations.

Production and Distribution

Compared to the large number of African video movies produced annually, the travel movie genre comprises a relatively small number of video productions.[4] The popularity of the genre in Ghana peaked around 2002, when the genre was new, but travel movies do still appear, in Ghana and Nigeria, regularly. Ghanaian videomakers shoot segments of their features abroad and at home and complete post-production in Ghana, where they have access to affordable and familiar editing facilities. Among the most prolific producers of Ghanaian travel movies are Bob Smith Jnr. and Socrate Safo, whose movies I focus on in this chapter. Both producers travel abroad regularly and have forged solid relationships with media professionals in the international locations where their films have been made.

Bob Smith's *Mamma Mia* series was one of the earliest and most successful attempts to give Ghanaians at home images of and stories about the European Ghanaian diaspora. In 1995, Smith produced *Mamma Mia* in Accra, Ghana, and Verona, Italy, where his wife lives and works and where he frequently stays for long periods of time. He followed with two sequels: *Double Trouble: Mamma Mia Part Two* (1998) and *Black Is Black: Mamma Mia 3* (2000). A few years later, Smith made another Ghana/Italy series: *Wild World: If Wishes Were Horses* (2002); *Wild, Wild World: Wild World 2* (2004); and *Wild World 3: What a World!* (2004). Smith's familiarity with Verona, his proficiency in the Italian language and Italian culture, his many friends and contacts in the Ghanaian community there, and his collaborative partnership with

(above) Figure 4.1. Portrait of Bob Smith Jnr. (© Carmela Garritano, 2009)

(right) Figure 4.2. Portrait of Socrate Safo (© Carmela Garritano, 2009)

the Italian videomaker Marco Bressanelli have enabled and sustained his Ghana-Italy movie projects. Smith's well-established contacts in Verona additionally have facilitated the inclusion of quite remarkable locations, characters, and even digitally mastered effects in his videos, despite his limited budgets. *Mamma Mia* showed Ghanaians images of African migrant workers picking grapes in an Italian grape orchard. Italian ambulances and police cars show up to deal with emergency situations in his movies, and Italian EMTs, cops, museum personnel, and tour guides often appear as minor characters.

Unlike other videomakers, Smith relies entirely on the resources available to him in overseas locations. Smith assembles a different crew, with its own style of videomaking and levels of expertise and experience, in each location, and each crew, of course, uses different cameras, microphones, digital tape, lights, and so on. What emerges is a bifurcated narrative in which significant variations shape how the audience experiences each place. In a Bob Smith production, the spectator's engagement with Italy is wholly unlike his engagement with Ghana precisely because the location and condition of the video's production inflects the materiality of the text. For the spectator, the material conditions of the movie's production undergird the back-and-forth movement of the video narrative. The texture of each place as rendered in the movie looks and sounds unlike the other. Because Smith is the only professional actor appearing in the overseas segments of his movies, the narratives can seem out of balance, relying too heavily on Smith's character, what he says and does, while other characters, such as Smith's Italian lovers or Ghanaian friends, rarely speak, and, when they do, they seem to lack depth and complexity because the amateur actors who play these parts fail to offer convincing performances.

In an interview with me in 2009, Smith explained that the high production quality of the Italian segments of his movies, a result of Bressanelli's participation, accounts, to some extent, for the high demand for his movies in Ghana. His example illustrates that networks of affiliations, which spread through various spheres of the foreign cities where the movies are made, make these movie projects possible. Videomakers who have been able to make more than one travel movie are those whose travel movies tend to be the most successful, and that success seems to be linked to the network the producer has access to in the West. Although many producers bring members of their cast and crew from Ghana, they depend on the cooperation of Ghanaians living in the diaspora, including friends and family. Their homes, businesses, churches, and community organizations feature as locations in the movies, and producers frequently recruit members of their cast and crew from among them.

The primary market for the first wave of travel movies was the ordinary African who lived in Africa, a person who had never been overseas and had little prospect of ever having the means to do so. Based in Ghana, the producer edited, printed, and duplicated his movies there, where he knew the local market and could readily distribute his transnational movies along with his locally made videos.

Though interested in developing a large market base in the diaspora, distributing movies abroad presented enormous difficulties. Without access to distributors operating from within an organized distribution system, most producers, in the early years, relied on informal business arrangements with African marketers who traveled back and forth frequently, obtaining African goods to market in the diaspora. Producers sold VHS or VCD copies of their movies to the marketer, and he, subsequently, carried these copies overseas where they finally were shelved next to fufu flour and plantains in the neighborhood African store. In later years, Ghanaian producers began working with African entrepreneurs in the diaspora, who owned and operated small African music shops and could reproduce and distribute their movies.

Over time, these distribution businesses have grown and become more formalized. Today, producers typically sell the international rights for their movies to these well-established African movie distributors, who transfer the movies from digital tape to DVD and arrange for high-quality replication and distribution to marketers.[5] In Amsterdam, the two main distributors are Quayson K and Agenim Boateng. In London, Money Matters, Wayosi, and Kumasi Market account for the largest percentage of African movie sales. Three very large distributors, Executive Images, Franco Films, and Sanga Entertainment, share the New York market and sell Ghanaian and Nigerian movies at wholesale prices to smaller distributors all over the United States. Through informal product placement arrangements, these businesses sometimes appear as locations in travel movies, giving Africans at home the chance to see that African businesses have become part of the global cultural landscape of London or New York.

As is the case in Ghana, piracy is an insurmountable problem in the diaspora. Nothing prevents duplicators from simply making copies of movies that someone sends them from Ghana, or that they buy for home use, and selling them without the proper rights and permissions. The wide availability of African movies on the Internet has further contributed to widespread piracy. The institutions that police international copyright laws disregard, or simply cannot account for, this minor cultural practice. The Ghanaian government lacks the resources to do much about piracy in Ghana let alone beyond its borders, and the producers themselves do not have the means to protect their own interests. Faced with these difficulties in collecting revenue for his movies overseas, Safo, who has made two movies in Amsterdam and one in New York, has concentrated his efforts abroad on distribution. In Amsterdam, he has partnered with Sankofa TV, an Afrocentric public access station, and in New York, Safo and other Ghanaian producers work closely with Rabiu Mohammed of Sanga Entertainment to organize the distribution of African videos and grow the US market. Mohammed has been relentless in his efforts to formalize the distribution of African movies in the United States. He has standardized the practice of buying distribution rights from producers and was instrumental in the establishment of a network of legitimate movie distributors, who buy from him and other New York distributors at wholesale prices. In an interview with me in 2010, he explained that customers and wholesalers do buy from his Bronx store, African Movie Mall, but his mail-order sales account for the biggest share of his business. He releases between five and ten new movies each month and can sell between five thousand and twenty thousand DVDs of each title.

Of far less importance, but still significant, have been contacts between Ghanaian producers and researchers who work on African popular video. The most noteworthy example is Birgit Meyer, whose assistance made possible the Ghana-Holland coproduction *See You, Amsterdam* (2003). Meyer's involvement gave the Ghanaian producers access to official institutions and resources typically not within the reach of Ghanaian videomakers. Sponsorship for the movie, unlike most, came from both countries: the independent, commercial producer HM Films in Ghana, and several governmental and nonprofit organizations in the Netherlands, including the National Commission for International Co-operation and Sustainable Development, the Amsterdam Fund for the Arts, and the Haëlla Foundation. Directed by Ashong Katai, at the time an employee of GAMA Film, this international project featured a Ghanaian cast and Dutch crew and was shot almost entirely in Amsterdam. The movie premiered in Amsterdam at the Cultuur op Drift (Culture Adrift) festival.[6] Meyer also has provided support to independent producers Socrate Safo, Albert Kuvodu, and Augustine Abbey, each of whom has made at least one Amsterdam movie. She acted in Augustine Abbey's *Idikoko in Holland* (2005) and allowed her home to be used as the movie's principal location.

Imaginary Travel and Virtual Tourism

Haynes (2003a) has used the term "African Abroad" to label the earliest transnational videos, but here I call them travel movies because their

plots hinge on travel. Characters craft elaborate schemes to escape
Ghana, and because they travel illegally or have had to do something
illegal in Ghana to find the money to travel, the trip itself becomes a
source of suspense and conflict. For Ghanaian audiences, the experience of international travel is a topic of curiosity, and the narratives
devote a lot of time to the banal details of airports and airplanes. The
earliest travel movies typically narrate the experiences of a male protagonist who leaves Africa to escape economic hardship in the belief
that Europe or North America promises better jobs, better work conditions, and the chance to make money. The traveler is always poor or
of modest means, and the movie usually narrates his first trip overseas.
These are not stories of the cosmopolitan transnational (Desai 2004)
or elite flexible citizens (Ong 1999), but of African subjects with little
knowledge of the Western world and with little money who make the
trip at great risk or cost. The protagonist must resort to illegality to
secure the money or papers he needs to get out of Ghana, and once
in the West, he maintains a precarious existence. Without the security of a legal immigration status or citizenship, he relies on personal
connections and the generosity of the Ghanaian community to help
him find work and shelter. In Bob Smith's *Mamma Mia* series, for example, Kwabena Dabo has worked as a bank teller in Ghana for nine
years. When his wife becomes pregnant, he decides that he must find
a way to take care of his family properly. He embezzles money from
the bank in order to buy a ticket to Verona. In other movies, travelers
might purchase illegal documents, as occurs in *See You, Amsterdam*
(2003) or *Koofori in London* (2005), pay smugglers to transport them
across borders illegally, as in *Amsterdam Diary* (2005) or the Nigerian
video *Europe by Road* (2004), or stow away as cargo, as seen, for instance, in *Wild World* (2002) and *Mr. Ibu in London* (2004). As Haynes
has noted of the Ghanaian and Nigerian travel video narrative, "The
process of establishing oneself abroad is presented as extremely arduous and as something that can be accomplished only with the advice and help of fellow Africans" (2003a, 27). Kwabena Dabo's plight
exemplifies the point. He spends his first four days and nights in Italy
in a public park in Verona, fighting off the cold and eating the gari he
has carried in his suitcase from Ghana. He speaks no Italian, and his
attempts to engage Italians walking through the park are met with
cold stares and annoyed expressions. In Socrate Safo's *Back to Kotoka*
(2000), Nat, a Ghanaian lawyer recently arrived in Holland, wanders
the streets of Amsterdam for days, hungry and cold and alone. His

situation improves when he encounters a fellow Ghanaian, who recognizes him from home and offers support and assistance. In many of the movies, romantic intrigue involving another Ghanaian's wife or a white woman inevitably spoils the fraternity shared by Ghanaian men and brings about central conflicts in the narratives. Working illegally and moving from house to house in search of a place to stay, the migrant's situation abroad is tenuous and finally unsustainable. The narratives, in all cases, are didactic, exposing the harsh realities hidden behind the myths of prosperity that lure Africans abroad. As a character in *Back to Ghana* (2008) says, "Auborokyire," the Akan word for "abroad," is "hell." Ghanaians tempted by the opportunities and conveniences of the global city are better off staying at home.

Amsterdam Diary, produced and directed by Socrate Safo, was one of four movies that emerged out of a collaborative effort among a group of Ghanaian actors, directors, and producers who traveled together to Amsterdam, with two cameras in tow, to shoot a series of movies quickly and inexpensively. Relying on well-established contacts in Amsterdam, including Safo's relationship with the media scholar Birgit Meyer, and on the generosity and curiosity of the Ghanaian diaspora there, the group managed to organize and shoot four movies in thirty-one days. Those movies were *Amsterdam Diary I* and *II, Idikoko in Holland, Twists and Turns,* and *Otolege.* To absorb the large expensive of bringing a small cast and crew to Europe, budgets had to be kept extraordinarily low. The group worked closely and cooperatively, and the cast and crew played multiple roles in the four productions. Actors in one movie became production assistants or costume designers in another, while directors doubled as camera operators and sound technicians.

As is characteristic of the travel movie genre, in *Amsterdam Diary* a spatial binary between an African city, here Accra, and a global city structures the narrative, which is organized through frequent crosscuts between the two locations. At the most immediate level, the narrative jostling back and forth produces for the spectator the travel and movement reiterated in the narrative. It also generates drama and suspense, withholding resolution in one place with a cut to the other. More than that, this use of parallel editing indicates simultaneity; the montage aligns the two locations in time and virtually inserts Ghana, and the Ghanaian spectator watching the movie, into the time of the global modern. It temporally and spatially constructs a relationship of proximity between Ghana and, in this example, Amsterdam, imaginatively relocating Ghana from a space of marginality to a global space of centrality.

The opening scene of *Amsterdam Diary* unfolds in Ghana and finds Abasaa's mother, attended by the family's pastor (played by the popular actor Nii Saka Brown) and Abasaa's sister Edinam, excitedly awaiting the return of her "been-to" daughter, who has gone to Holland to marry Kobby, a rich and handsome Ghanaian. Expectations are high as Abasaa's return promises to bring wealth and prestige to her family. But when Abasaa arrives, the audience knows immediately that something has gone terribly wrong. Abasaa does not speak. She trembles, her clothes and hair disheveled. Her mother, horrified, asks, "Who is this? Is that my daughter?" When the pastor hurries off to pray, Abasaa's mother must go to her room because she is so distraught. Alone with Abasaa, Edinam finds a small notebook in Abasaa's bag, which she searches after Abasaa falls into a fitful sleep. She opens the book and realizes it is her sister's diary. Abasaa's Amsterdam diary, now an emotionally charged object, must speak for Abasaa, who has been so traumatized by whatever transpired in Amsterdam that she is unable to voice her experiences. Through Abasaa's day-by-day account of her journey to the Netherlands as written in her diary, the audience comes to see how the beautiful Abasaa was transformed into a twitching, shivering mess.

The camera zooms in to an extreme close-up of the first page of the diary and then dissolves to the streets of Amsterdam, signaling a transition in space (from Ghana to Amsterdam) and time (from the time of the reading of the diary to the past when it was written). Travel movies rely excessively on the cityscape establishing shot to signal location. Here, Safo shot his own street footage in Accra and Amsterdam, and he uses the same city scenes throughout the movie. Other directors pirate city scenes from other films or from tourist videos. The movie cuts to an interior location, a small and well-furnished apartment, where Kobby opens a package from his sister Diamond in Ghana that contains photographs and a video. Among the photos, Kobby finds a snapshot of Abasaa and using his tiny cell phone, immediately calls his sister and asks her to "Hook him up." When his sister wants to know why Abasaa, he explains that she is beautiful and that he "[doesn't] find the girls here attractive." "I want to date a girl from home," he continues, "a home-brewed girl." Diamond agrees to help Kobby convince Abasaa to come to Amsterdam to meet and marry him on the condition that Kobby send Diamond money.

Diamond, appropriately named, becomes the agent of the trafficking of Abasaa's body. Attempting to persuade Abasaa to consider her brother's proposal, she tells her friend, "This is an opportunity every young woman our age is dying for." Abasaa, seriously involved with a young Ghanaian man, refuses, asking, "What does Europe have to do with love?" Determined to get her reward, Diamond visits Abasaa's mother, who is thrilled by the prospect of Abasaa going abroad and greedily anticipates the remittances she'll receive. She says to Diamond: "You mean your brother is in Amsterdam, and he is rich, and he wants my daughter? . . . God has just answered my prayers. Give your brother a positive answer."

After much manipulation and persuasion, and after discovering that her lover is already married, Abasaa relents to the wishes of her mother, who advises her to use the beauty God gave her to secure a future for herself and her family in Holland. Diamond arranges for Abasaa to meet with a visa contractor, who secures a fraudulent Turkish visa for her. The contractor assures Abasaa that once in Turkey, she will be transported to the Netherlands safely. He has arranged for her to meet with a smuggler, who will drive her and several other women to the Netherlands. Frightened and uncertain, Abasaa goes along with the plan. She flies without incident to Turkey where she and five other African women who have paid to be smuggled into Holland are packed into a windowless van by four dangerous and devious African men. When they arrive in Holland, the men order them out of the van and try to rape them. Abasaa manages to break free and escape, but while fleeing from her assailants loses her passport, address book, suitcase, and money. (Conveniently, she has her diary in her pocket.)

Running through a park, Abasaa comes upon a Ghanaian couple who have pulled to the side of the road because their car has stalled. Abasaa pleads for help, and the couple quickly gets her into their car, which miraculously starts, and drives her to the safety of their home. Mrs. Anim assures Abasaa that "God made this happen." She and her husband, who is a pastor, stopped there because God wanted them to find and help her. The Anims take Abasaa into their home, and Abasaa quickly makes herself useful, preparing meals for Mr. Anim and performing other household duties. Mrs. Anim, the Westernized bad wife figure, is rarely at home because she is unsuccessfully balancing her obligations as the leader of the women's fellowship at her husband's church and as the owner of a small food shop. Pastor Anim complains that his wife fails to "take care of [her] wifely duties." "This is Europe," he tells Abasaa, where a wife is allowed to put her work before her husband.

Pastor Anim is a reprehensible figure. When his wife is out of the house, he continually attempts to seduce Abasaa, despite her tears and protests. Relying heavily on melodramatic emotional codes, these scenes elicit sympathy for Abasaa and cast a disapproving eye on the hypocritical Christian pastor who exploits her for sexual gain. But the movie's critical stance is compromised by its misogynistic gaze. The movie's blatant sexism becomes most apparent in the scenes set in the Anim household. Pastor Anim's repeated attempts to accost and rape Abasaa are rendered as comedy. In one of the most disturbing episodes in the movie, the comedic actor Augustine "Idikoko" Abbey, cast as Pastor Anim, performs a rape scene for comedic effect. While Abasaa sleeps, Anim struggles to undress her. He grimaces, groans, and writhes around in an overstated manner; his desire for Abasaa and his fear of her waking and catching him are communicated by his comic and exaggerated facial expressions. The violation as performed showcases Abbey's exaggerated and buffoonish acting style and is meant to provoke laughter. But one can laugh only if disregarding Abasaa's attempted rape by a man posing as her protector. In another episode, Anim sneaks into the bathroom while Abasaa is showering. Again, Anim's clumsy movements and contorted facial expressions invite laughter. These episodes open up two very different readings. The spectator either laughs at Anim's antics and diminishes Abasaa's violation, or finds Anim's behavior disgusting and aligns themselves with Abasaa. Either option has the potential to generate discomfort or uncertainty, or for a spectator expecting a unified and didactic narrative, this tension might compromise the video's pedagogical purpose. The lesson the movie wants to teach relies on Abasaa's victimization and on the spectator's affective response to her extraordinary plight. To laugh at Anim's violation of Abasaa is to disturb that affective connection with her character and to diminish the crime of rape against a vulnerable victim.

Finally unable to tolerate Pastor Anim's advances, Abasaa leaves. But without her passport and money and with no way to contact Kobby, she can do nothing but wander the streets of the foreign city. She tries to reach her mother by phone, and when she finally manages to speak with her, her mother refuses to help and instead angrily instructs Abasaa to start sending her money. While waiting at a bus stop, she meets one of the African women (a French speaker referred to in the credits as "Frenchwoman") with whom she traveled by van from Turkey to Holland. The woman, who is marked by her accent and language as someone who is African, but not a Ghanaian, invites Abasaa to stay with her. With no other option, Abasaa agrees and finds herself, again, victimized by a stranger. The French woman lures Abasaa into the dark evils of Amsterdam: sex shops, exotic dancing, prostitution, and drugs. Abasaa slowly turns into a junkie, and when unexpectedly on the street she bumps into Kobby, the husband she came to the Netherlands to meet, he fails to recognize her. Once he realizes that she is *his* Abasaa, he decides that the only thing for him to do is to send her back to her family in Ghana.

Focalized through the point of view of a female subject, *Amsterdam Diary* veers slightly from the formulaic plot of the typical Ghanaian travel movie. Still, it reiterates the gendered logic of transnationality that informs most travel videos. The movie relegates women to the status of symbolic objects, whose bodies do little more than act out the movie's larger meaning. Abasaa is an unwilling traveler, a victim of human traffickers, whose agency is always compromised. Men enable and limit her movement. She goes abroad only because Kobby has sent for her. He is the traveling subject, while her function is largely symbolic; she embodies the dangers and vices of the European city. Her unhappy encounter with the world city transforms her body. Traumatized and addicted to drugs, she returns to Ghana without the ability to speak. Here, as in many transnational video movies, the space of the diaspora is sexualized and gendered. African women who live in the diaspora, like Mrs. Anim and the French-speaking prostitute, are bad wives or loose women. Ghanaian men, in response to their wives' provocations, are adulterous and jealous, and family ties become increasingly tenuous, signifying the homeland's weakening hold on the migrant. Perhaps indicating points of affinity with Bollywood diasporic cinema, it is marriage to a woman from home that, in many movies, sutures the male African traveling to or living in the diaspora, like Kobby, to the homeland (see Desai 2004). The Ghanaian man living abroad looks to the homeland for his wife, his Mother Africa figure. The homeland, however, is anything but a stable and homogenous site of origin or safety. Abasaa's plight serves to harshly criticize families that pressure their loved ones to go abroad. Crosscuts between Abasaa's slow downfall in Holland and her mother's excruciatingly long prayer meetings with her pastor in Ghana, where they pray to God to let Abasaa send lots and lots of money, emphasize the point.[7]

The most striking, and sometimes irritating, feature of the first travel movies is the unsystematic deployment of the codes and conventions of classical narrative cinema. The movies violate expectations of temporal unity and spatial coherence, particularly in the placement and extended duration of location shots, shots that index location and situate the narrative in a specific setting. Unnecessarily long takes of the global city frequently interfere with the cause-effect logic of the narrative. Location or establishing shots grow to be scenes, spilling into and submerging the video's narrative, while the plot is put on hold for an extended look at and tour of a place or site that may have only passing relevance to the story. During these segments, the camera adopts the tourist's gaze, putting exotic locations on display for their own sake. These to-be-looked-at spaces and sites are usually associated with global travel and the global cityscape: international airports, tourist attractions, city streets, and public spaces populated by other tourists. The audience, like the main character of the movie, experiences the global city as a sight-seeing adventure.

Two examples illustrate the point. *Amsterdam Diary* includes a long segment that depicts in great detail Abasaa's movement through an unspecified international airport. Safo assembled this segment from actual footage he captured with a small hand-held camera that he concealed in his coat when he and the cast and crew traveled to the Netherlands. Viewers travel with Abasaa as she sits on the airplane, disembarks, walks through the airport, passes through immigration, picks up her luggage, queues for her customs interview, and, finally, after what seems a long time, leaves the airport. In Augustine Abbey's *Idikoko in Holland* (2005), one of Idikoko's Ghanaian hosts, Vera, treats him to a tour of Madame Tussaud's wax museum in Amsterdam. The camera follows the characters as they leisurely stroll through the museum, posing next to a variety of well-known African American cultural icons, including Martin Luther King Jr., Oprah, Tina Turner, and James Brown. Idikoko, enchanted by this excursion into simulacra, exclaims, "Auborokyire yɛ dɛ. This is a nice country; I am not going back to Ghana." Leaving the museum, he and Vera feed pigeons in an open plaza, buy trinkets at a tourist boutique, and enjoy a horse and buggy ride through the city. Rendered mainly in long takes, these excursions through global spaces extend temporally beyond what is necessary for narrative coherence or plot development and disrupt the narrative by introducing a different temporality and by engaging the spectator directly.

Although these breaks with well-established narrative conventions might be taken as aesthetic failures or amateurish mistakes, they are, nonetheless, meaningful. Safo and Smith both explained that travel movies sell because Ghanaians in Ghana want to see how their compatriots, their people, are faring overseas. As the camera moves through the streets of the global city, it casts a curious and desiring gaze on the city's sites and spectacles. Here, the spectatorial investment involves, for the spectator in Africa who desires but has no way to experience life abroad, the space to temporarily occupy a transnational subjectivity. Mayfair Mei-hui Yang (2002), in her analysis of Chinese modern mass media, uses the phrase "imaginary travel" to describe the pleasures Chinese national subjects derive from watching television programs about Chinese characters living in Japan or the United States. Likewise, African subjects might be said to "inhabit transspatial and transtemporal imaginaries" (Yang 2002, 190) as they watch other Africans navigate the journey overseas, tour famous places, and consume the experience of living or visiting elsewhere. Spectators identify with someone like them walking through the Red Light District of Amsterdam or, as in *Mamma Mia* (1995), visiting a McDonald's in Verona and share with the characters of these movies unfamiliarity and fascination with the global city. As Vijay Mishra (2001) has noted in his writings about the diasporic cinema of Bollywood, imaginary travel "brings the global into the local, presenting people in Main Street, Vancouver, as well as Southall, London, with shared 'structures of feeling' that in turn produce a transnational sense of communal solidarity" (238). Not only do African movies bring the global into the local, however; they go further, inserting the local into the global. Travel movies create an imagined transnational community among Africans, and more, they assert African membership in the global community.

One of the ways African characters express their global membership is through consumption. In *Window Shopping: Cinema and the Postmodern* (1993), Anne Friedberg demonstrates a correspondence between the "mobilized virtual gaze" of cinema and television and other commodified forms of visual mobility, specifically the look of the tourist, who visually experiences foreign spaces, and of the shopper, who examines goods on display. Friedberg describes shopping and tourism as metaphors for cinematic and televisual spectatorship. Much like watching a dynamic world unfold on a screen, these activities bring together movement and visual consumption and produce "a perceptual displacement" that "defers external realities, retailing instead a controlled, commodified, and pleasurable substitution" (Friedberg 1993, 122). The earliest African abroad movies play on cinema's capacity to offer, virtually, pleasures associated with mobility and consumption. The African protagonist's introduction to the global city brings these pleasures together in the presentation of an extravagant shopping excursion. These episodes present the global city as a consumerist space experienced through a variety of virtual mobilities and imaginary acts of consumption. Using actual locations in which real tourists shop and look, the shopping scene embeds consumption into the fabric of the everyday and allows the African spectator to take on the identity of a tourist, visually consuming the signs and commodity spaces of the global city as she or he moves across its landscape. Typically, the African protagonist and his female guide, whether she is African or European, embark on this outing together, and their romance, too, finds expression as a commodity-experience. To be in love in the global city is to consume tourist sites, foreign food, and goods as a hand-holding, heterosexual couple. In Bob Smith's *Wild World*, a shopping mall in Verona is the setting for a romantic interlude shared by Jojo, the Ghanaian tourist in Verona, and Gianna, his Italian hostess. The segment includes neither dialogue nor consequential actions. Set to cheerful Italian pop music, the characters stroll through the mall. They smile and shop, signaling to the audience that they have fallen in love.

Amsterdam Diary modifies this formula, sending Abasaa and her female Francophone guide through the Red Light District of the city. They walk, shop, look, buy, and eat. The montage cuts between two shots: the first, from afar, places the women in the midst of the city crowds that move along the busy streets; the second is framed more tightly and follows the two characters as they window-shop. The window that holds the camera's interest for the longest period of time advertises "sex for sale," and behind it are exhibited pornographic videos, pink vibrators, and lacy lingerie. Another sign announces "private cabins." The spectator who watches the women meander through the streets of Amsterdam virtually encounters the global cityscape as a shopper encounters a display window; it presents a range of pleasures made available to the tourist, or anyone, for a price. The appeal of the movies involves, it seems, an imaginary "visual excursion and a virtual release from the confinements of everyday life" (Friedberg 1993, 28). For the ordinary Ghanaian spectator who does not have the

Figure 4.3. Consuming pleasure virtually (*Amsterdam Diary*, 2005)

means to travel as a tourist or to treat shopping as leisure, the movies provide, if only virtually, the chance to be a tourist and adopt a globally mobile subject position and to consume exotic and titillating pleasures from elsewhere.

Inadvertently, African travel movies upend the power relationship naturalized by the tourist gaze and write back to tourist discourses that "other" Africa. Deborah Shaw (2011) explains that the tourist gaze "often rests upon an assumed viewer of the developed world observing a 'third world other' or objects of their culture which are often deemed to be more desirable than the people themselves" (18). Detached and voyeuristic, the tourist gaze positions the foreign subject as an exotic object of Western curiosity. In these movies, the African "other" points his camera at the Western "foreigner," who is usually part of the tourist landscape, and if he is incorporated into the narrative at all, the foreigner is little more than a stereotype. The white Italian police officer in *Mamma Mia* hates blacks. The white woman who loves the African protagonist in *Back to Kotoka* is jealous and possessive and totally ignorant of African culture. The traveler's encounter with the global city is, then, superficial and limited. The narrative moves back and forth between the tourist landscape, where the migrant laughs and enjoys the tourist experience, and unmarked interior locations, where melodramatic domestic conflicts among Ghanaian migrants unfold.

At Home Abroad

For the Ghanaian traveler in the first wave of Africans-abroad movies, arrival and integration into the global city are continually deferred, obstructed by legal and economic barriers that prove impossible to avoid or scale. The movies' plots, as my discussion has shown, spin conflict, romance, and humor from the travelers' encounters with dire poverty, immigration laws and officials, unscrupulous visa dealers, racist Europeans and North Americans, greedy and deceitful hosts, immoral employers, and human traffickers, and resolution is achieved when the Ghanaian returns to Ghana. The latest travel movies represent life in the diaspora differently. They feature African characters who do not go back home, who seem more at home abroad. No longer centered on the travel undertaken by the migrant and his/her uncertain arrival in the global city, titles such as *London Got Problem* (2006), *Coming to Ghana* (2005), *Love in America* (2008), *Run Baby Run* (2008), and *Abrokyire Bayie* (2009), narrate the experiences of Ghanaians who are well established in the diaspora. Turning their focus away from tourist sites and spectacles, the latest transnational movies, made by videomakers now familiar with the "foreign" city, focus attention on the experience of living aboard. As producers and directors spend more time making movies outside of Ghana, their movies have become more integrated into the landscape of the world city and its African diaspora. Furthermore, the development of more formalized distribution networks overseas have allowed producers to make movies for African migrants living in the West.

Coming to Ghana, another movie by Bob Smith Jnr., was among the first travel movies to center on a Ghanaian living in the diaspora. Kwabena, played by Smith, is a Ghanaian who has lived in the United States for twenty-six years, working in a mortuary. At the start of the movie, Kwabena's boss informs him that a finger was discovered missing from one of the bodies kept in the mortuary and that until an investigation clears his name, he should not return to work. Without work, Kwabena decides to return to Ghana to search for a wife because, he explains, no Ghanaian woman in the US would marry a mortuary man. Kwabena's very successful and rich Ghanaian friends who live in the US advise him to return home and perform the role of a rich "been-to" in order to attract a beautiful and faithful Ghanaian wife.[8] Once back in Ghana, Kwabena realizes, however, that most of women want him only for his money and the possibility that he might take them to America. Disappointed and close to giving up, Kwabena, while driving through the streets of Accra, sees a woman selling nuts on the side of the road and offers to give her a ride. The woman, called Comfort, is beautiful and modest, and Kwabena invites her for a drink. Over time, the two fall in love, and Kwabena asks her to be his wife. When Comfort accepts, he buys her a home and her father a new taxi.

In *U Gotta Go Home* (2007), the second part of the series, Kwabena is called back to the United States by his employer. There, he finds himself embroiled in a Ghanaian friend's marital problems, wrongly and improbably accused of murder and, near the end of the movie, visited rather unexpectedly by his mother's ghost. (She is furious because while her son was in Ghana after a long absence he was too busy chasing women to come see her.) Amid the tortuous twists of Smith's convoluted plot, frequent crosscuts shuttle the audience back to Ghana, where Comfort has rather too quickly spent the money Kwabena left with her. She continually tries to call him, but cannot get through. In the meantime, in New York, Kwabena too is unable to reach Comfort by phone. As is often the case in these travel movies, technological malfunction and breakdown produces suspense and conflict. Hunted by the police, haunted by his mother, and at risk of losing his wife, Kwabena at the end of the film decides he's "gotta go home."

In this movie as in several other recent African-abroad movies, the mise-en-scène narrows the gap between the global city and Africa. No longer is the city displayed as a curious spectacle and rarely do characters tour its sites and amusements; in most cases, few scenes take place in exterior locations, and the cityscape merely frames the dramas happening inside domestic spaces. Many of movies set in the diaspora, especially the most cheaply produced, including *Coming to Ghana, London Got Problem,* and *Abrokyire Bayie,* rely on a similarly assembled montage in which an establishing shot of an exterior, urban location in a global city cuts to an unmarked interior space, usually a living room or kitchen, of a neatly and inconspicuously furnished home. These domestic scenes, though set in the home of Ghanaians living in a global city, often are shot in Ghana. In *Coming to Ghana* and *U Gotta Go Home,* a compilation of multiple locations in the

Figure 4.4. A tourist's view of the New York cityscape (*U Gotta Go Home*, 2007)

United States, Italy, where Smith visited on his way back to Ghana, and Ghana is presented as the New York City setting. In the first scene, set in the New York morgue where Kwabena works, an establishing shot of the morgue's exterior, identified by a large sign that reads Hennepin County Morgue, was shot in downtown Minneapolis, Minnesota. Because Smith's crew was not granted permission to videotape in the Minneapolis facility, scenes set inside the morgue were strung together from various unremarkable rooms, hallways, and offices along the path Smith traveled in the production of the video. The morgue's interior, where we see Smith getting dressed for work and walking down the hall, was shot in Verona, Italy, while the following scene, where Kwabena enters the temperature-controlled holding room and pulls out a drawer containing a body, was shot in Accra, Ghana. Only the last scenes of the film, which transpire in Manhattan against the backdrop of the site of the World Trade Center, offer a tourist's view of the New York cityscape. Smith explained to me that he had intended for this site to be the movie's big selling point (personal communication). Indeed, he chose New York as a location because Bob Santos, the famous Ghanaian concert party actor who had appeared in many videos, was living there and had agreed to participate in the movie and because of the opportunity to take Ghanaians to the former location of the Twin Towers.

Producers hoping to appeal to viewers who want to see movies about Africans living abroad have pushed this fakery to its furthest extreme, presenting movies shot entirely in African locations as if they were also set in a foreign country. The Ghanaian movie *Agya Koo in Libya* (2009) and the Nigerian movie *Love from Asia* (2004) are two examples. In these movies, global spaces in Africa are presented as global spaces abroad. *Agya Koo in Libya* relies on the most superficial Orientalist markers to encode a location as Libyan. Characters that are in Libya wear head scarves, and scenes that transpire in Libya are set in the same location, the outside porch of a large house that is tiled in a Middle Eastern design. A picture of Gadhafi has been hung conspicuously on the wall. An Asian restaurant in Lagos, frequented by Asian customers and decorated in Asian decor, is put forward as Asia in the Nigerian movie *Love from Asia*. These tricks play on Africa's real and imagined worldliness, exploiting the actual intermingling of the local and global that is a feature of African cities to create an imaginary, deterritorialized landscape.

In the most recently produced transnational movies, the central conflicts stem from the strained relationship between the Ghanaian in the diaspora and his family at home. Starring well-known comedic actors Abeiku Nyame (Jaguar P) and Agya Koo, Albert Kuvodu's *London Got Problem* (2006) focuses on a Ghanaian couple, Adams and Ayeley, who have lived in London for many years. When Adams's cousin Edem arrives at their London flat late one evening, unannounced, the couple receives him reluctantly and coldly. Adams explains to his wife, who demands to know who Edem is and what he wants: "I didn't know he'd get the visa. I gave him an empty promise." Adams is a sleazy character who cheats on his wife, lies to his mother about the money he intends to send her, and loses his job in a travel agency because he is lazy. Edem, on the other hand, works two jobs so he can send money home to his mother and fiancée. When, back in Ghana, Adams's mother discovers all that her nephew has done for her sister, she is furious and calls Adams continually to demand that he send her money, too. Worried that, back in Ghana, Edem's good example reflects negatively on them, Adams and his wife scheme to get rid of Edem. When their various sinister and misguided plans fall apart, they decide to exploit him by convincing him to deposit his income into their account. Because Edem is in the country illegally and cannot open his own account, he is easily persuaded to hand his money over to his cousin for safekeeping. This scheme, too, collapses after Edem has been granted legal status in London. With no other alternative, the couple decides they must have him deported. They plan to drug him with sleeping pills and call the police, claiming that he has robbed them. The pills, however, kill Edem. (Ayele reads the box after she realizes that Edem is dead and discovers that the pills have expired.) Adams buries his cousin's body in his backyard, but the ghost of Edem refuses to rest and returns to drive the greedy and scheming couple mad. Like many African popular forms, these transnational video movies from Ghana reiterate a moral economy that contrasts two types of wealth: one type, in the words of James Ferguson, is "a kind of collective wealth bound up with a prosperity that is general and shared" while the other is "selfish, antisocial, exploitative" (2006, 73).

Two competing narratives structure Parts I and II of Socrate Safo's *Love in America* (2008). The first details the efforts of Daniel, a Ghanaian living in New York, to obtain a green card, and the second concerns the power of witchcraft and "tradition," forces that dwell in Africa, but negatively influence Daniel's new and modern life in the global city. Like Edem, Daniel is residing in the United States illegally; his precarious status generates the humor and action in the first part of the two-part movie. After Daniel loses a bundle of money to an unscrupulous visa contractor, Mr. Ofori, Daniel's host, tells Daniel that he has found an American woman who will marry him and help him obtain his papers, and for a mere $30,000. Daniel reluctantly agrees to the plan, and Ofori brings the American woman, Lydia, to the house, and she and Daniel discuss the terms of their agreement. The two spend time together completing paperwork, sharing meals, and visiting the immigration office, and Lydia falls in love with Daniel. She continually tries to seduce him, threatening to pull out of their agreement if Daniel rejects her. Daniel, during the same period of time, has met and fallen in love with Sarah, a Ghanaian woman living legally in New York, who happens to be from Daniel's village, Sanga, although the two had never met. Overcome by love, Daniel risks everything and walks away from Lydia. He proposes to Sarah, and the two make plans to marry. But when Daniel calls his mother in Ghana to tell her that he wants to marry a woman from the North of Sanga, his mother forbids it, explaining to her son that the marriage would violate a centuries-old curse prohibiting marriage between residents from the North and the South of Sanga. Daniel refuses to respect this interdiction: "How can I not marry somebody I want to marry because of some ancient belief," he asks. Her mother insists that to marry Sarah will be to bring "calamity" to his family.

In this movie, as in *U Gotta Go Home, London Got Problem*, and *Amsterdam Diary*, the mother in Africa signifies burdensome obligations to family and community; from back home, she reminds her son of his familial duties, which typically impede his desires for success or love. In *London Got Problem*, Adams's mother calls incessantly to ask for money, and in Ghana, she seeks the help of a fetish priest, whom she asks to transfer Edem's luck to her son, an intervention that does not appear to work. In *Love in America*, it is Daniel's mother who objects to his marriage; hers is the voice of tradition and sanction. When Daniel assures her that "this is America," a place where curses and witchcraft cannot touch him, she answers, "Tradition is tradition and you have to abide by it." Like the cultural style James Ferguson describes as "local," the tradition portrayed in this movie is an urban invention, here constituted by its difference and distance from the lure of America. Tradition, located in the Ghanaian village, where his mother travels from Accra to consult with the elders and a fetish priest, signifies the family commitments, social obligations, and poverty that burden the Ghanaian in the diaspora. Tradition holds Daniel, not Sarah, responsible for the violation that their marriage represents, and it enforces a similarly gendered punishment on the villagers, those furthest from the economic prosperity located in the global city. In Sanga, young girls fetching water are swallowed by the river in a flash of light, and Daniel's closest male relatives, his uncle and father, contract a gruesome skin ailment. With each disappearance and when his uncle dies, Daniel's mother phones her son, finally convincing him to separate from his wife until another solution can be found. Though initially Daniel tries to extricate himself from his responsibilities to his family in Ghana, he ultimately cannot. His mother informs him that he must obtain a sample of his wife's menstrual blood and send it to her in Ghana so that she can present it to the fetish priest. The priest then frees the family from the curse, but he informs Daniel and Sarah that they can conceive and give birth to only one child. Different from earlier films set abroad, here, it is not the return home that marks the movie's resolution. Instead, the plot concludes when the Ghanaian migrant learns that he cannot deny his ties and responsibilities to those who remain in Ghana.

In 2000, Ghanaian migrants transferred over forty million dollars to Ghana as remittances, and after gold and cocoa, remittance was the largest source of foreign exchange in Ghana (Oppong 2002). The latest transnational movies about Ghanaian migrants speak to Ghanaians living in the diaspora, reminding them of their moral and financial obligations to family in Ghana. Protagonists who put their own desires before the needs of their families unleash conflict and suffering on their families and themselves. The intense focus on remittances and connections to home in these and earlier travel movies demonstrates that in the postnationalist, postcolonial era of global capitalism, citizens of the African postcolony no longer look to the nation-state to ensure their livelihoods. The nation-state has failed to meet its promises of modernization and national development, and individuals, on their own, seek a better life elsewhere.

5

Transcultural Encounters
and Local Imaginaries

*Nollywood and the Ghanaian Movie Industry
in the Twenty-First Century*

In his widely anthologized essay "Toward a Regional Imaginary in Africa" (1998), film critic Manthia Diawara argues that in the context of globalization and liberalization, regional zones of exchange in Africa, and the transnational flows of capital, people, imaginaries, technologies, and commodities that produce and sustain them, generate a type of "disorder" that challenges the homogenizing forces of multinational corporations and resists the state's complicity with global capitalism. Diawara points out that because cultural nationalism "has lost some of its explanatory power in the era of globalization" (77), what is needed in Africa is the cultivation of "regional imaginaries" that are built on "linguistic affinities, economic reality, and geographic proximity, as defined by the similarities in political and cultural dispositions grounded in history and patterns of consumption" (81). Diawara says little about transnational or regional cultural production in Africa, focusing instead on African markets as transnational spaces of trade and consumption, but as Moradewun Adejunmobi (2007) has shown, Nollywood functions in precisely this way. It has emerged from and contributed to the production of a regional identity and to regional movements of culture and commodities in Africa, and as a minor transnational and popular commercial form detached from formal networks, she argues, it presents local or regional cultural producers with "the best chance for competing with or even displacing cultural products circulating through the official global economy within national and regional contexts" (11). Put differently, Nollywood's informal and fragmented networks exploit the kind of disorder and chaos that Diawara credits with holding off cultural homogenization and bypassing state control. In both Diawara's and Adejunmobi's accounts, then, regional cultural economies in Africa have resisted assimilation into dominant economies and given expression to local voices, concerns, and desires.

Though both critics celebrate the regional generally, they tend not to look very closely at particular regional configurations in Africa or the many dynamic and heterogeneous horizontal movements of culture that contribute to regional cultural formations, instead adopting a vertical sightline that places a unified and static conception of the regional in opposition to multinational corporations or American mass media. This perspective positions the marginalized African cultural region in relation to the Western center, and from this point of view, regional African culture becomes synonymous with local African culture. In this chapter, I want to suggest another way of seeing regional zones of culture. Here, we adopt a lateral and transnational view of Nollywood from within Ghana's national borders, a position from which Nollywood appears far more ambivalent than Adejunmobi suggests. According to many Ghanaian producers, whose national market has been inundated with Nollywood movies, Nollywood has had a deep and lasting impact on the "local" industry. A regionally dominant cultural force, it has pushed Ghanaian videomakers out of production and exerted significant control over their more minor industry. For others, however, collaboration with Nollywood videomakers has allowed their products to travel far beyond national borders, providing access to transnational circuits of distribution and facilitating the creation of new transnational forms of African cultural expression.

At the level of the text, too, the opposition between the regional and the global imposes limited visibility. It overlooks the incredible mingling and mixing that contribute to the locally made movie's appeal. African video movies continually dialogue with global mass media. They are extroverted (Julien 2006), but unlike the African literary text, video movies have no interest in presenting African worlds to outsiders. Instead, they are extroverted in style and, to borrow Eileen Julien's term, in their "mood" (689). They enthusiastically embrace aspects of global mass culture and reinvent it for presentation to African audiences. As Karin Barber (1987) noted, syncretism is perhaps the most pronounced feature of African popular arts. They seek elements of foreign cultures as a renewable source of innovation and creation.

This chapter describes the affiliation, imitation, and competition that characterize the Anglophone West African video economy in the twenty-first century and discusses the types of movies that have emerged from it. It first examines the regional flows of financing, people, ideas, and media that move between the Nigerian and Ghanaian movie industries and describes the collaborations and coproductions that have resulted in unique transcultural practices. Within this regional economy, the English-language "professional" movie described previously becomes more deeply intertwined with transnational processes and global mass media forms. Its development outward, however, is coincident with the appearance of new types of Ghanaian movies that strategically articulate "localness" by taking up current and sensational debates and rumors, or in other ways signaling their relevance to their immediate context. The last section of the chapter compares the glamorous domestic dramas of Shirley Frimpong-Manso with a series of quickly made movies about Internet fraud and magic. Though not transnationally produced, Frimpong-Manso's movies circulate transnationally and address a transnational viewership. The movies about Internet magic are strategically topical, addressing current and local narratives. The comparison suggests a correspondence between these types of movies, which speak of similar desires and aspirations, but at markedly different registers.

Minor Transnationalism: Nollywood in Ghana

Like earlier cultural forms, such as the Ghanaian concert party and Onitsha pamphlet literature, video movies have spilled across and blurred national borders in West Africa. Following paths well worn by a long history of migration, trade, and cultural exchange between the two Anglophone West African countries, Nollywood movies have poured into Ghana as legitimate and, to a much larger extent, pirated commodities. It was in the 1990s that Nigerian movies on VHS cassettes first made their way into Ghana, carried by itinerant Nigerian traders, primarily electrical parts dealers, who supplied merchants in Accra. These traders created an individualized and underground network of pirate video distribution that stood on top of already organized commercial trade circuits. Soon after, Ghanaian video distributors and marketers, who had been trading in local video and pirated global media, became involved in the wide-scale bootleg duplication and distribution of Nigerian features on videocassette, and Nigerian videos quickly became embedded in the decentralized and widely dispersed Ghanaian video distribution economy, muddying already unclear lines separating the legal from the nonlegal and the local from the regional. Nigerian videos appeared in many of the unofficial commercial video parlors scattered throughout the cities of Accra and Kumasi, alongside their Ghanaian counterparts. Although some of the early traffic and trade in Nollywood movies in Ghana was legal, much of it operated within the pirate economy.

Since the early years of the industry, when the first Ghanaian videomakers exploited the pirate exhibition infrastructure to show their features, the pirate and legitimate video economies have been entangled. Ravi Sundaram has used the phrase "cluster[s] of legality and non-legality" to describe the electronic space of Indian technoculture (1999, 61). This phrase, I think, aptly captures the messiness of the video economy in Ghana. Locally produced videos were duplicated, sold, and projected, legally and illegally, in the same small venues as pirated foreign films and television programming that were copied onto video cassettes and, more recently, burned to VCDs. But whereas this entanglement, in the early years of the industry, buoyed local production, between 2000 and 2004, the influx of legal and illegal Nigerian videos nearly strangled the making of video features in Ghana. In 2000, Nigerian videos were exerting significant pressure on the Ghanaian video market, but Ghanaian production was holding its own with as many as forty-nine videomakers registered with the Film and Video Producers Association, and, of those, more than fifteen producing videos on a regular basis. GAMA Films continued to produce videos, and independent television station TV3 and the state-owned TV station GBC (Ghana Broadcasting Company) featured in-house and independently produced Ghanaian movies weekly. Each month, approximately four new videos opened at the Executive Theatre, the main venue for video projection in Ghana. In no more than five years, this situation declined precipitously. By 2005, local production in Ghana had almost died off completely, strangled by the predominantly, although not entirely, illegal traffic in Nigerian videos. Many producers had gone out of business; some were now involved in distributing Nigerian videos. GAMA Film Company, too, had discontinued video movie production, and TV3 and other independent local TV stations had stopped purchasing the broadcasting rights to Ghanaian features and, instead, began showing Nigerian videos, in many cases without purchasing the rights to do so. Then, in

2003, came the inauguration of Africa Magic, a digital satellite television station that aired Nollywood movies seven days a week. By this time, several video marketers from Nigeria, such as Infinity Films, had opened shops in Ghana, which distributed Nigerian videos exclusively, exacerbating the difficulties of Ghanaian producers in a market already saturated with Nigerian movies. Ghanaian productions almost completely disappeared from the local cultural landscape.

Various factors coalesced to create this situation. Jonathan Haynes (2007c) has suggested that audiences stopped purchasing Ghanaian videos because they preferred the racier and better quality videos that Nollywood's high production values supported. He argues that Nigeria's huge domestic market

> permits relatively large budgets, which lead to relatively higher production values—better equipment, better acting from more professional actors, fancier sets and special effects, etc. Relatively higher production values means it is easier to export, which leads to more profits and still higher production values, and soon one film industry can afford car chases while the other is stuck with domestic dramas filmed in modest homes. (Haynes 2007c, 4).

Demand for Ghanaian videos contracted, and production slowed to a stop. My research verifies Haynes's assertions, and I discuss the appeal of Nollywood movies in Ghana later in the chapter.

Nonetheless, focusing on quality runs the risk of diminishing the crushing impact the rampant and unchecked piracy of Nigerian features has had on local Ghanaian production. With no mechanisms in place to police or prosecute the smuggling of pirated media or to censor or regulate foreign films and videos sold and exhibited in the country, the state left local video producers completely vulnerable to the onslaught of Nigerian videos dumped into the market. In 2002, a VHS copy of a Nigerian feature could be purchased for as little as two dollars; a Ghanaian producer had to sell his feature for at least twice as much, and Ghanaian movies simply could not compete with the huge quantities of cheaper Nollywood movies flooding the market.[1] Without recourse to effective piracy protection, Ghanaian producers first turned to the National Censorship Board and demanded that it more effectively censor and police Nollywood movies, which were alleged to contain violent content that violated Ghanaian censorship laws. They hoped that censorship might, at the very least, restrict

Figure 5.1. Ibrahim sells pirated DVDs in Osu, Accra (© Carmela Garritano, 2009)

the number of Nollywood movies circulating in the system.[2] They also appealed to the National Anti-Piracy Committee, lobbying successfully for the formation of a national piracy task force. The task force, made up of producers, copyright officials, and border guards,

Figure 5.2. Socrate Safo sifts through pirated CDs confiscated by the piracy task force (© Carmela Garritano, 2007)

traveled to border checkpoints across the country to educate officers of the Customs, Excise and Preventive Service in copyright enforcement and to assist with the enforcement of copyright laws. In its first week of border visits, no fewer than eighteen thousand VHS tapes, CDs, and VCDs were confiscated, and between 2005 and 2007, the assistant director of the Ghana Copyright Office, Alfred Kumi-Atiemo, estimated that his office seized pirated audio and visual materials worth over eighty thousand dollars (personal communication).[3] Yet these efforts were expensive to bring about and not particularly effective against the tidal wave of piracy. Eventually, the task force was disbanded.

Policing the national borders also did little to curb piracy occurring in Ghana. Early on, a few Ghanaian distributors and producers managed to "beat the pirates," a phrase used to describe the strategy of purchasing the exclusive rights for VHS reproduction of a Nigerian movie in Ghana well before it had been released in Nigeria.[4] This strategy worked only for Ghanaian producers who had links to Nigerian producers and marketers. And still, its effectiveness was limited because once the Nollywood feature was made available in Ghana, nothing prevented distributors and marketers from immediately making and selling illegal copies of a legally obtained video. Making matters worse was that Ghanaian television stations were broadcasting far more Nollywood than Ghanaian movies and without purchasing the rights to do so. If a station could obtain a Nigerian movie for the price of a single copy, why would it pay hundreds or even thousands of dollars to buy the rights to broadcast from a Ghanaian producer? The Nigerian movie came unencumbered, as it were, and much like a video cassette copy of a Hollywood or Hindi movie, it was bootlegged without fear of prosecution, and pirates easily "chopped" profits from legitimate producers and distributors in both countries.[5]

In the past decade, Ghanaian movie producers have been further disadvantaged by Nollywood's faster transition from analog VHS to digital video compact disc (VCD) production and replication technologies. As early as 2001, inexpensive VCD players imported from China and Singapore were widely available in West Africa, as were VCDs and DVDs that contained pirated movies and television programs from the United States and India. Nigerian producers and distributors moved to digital release very rapidly and began importing and selling Nollywood movies on VCD years before Ghanaian producers had access to facilities that could mass produce VCDs.[6] It was not until 2005 that the first VCD factory, called Atlas, opened in Accra. Before that, the only alternative available to Ghanaian producers who wanted to do digital release was to purchase several CD duplication towers and burn copies of their features to individual CDs. But the process proved too slow, and the machines and blank CDs too expensive to be profitable. Lacking robust hardware and working in hot and dusty studios, the VCDs duplicated in this way were often faulty, and customers frequently complained that they did not play in their home machines.

Around 2005, the few Ghanaian producers who had the capital to invest in digital cameras, personal computers, editing software, and the assortment of digital technologies required to facilitate digital production initiated a slow but strong resurgence in the making of Ghanaian movies. The shift from analog to digital technologies, furthermore, has reshaped the industry, fragmenting and realigning what had been developing into a stable, though decentralized, network for video movie production and distribution. The integration of digital technologies into movie production, for example, individualized postproduction, expanding and loosening the links of what had been a widespread, but at key points concentrated, network. Now producers could purchase the personal computers, hardware, and software required to set up their own editing and sound studios. Previously, the size and expense of the analog editing system made individual ownership impractical. Producers typically outsourced the editing of their movies to GAMA Film Company or one of several private analog editing studios. These shared spaces, frequented by all Ghanaian video-makers, functioned as centers of the industry and facilitated a great deal of interaction and exchange among those involved in moviemaking. The availability of low-cost and user-friendly personal computer editing technologies eliminated the cost of renting time at GAMA or a commercial editing studio and, indirectly, disbanded these commonly held sites within the industry.

The transition from VHS cassette to VCD also rerouted the path that a local feature traveled from its production to its distribution and gave the producer more control over his commodity. As previously explained, in the 1990s when producers output their features as VHS cassettes, movie reproducers, such as Alex Boateng, also acted as movie distributors. Producers brought their finished VHS movies to a movie distributor who was responsible for copying the movies and then distributing those copies to marketers and traders. Working within this system made the producer dependent on the distributor/reproducer for both the production of his commodity and for its distribution and sale. The distributor refused to purchase the rights for the movie but sold it in his shop on behalf of the producer for a sizable percentage of the profits. Under these terms, the return the producer received on his investment was determined by the distributor. The integration of VCD replication technologies into the reproduction and distribution of local movies in Ghana altered this setup, giving the producer greater control over the production and circulation of his commodity. Instead of delivering a master copy of his movie to a distributor and relying on him to duplicate and distribute it, the producer was able to work directly with the VCD factory to replicate his video, a process that was far less expensive than VHS reproduction.[7] This setup allowed the producer to distribute his or her own movies or to organize and negotiate for their distribution with local marketers.

The technological innovation that has spurred growth in local production has also fostered the development and delivery of new forms of pirate media, like pirated combination-DVDs, commonly called combo-DVDs. The combo-DVD, a single DVD that contains as

Figure 5.3. Sign that explains the transition from VHS to VCD (© Carmela Garritano, 2009)

many as twenty highly compressed movies, is replicated in China and transported along global routes recently forged between West Africa and Asia. The DVDs are bundled with other products and shipped in large containers, which allow massive quantities of goods to be transported long distances at reduced costs, through the ports at Tema, in Ghana, and Lome, in Togo. (From Lome, traders smuggle the DVDs in much smaller quantities into Ghana by road.) As one might expect, much of the media and movie content duplicated on the DVDs originates in the United States, giving viewers in Africa almost immediate access to the films and popular television programs current in the West. Astonishingly, since 2009, combo-DVDs featuring locally made Nollywood and Ghanaian movies are everywhere available on the streets of Accra. A regional cultural flow between Nigeria and Ghana has expanded globally, toward Asia. Kumi-Atiemo mapped the circuit this way: individual movies are carried from West Africa to several Asian countries, but principally China, by itinerate traders who illegally compile, compress, and replicate the movies on combo-DVDs in Chinese factories and then transport them back to West Africa in large quantities (personal communication). The combo-DVD sells for as little as one or two dollars, while a locally produced movie, output as a single title, might cost as much as five.

Figure 5.4. Combo DVD (© Carmela Garritano, 2009)

The Nigerian and Ghanaian industries have launched several joint initiatives to diminish the impact of piracy on local markets by promoting regional collaboration and coproduction. In 2008, for instance, delegations from Ghana and Nigeria met twice, in May in Abuja and in July in Accra, to discuss strategies for legitimizing and regulating the marketing and distributing of movies in both countries. The Ghanaians voiced concerns about pirated and uncensored Nollywood films flooding their market and about their difficulties with breaking into the far larger and more organized Nigerian market. The Nigerian stakeholders, not surprisingly, were most concerned about the number of unlicensed and illegal distributors selling Nollywood movies and the rights to broadcast and reproduce those movies in Ghana. According to the official report of the meeting, they made no concessions to Ghanaian producers, who asked for "assurances from the Nigerians that their films will be accepted in the Nigerian market"; the "only assurances given the Ghanaians was that their films must be made more competitive and meet the quality of the Nigerian audience." The meetings, like others before them, concluded with elaborate strategies to facilitate the creation of transnational clearing houses to register imported movies and committees to resolve copyright and other disputes, but without detailed plans to fund these initiatives and without any financial support from official government ministries or offices in either Ghana or Nigeria, these ideas and recommendations have brought about no significant modifications in either industry.

Coproduction and Collaboration:
The Emergence of a Transnational Aesthetic

Commercial videomakers in Ghana and Nigeria now find themselves contending with the structural and economic conditions that have thwarted national cinema industries in the developing world for decades, the conditions, paradoxically, that facilitated the emergence of these industries in the late 1980s: increased market liberalization and the withering of state support and the expansion and escalation of global media flows and technologies (Alvaray 2008; Dovey 2009; Hoefert de Turegano 2004; Iwabuchi 2002; Tcheuyap 2011; Tuomi 2007). In Latin America and Africa, where national film industries have experienced significant contraction, entry into global commercial distribution networks and transnational collaboration have proved viable survival strategies for filmmakers. Most commonly, collaboration and coproduction between cinema industries join a major commercial distributor or a larger film producing country and a smaller, more minor national or regional industry. Borrowing terminology from Françoise Lionnet and Shu-mei Shih (2005), we might describe these collaborations as major-to-minor forms of transnationalism. Walter Salles's hit film *The Motorcycle Diaries* (2004) exemplifies this kind of transnational, transcultural articulation. Salles used a Latin American cast and crew and distributed the movie globally through the multiplex commercial circuit. In other cases, international coproduction brings a major or national film industry into contact with a smaller, more minor industry. Spain's support of cinema in Latin America and, though not a recent development, France's ongoing involvement in filmmaking in Francophone Africa are examples of this type of major-to-minor collaboration and coproduction. Though state-subsidized filmmaking in neither Spain nor France is major in the same way that Hollywood might be described as major, these industries function as dominant partners in their interactions with minor industries in the global south.

Unlike the major-to-minor international collaborations described above, movies coproduced or made collaboratively by commercial videomakers in Ghana and Nigeria represent an instance of what might be called minor-to-minor transnational collaboration; these minor transnational practices operate independent of partnership with a former colonial power or reliance on international multiplex distribution. And yet, though they transpire within the regional economy and outside of dominant economic networks, in form and content, they are deeply interpenetrated with globalizing forces. Minor transnational practices in Anglophone West Africa seem to confirm the findings of Koichi Iwabuchi (2002), whose study of Japanese popular culture in Asia shows that instances of regional transculturation are best understood within the context of the homogenizing power of American mass culture, where intraregional cultural interactions negotiate with and recontextualize global popular culture, creating contesting sites of "local cultural meaning" (40). Nollywood's regional impact is enmeshed with Western cultural influence, not entirely determined by or free of it, and, moreover, the cross-fertilization between the Ghanaian and Nigerian industries enacts what Iwabuchi (2002) calls "the intertwined composition of global homogenization and heterogenization" (16). The history of interaction between the Ghanaian and Nigerian video industries replays this double movement, the imitation and reinvention characteristic of transcultural practices occurring under asymmetrical global cultural relations.

Coproduction and collaboration between the two commercial industries has emerged in response to intensified competition in the media market and, for Ghanaian producers in particular, as a strategic response to Nollywood's regional dominance. Transnational production of video movies grew from transnational distribution, which required ongoing communication and travel between the two countries. It was the networks erected to facilitate the transnational circulation and sale of media that enabled, early on, coproductions between Nigerian and Ghanaian producers and, later, made possible the exchange of actors, cinematographers, set designers, makeup artists, and directors. Opa Williams, a producer and distributor from Nigeria, had been marketing Nigerian movies in Ghana for several years before he teamed up with the Ghanaian producer Hammond Mensah of HM Films to make *Mama* (1999), the first Ghana-Nigeria coproduction.[8] Macdavis Odikah, a Nigerian entrepreneur who had relocated to Ghana, established Gupado Films in 2001 as a Nollywood movie distribution outlet. In 2007, the company began producing transnational movies. The Ghanaian Abdul Salam Munumi, CEO of Venus Films, traded currency, VHS tapes and players, and video movies between Ghana and Nigeria for years before he began to make movies between the two industries.

Coproduction expanded legitimate markets, and in both countries, the movies that grow from the creative exchange between the industries have appealed to audiences' appetites for fresh and exciting stories, faces, locations, and genres. But, initially, for Ghanaian producers, affiliation with Nollywood also provided the chance to increase a movie's value in a distressed local market. Starting from the earliest productions, Ghanaian and Nigerian videos have exhibited a fascination with sensationalism and glitz. Producers from both industries have consistently expressed their ambitions to make African movies for African audiences that are as entertaining and glamorous as Hollywood movies. This aspiration has animated not only the "professional" movies described in the previous chapter. More recently, it also has contributed to the creation of an aesthetic of excess that is displayed, in differing degrees and modes of articulation, by most Nollywood and Ghanaian videos. Whether an epic set in a precolonial village or a domestic drama set in contemporary Accra, video movies commonly deploy an aesthetic characterized by flamboyant and extroverted

Figure 5.5. Portrait of Abdul Salam Munumi (© Carmela Garritano, 2009)

modes of self-styling, putting on display refashioned elements of global mass culture. This loud remixing of borrowed riffs signals modernity and makes a claim of membership in the global field of culture. In the late nineties, when the first coproductions appeared, the most successful Nollywood producers, benefiting from a much larger market than their Ghanaian counterparts, could afford more glamour and glitz; Nollywood movies featured bigger houses and SUVs, more extravagant costumes and props, and the most spectacular special effects.[9] Merely the inclusion of Nigerian actors, locations, or special effects was thought to significantly bolster a movie's local appeal. It was as if the imprint of Nollywood brought the Ghanaian movie closer to achieving first-class, Hollywood status. The Ghanaian director E. Dugbartey Nanor, who was involved in coproductions made by Ghanaian producer Samuel Nyamkye and Nigerian producer Ifeanyi Onyeabor, explained that he wanted to work with a producer from the Nigerian industry so he could make Ghanaian films with Nollywood "style" (personal communication). The movies that emerged from the collaboration were *Asimo* (1999); *The Visitor* (1999); *Time* (2000); *Lost Hope* (2000); and *Web* (2000).[10] Featuring big-budget stars from both industries and sophisticated special effects, the movies, which were promoted as Ghana-Nigeria productions, attracted a lot of attention in the media and among professionals in the Ghanaian industry, and at a time when movie production in Ghana had slowed considerably, the movies consistently drew large crowds to the cinema halls.[11]

In the twenty-first century, cross-pollination between the two industries has engendered unique and unexpected types of transnational African movies, the success of which have supported the Ghanaian industry's resurgence and growth. These forms have emerged from transnational modes of production and address, although today they also are produced discretely in both countries. Notable among them is the "epic," which, according to Birgit Meyer (2010), migrated to Ghana from Nigeria around 2001. It was Samuel Nyamekye, discussed above, who made the first Ghanaian epic, *Asem* (2001), and as Meyer notes, he worked in consultation with the Nigerian costume designer Emeka Nwabueze. Conventionally, the epic movie is set in a village kingdom in an unspecified precolonial time period. Narrative conflict often involves "traditional" beliefs or taboos that are violated or undone. In *Wedlock of the Gods* (2007), an all-powerful king casts a young mother's baby girl into the evil forest because she is born with a hump on her back, a sign that she has been cursed by the gods. The king also accuses the baby of causing the sudden death of her father on the night of her birth. The distraught young mother defies the king and rescues her baby from the forest with the help of a kind hunter, and the three of them make a life together outside the village walls. The baby, Sarpoma, grows to be a beautiful woman, and twenty years after her birth, a handsome young wrestler, Kofi, who happens to be the best friend of the village prince, meets and falls in love with her. Determined to "make her normal," Kofi enters the evil forest to find the enchanted cream that will break the spell that has deformed her body. There, with the help of the gods, he prevails over the many supernatural ordeals placed before him. (These battle scenes are rendered in dazzling digital graphics.) He returns and heals Sarpoma, and the two make plans to marry. Until, that is, the prince sees the beautiful young woman and proclaims that he wants her for himself. The king orders Kofi to release Sarpoma to his son. But the two lovers decide instead to leave their families and flee their village so that they can stay together.

There is an obvious and overdone critique of patriarchal power here, but, as Meyer (2010) remarks of the epic genre more broadly, the appeal involves the sumptuous and excessive display of "traditional" life. This rendition of tradition is entirely imagined, a chaotic assemblage of ornaments from a hodgepodge of sources. Bodies beautifully display "traditional" adornments, including delicate body paintings, printed textiles, feathers, animal skins, and beads. Drums, flutes, and dancing figure prominently, and I have identified motifs that might have originated in African tourist art, *Tarzan* or more recent Hollywood movies, Chinua Achebe's *Things Fall Apart*, Yoruba video movies, or African folktales. But, clearly ethnographic authenticity is not the point. "Tradition" as represented here is unapologetically invented and, moreover, meant to signal the movie's modernity. This is a past that could only be conjured and performed by modern subjects who are placed outside of it.

Transnational collaboration and competition also have given rise to a wave of flashy, big-budget, English-language domestic dramas popularly known as "glamour" movies. Venus Films' *Beyoncé: The President's Daughter* (2006) was perhaps the most successful and influential of the transnational glamour movies. Nothing of its scale had been seen before, and Venus sold close to a million copies in Africa and the diaspora. Produced by the Ghanaian Abdul Salam Munumi and directed by the Nigerian Frank Rajah Arase, the movie launched the Ghanaians Van Vicker and Jackie Appiah, two emergent stars, and a newcomer, Nadie Buari, into big-name fame and lucrative careers in Nollywood and the Ghanaian industry. Despite its title, the film has little to do with politics. Beyoncé, played by Nadia Buari, is the rich daughter of the president and in the course of the film becomes a

Member of Parliament. But we never see her do any actual work in this capacity. Instead, her political position seems intended to explain her unfathomable wealth and power. Melodramatic and excessive, the movie centers on Beyoncé's ruthless determination to have Raj, the man she loves, but who loves Ciarra, a poor singer who saves Raj's life when he is gunned down by unknown assailants. The meandering and improbable plot chronicles Beyoncé's fight with Ciarra for Raj. At the end of the film, Beyoncé pays her thugs to burn Ciarra's face with acid, forcing Ciarra to agree to accept Beyoncé's offer to rebuild her face only if she stays away from Raj. In *Beyoncé II* (2007), Raj believes that Ciarra is dead. Although initially he suspects that Beyoncé was involved in Ciarra's death, he eventually falls in love with Beyoncé, and the two make plans to marry. Ciarra turns up at the wedding with a gun and shoots Beyoncé. Raj is tried and found guilty of the crime, and the film ends with his (poorly executed) execution by hanging.

Ghanaian and Nigerians have been making melodramatic English-language domestic dramas since their industries' inaugurations, but this recent iteration is groundbreaking in its glamour and excess and because its appropriation of global styles and idioms is more pronounced than ever before. Glamour movies, like *Beyoncé*, showcase fantastically luxurious urban locations. They typically feature big-name actors, many of whom are biracial and model Western standards of beauty and sex appeal, sometimes displaying their international credentials by adopting contrived and poorly executed British or African American accents. Their aesthetic is also marked by ostentatious and extroverted stylization of the body (dress, hair, and makeup, for example), which draws inspiration from music videos by American hip hop artists, fashion magazines, and soap operas, and by a fascination with expensive and superfluous commodities such as cell phones, flashy cars, computers, and designer sunglasses. Achille Mbembe's ideas about "an aesthetic of superfluity" (2004) apply perfectly here. The pleasure and fantasy visualized in these movies reiterates "the logic of the commodity" (Mbembe 2004, 401). Spectators watching glamour videos can imaginatively consume the luxuries displayed before them and are invited to temporarily inhabit the subjectivities of glamorous and wealthy characters, whose lives are sealed off from the materiality of the postcolony, which stays safely out-of-frame. These movies produce desire to possess the things exhibited and showcase modern subjects who craft identities through consumption. The subtext of these movies promotes, in Mbembe words, "a stylization of consumption"

(2004, 400) that is not sutured to a specific context and instead is meant to appeal to a broad audience of English-speaking Africans.

Combining elements of the epic and glamour forms are so-called royal movies. These are narrative epics, like *Asem* and *Wedlock of the Gods*, but they are removed from the village of the distance past and set in contemporary, urban locations. Produced in English and characterized, once again, by lavish display and self-styling, this type of movie takes the performance of modernity to an extreme. Here, African "tradition" has been quite literally detached from any historical reference and moved into the present. It has been "de-temporalized," a term used by James Ferguson (2006) to capture what Africans means when they talk about being modern. For most Africans, Ferguson argues, modernity is not about historical progression as in modernization theory. Nor does being modern refer to "a set of wonderfully diverse and creative cultural practices," as he suggests it is often treated in anthropological discourse. As African video movies clearly demonstrate, being modern describes arriving at a particular economic position, of reaching a high standard of living or obtaining a first-class global status (Ferguson 2006). Here the fantasy of being modern and being African is played out in a baroque theatrical pageant led by traditional kings who wear beads and Kente cloth and drive BMWs.

The Ghanaian Industry in the Twenty-First Century

Since plummeting to a nadir in 2005, the Ghanaian industry has slowly rebounded. In 2011, over one hundred movie producers were registered with the Film and Video Producers Association (FIPAG), and Kumasi has become a second movie-producing city, rivaling Accra for the most movies made. Many producers work in both cities; some, like Miracle Films, are more rooted to one, in this case Kumasi, though because Accra remains the center for movie distribution, producers travel back and forth regularly. There have been significant structural changes in recent years, too. Producers and distributers have organized to more effectively control the number of movies circulating in the national market. Only eight Ghanaian movies and two Nigerian movies are released each month. Transnational collaboration has been another factor in the resurgence in production, creating new attractions for audiences in Ghana and abroad.

Concurrent with this wave of movies with transnational reach has been a surge of Akan-language movies made for local audiences.

Movies made in Akan have supplanted English-language movies in popularity and number of movies made. Producers explained that using Akan purposefully restricts the movie's audience and limits the bootleg distribution of the movies outside Ghana, where policing piracy is impossible. These movies "are like magazines," to borrow a phrase from Socrate Safo (personal communication). Often topical in focus and made and consumed quickly, they dialogue directly with local publics. The narratives rely on various forms of local knowledge and make assumptions about shared experiences, values, or beliefs. Perhaps the most popular genre of the Akan-language movie is the local comedy, a form which incorporates narrative conventions and character types associated with the Ghanaian concert party and features actors like Kofi Adu, known as Agya Koo, who formerly appeared in the Key Soap Concert Party on Ghanaian television, and Rose Mensah, known as Akua Kyeiwaa, who previously stared in two popular Akan-language television programs, Akan TV Drama and Cantata TV Drama. Many of these movies are made in Kumasi, and they are sometimes referred to popularly as "Kumasi movies." Commercial success here depends on the audience's understanding and appreciation of older forms of Ghanaian popular culture and the character types, narrative structures, and cultural idioms specific to them. Although the movies might appeal to non-Ghanaian audiences, it is a national audience that producers seek. This type of movie, nonetheless, has also sold well in the Ghanaian diaspora. Rabiu Mohammed, founder of Sanga Entertainment, one of the three largest African movie distributors in New York, claims that among his customers, local movies, such as Akan-language dramas, are in high demand because they offer Ghanaians living abroad the virtual experience of "home." The stories, humor, and speech, he explained, portray their home and their culture, which they miss and want to share with their children, many of whom have never been to Ghana (personal communication).

In 2011, spread between two urban centers, Accra and Kumasi, and interlaced at various points with Nollywood, the Ghanaian movie industry is more like a sprawling and shifting network of individual producers than a unified, national configuration. And while unwieldy levels of change and diversity and tremendous amounts of generic blending confound efforts to strictly categorize the types and genres of movies produced in Ghana, it is of course possible to describe the broad and meaningful differences that distinguish one movie from another. We have already identified target audience as one significant area of difference. Budgets, too, vary considerably, and there is typically, but not always, a correspondence between these categories. Movies made for local consumption tend to have lower production values than movies made for transnational distribution. The total cost of most Ghanaian productions likely falls between $30,000 and $60,000; these figures include all costs associated with a movie's production as well as with its replication, distribution, and promotion. In the area of production budgets, that is, the total amount spent on making the movie, two models anchor opposing ends of a lengthy continuum. On one end is Socrate Safo's Movie Africa Productions. An industry pioneer, Safo has made hundreds of movies and is one of the most successful producers working in Ghana today. His movies tend to be made as quickly and cheaply as possible. Movie Africa operates like a small, high-volume production house, releasing about two movies on VCD in the local market each month. Though he spends a lot of money on advertising and promotion, Safo keeps production costs very low, spending, on average, about seven days shooting a movie, and editing it in as few as five days. He shuns what he calls "unnecessary affluence" in costuming and sets and rarely uses big-name actors in his movies (personal communication). In 2006, Safo established the Movie Africa Artists' Club, a training school where he convenes acting and directing classes two nights a week, in the backyard of the building that houses his modest office and editing studio. At its peak, the school enrolled as many as one hundred and fifty students. Safo does not charge students to attend classes, but of the many inexperienced young actors and videomakers who participate, only the most disciplined and talented are given roles in his movies or hired to work as members of his crew. For Safo, the school provides an almost endless supply of cheap labor.

Safo is closely connected to local audiences and has been especially effective at anticipating audience interests and at generating buzz around his movies even before they have been released. His target audience includes market women and street hawkers—those, he explains, who always have cash on hand to spend on the hottest movie. Because he releases movies so quickly, he can link his movies to the most recent rumors or scandalous stories circulating through Accra or Kumasi, and in recent years, he has shocked and enticed viewers with scantily dressed women and sexually explicit romantic encounters.

One the other end of the continuum are the movies of Shirley Frimpong-Manso's Sparrow Productions, which are among the most professional features, with the highest production values, ever released in Ghana. While Safo relies on speed and sensationalism, Frimpong-Manso, a graduate of the National Film and Television Institute (NAFTI), produces about one top quality feature film each year. Her titles include *Life And Living It* (2007); *Scorned* (2008); *The Perfect Picture* (2009); *A Sting in a Tale* (2009); *Checkmate* (2010); and *Six Hours to Christmas* (2010). The English-language movies adopt the professional style described earlier, but supported by much bigger budgets and better technology; they achieve a style closer to that made popular globally by Hollywood than did their predecessors. Frimpong-Manso's critics, in fact, consider her movies unoriginal because they imitate Hollywood romantic comedies and drama; they accuse her of remaking Tyler Perry films for an African audience or producing movies that are too Western.[12] Perhaps because they so successfully shadow and reimagine Hollywood, capturing Ghanaian aspirations to be as good and as modern as the characters in Hollywood films, Frimpong-Manso's movies have been well received in the local market, and like many of the higher quality Ghanaian-Nigerian coproductions, they have achieved a substantial regional and international viewership, in Africa and the diaspora. Adopting a model of production and distribution more common to major, international independent and commercial film industries, Frimpong-Manso has rejected the straight-to-DVD/VCD model of distribution, which has been dominant in both Ghana and Nigeria since the mid-1990s.

Other Ghanaian filmmakers like Leila Djansi and Francis Gbormittah as well as "New Nollywood" directors Kunle Afolayan and Mahmood Ali-Balogun have made a similar shift, investing a great deal more time and money in far fewer, high-quality productions made chiefly for the cinema screen. With access to digital cinematography cameras and professional, computer-based editing suites, these producers are releasing film-quality movies, which have significantly diminished the gap between locally made popular videos and Hollywood or Bollywood productions. The profitability of this model of distribution for many of these emergent filmmakers has opened up new sources of revenue: bank loans, corporate sponsorship, and international, private investors.

The next section of this chapter focuses close attention on two types of movies: the professional, English-language domestic dramas of Shirley Frimpong-Manso, which address a transnational audience, and a series of lower-budget, quickly-made local movies about "sakawa," a term that describes Internet crimes believed to involve the occult. I suggest a correspondence between these two types of movies, arguing that sakawa movies expose what Frimpong-Manso's movies hide.

Sparrow Productions and the Pleasures of Consumption

In July 2008, the Accra Mall opened for business in Ghana. The mall's website boasts that the Accra Mall, with sixty-five retail stores, including the South African chains Shoprite and Game Stores, a large food court, and a five-screen cinema complex, offers its patrons "the goods and services widely available elsewhere in the world." It stands as "a symbol of the growth, modernization and progress of the nation."[13] I first visited the shopping center in 2009, and though many of the specific stores were unknown to me, the mall seemed an utterly familiar place, its geography and atmosphere replicating any shopping mall I might visit in the United States. And this, of course, is precisely the point. The Accra Mall offers patrons the opportunity to participate in a globally homogenized shopping experience in Africa. Gregor Dobler (2008) has noted that although consumer goods have been available in Africa for centuries, economic liberalization and the emergence of new trade networks have contributed to the expansion of the consumer landscape. He suggests that in the African context of economic deprivation, consumption functions as a mode "to express personal identity in relation to the wider world, with all its social and economic discrepancies" (Dobler 2008, 410). The mall becomes an arena for articulating a modern subjectivity.

The first Ghanaian movie to be screened at the Accra Mall in the state-of-the-art Silverbird Cinema was Shirley Frimpong-Manso's *The Perfect Picture*.[14] The film was hugely successful, outselling Hollywood films that were featured concurrently. The first weekend, over fifteen hundred people purchased fifteen-dollar tickets to see the film, and the showing at Silverbird was held over to accommodate the extraordinary and unexpected demand.[15] The movie's extended run was followed by screenings in Silverbird's Nigerian theaters and a string of cinemas in other parts of Africa and the diaspora. After its cinema circulation had concluded, it was released locally on VCD for individual sale.

Near its conclusion, *The Perfect Picture* includes a scene filmed and set in the Accra Mall and at the Silverbird Cinema. It is a moment when the boundary between the film and the spectators watching the film blurs, when the characters and the audience at the Silverbird share the same space. For spectators, the experience of watching the women in the mall is a bit like window-shopping. To a backdrop of Ghanaian hip-life, a musical fusion of Ghanaian highlife and hip hop, the three main characters, Aseye, Dede, and Akaysie, stroll leisurely through three different venues in the mall: Aseye moves in front of a clothes shop, Dede shops for books in a bookstore, and Akaysie purchases a tub of popcorn at the cinema. The film then cuts to a three-way phone conversation, playfully initiated by Aseye, and captured in a three-way split screen shot. The women chat and giggle before deciding to meet at the cinema and catch a film. The gorgeous women, each wearing a chic, color-coordinated ensemble, each made-up flawlessly, each with a slim and stylish cell phone, model the clothes, accessories, and entertainments that the mall offers. This scene functions as a metonym for the aesthetics of superfluity that all of Frimpong-Manso's movies deploy impeccably. Like the mall, these films work like "synthetic spacetimes" (Mbembe 2004, 401), provoking desire not only for the goods on display, but for the characters' lifestyles. The spectator's pleasure derives from leaving the banality of the everyday and vicariously fashioning a new, modern self through consumption.

Much like the professional movies discussed in the third chapter, Frimpong-Manso's movies are generic and secular, sanitized, including no markers or mention of historical or cultural specificity, nor any trace of poverty or hardship, and stripped of any references to juju priests or charismatic preachers. Yet, these features possess a certain "spectral power" (Mbembe 2004, 401); they captivate through their power to produce entire fantasy worlds built around consumer goods. Frimpong-Manso, whose company, Sparrow Productions, also produces videos and commercials for corporations and businesses, composes shots like advertisements; they appear as highly stylized visual displays that aestheticize consumption. Two shots from *The Perfect Picture* illustrate. In the first, a pair of hands with manicured nails gently touches a gold and diamond necklace. The shot, taken at an angle from above, represents Akaysie's sight, and the necklace, positioned in the middle of the shot, is the focal point of the gaze. Displayed in its box with the brand name conspicuous, the necklace is intended to attract and amaze the spectator. In the second shot, also from *The Perfect Picture*, a vertical line, created by the edge where a mirrored dresser meets a mirrored door, splits the frame. On the

Figure 5.6. Commodity aesthetics (*The Perfect Picture*, 2009)

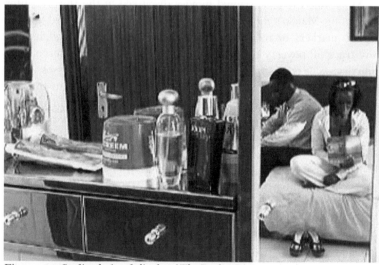

Figure 5.7. Stylized visual display (*The Perfect Picture*, 2009)

left side and prominent in the foreground of the frame on top of the dresser sit several bottles of brand-name perfumes and colognes. The elegant and expensive bottles face the camera directly, their labels clearly visible. Reflected in the mirrored door from a distance, sit Aseye and Larry, the newlyweds, on their large bed, each dressed in a well-accessorized ensemble; Larry wears a suit and tie, and Aseye sits cross-legged in her pajamas, her matching pumps on the floor. As in the previous shot, the sensuous products exhibited here dwarf the human figures, which appear at a distance and in the mirror's reflection.

The narratives and aesthetics of Frimpong-Manso's movies are very similar: each movie resembles an abridged soap opera; its plot moves quickly among several distinct but intersecting story lines that center on the romantic travails of young, well-educated, excruciatingly beautiful and prosperous Ghanaian couples. Men and women talk about love and sex very explicitly and in great detail in these videos; they drive posh cars, work in shiny and modern offices, and dance and make love to American and Ghanaian pop music. In each of Frimpong-Manso's movies, multiple narratives unfold and interact. The opening segment of a Frimpong-Manso movie typically introduces the narratives, central characters, and conflicts. In the first scene of *Life and Living It*, Kente has come to the home of Erica, the mother of his child, Eric, to see his son. Erica sends him away, and when Kente threatens to take her to court so that he can spend time with his son, she asks, sarcastically, how he could ever manage that on his "measly salary." In the next scene, set at the same time of day, Jerry Klevor, a doctor, has breakfast with his mother. They discuss the upcoming return of Jerry's sister, Lailah, who has been abroad for several years, and Mrs. Klevor worries that both of her children are unmarried. The third scene introduces the womanizer Ray. He smokes a cigarette while running on a treadmill, when his lover appears from the bedroom. She suggests that he travel with her, and he responds by asking what her husband would think. Finally, in the fourth segment, the movie presents the workaholic husband Ato Yawson and his stay-at-home wife, Karen, whom he disappoints when he pulls away from her embrace to speed off to work. After Ato's hasty departure, Jerry knocks on the door. The brief interaction between Jerry and Karen makes it clear that they have been lovers and that Ato, who is one of Jerry's best friends, is not aware of this. Throughout the movie, synchronous editing and the intersection of story lines, as represented here through Jerry's visit to Ato's, create the illusion of a self-enclosed world that spins outside of history and economy in a state of perpetual plentitude.

The movies fetishize individual agency and choice. Each of the multiple narrative threads of a Sparrow Productions movie is structured around a key, personal decision, which is presented as monumental and life-altering. After much deliberation, Kente resolves to pursue his case against Erica for custody of his son. (The judge decides in favor of his petition.) Jerry chooses to express his love to Karen and then decides to help Karen and Ato reconcile. Ray reconsiders his policy of dating only married women. Karen is determined to go back to work, and Ato finally decides to accept and support her decision, which he initially resisted. The movie resolves and concludes after each character has made and announced his or her decision.

In the dark comedy *Six Hours to Christmas*, the entire film hinges on Reggie's belabored decision to cheat on his girlfriend on Christmas Eve and sleep with his hot office co-worker Pebbles. His bad choice sets off a chain reaction of deception and violence. The point of the film, as Frimpong-Manso stated in an interview, is that "one indiscretion on our part could lead to errors capable of ruining one's life forever" (qtd. in H. L. Smith 2010, 2). As these examples are intended to demonstrate, it is through individual choice that characters solve their problems and plots achieve closure. These are lives free of economic and political constraint and without disability or disadvantage. Family or social obligations that might complicate the idea of individual preference are either absent or reduced to moral choices about infidelity, and the movies erase economic obstacles that might impede choice or get in the way of fulfilling desire.

This representation of individual autonomy perfectly aligns with neoliberal rationalities and the dominant ideologies that undergird them. Neoliberal rationality, as defined by Wendy Brown, "involves extending and disseminating market values to all institutions and social action" (2003, 3). Brown argues that since the 1980s, this rationality has functioned "as governmentality—a mode of governance encompassing but not limited to the state, and one that produces subjects, forms of citizenship and behavior, and a new organization of the social" (1). Neoliberal rationalities extend the free-market principles of global capitalism into all dimensions of human life and create the individual as an autonomous, rational agent who "bears full responsibility for the consequences of his or her action no matter how severe the constraints on this action, e.g., lack of skills, education, and childcare in a period of high unemployment" (6). Subjects are understood "as entrepreneurial actors in every sphere of life" (6). In that the movies conceal the economic advantages these characters enjoy and embody, they participate in disseminating neoliberal governmentalities. The narratives build entire fantasy worlds around personal choices made and realized. It is individual will alone that brings love, happiness, fulfillment, or, as in *Six Hours to Christmas*, disaster.

Perfect Picture (2009) is a movie centered on three modern Ghanaian women. Like Quarshie, Frimpong-Manso has made an effort to privilege women's perspectives on love, marriage, and work. The movie represents Aseye, Dede, and Akaysie as fiercely independent, defying gender conventions that stigmatize women who seek pleasure and personal fulfillment without men. Each expresses her agency through sex, sexy talk about sex, and shopping. In the end, however, the patriarchal economy domesticates the women, although the narrative insists that each woman chooses to conform to gender norms because it makes her happy. (This, of course, is how dominant ideologies work. The coercive social mechanisms that influence choice are coded as expressions of personal happiness or will.) Dede adopts a child, fulfilling her deep desire to be a mother. Aseye reunites with Larry, despite their sexual problems, and Akaysie, the rich career woman who vowed never to marry, eschews class prejudices and her own doubts and accepts the marriage proposal of Fela, whom she believes is a lowly air-conditioner repairman. Even this muted acknowledgment of class is erased in the last scene of the movie when Fela reveals that he *really* is a rich attorney who enjoys manual labor and works on air conditioners for fun. These narratives, masking gender and class ideologies as the whims of freely made personal choice, conceal the coercive pressure of gender norms.

In a different context, Nivedita Menon uses the phrase "beauty parlor" feminism to describe an iteration of feminism that sets itself in opposition to conservative practices coded as "cultural," such as veiling (2005). It is this version of feminism, without an obvious opposition, that we find in *Perfect Picture*. Here, beauty, consumption, and sexually explicit talk and behavior are configured as expressions of women's liberation. Menon points out that such a feminism is extremely limited in its reach and articulation, available only to the global elite, and that, additionally, it fails to acknowledge the commodification of women's bodies and the stringent regime of beauty standards it participates in legitimizing. The "choices" made "freely" here reinforce dominant gender ideologies. In the end, these progressive and liberated women behave as women are supposed to behave. In *Perfect Picture* we see, too, that gender difference structures every choice a woman makes. Should she cheat on her husband? Should she marry? Should she get involved with a married man? A woman's "freedom" relies on a man for its expression.

Frimpong-Manso's movies fetishize personal choice much as they fetishize consumer goods, repressing the material and social conditions that enable or limit autonomy and free will and removing subjects from history by placing them in a mall-like, synthetic world. In sakawa movies, which we turn to next, the repressed dimensions of neoliberal capitalism return.

Sakawa Movies

In part, it is the luxurious lifestyle projected in Frimpong-Manso's movies that lures Kingsley, the protagonist in Trisha Adaobi Nwaubani's novel *I Do Not Come to You by Chance* (2009), into the world of 419, the e-mail scam named after the section of the Nigerian penal code developed to address it. In the award-winning Nigerian novel, Kingsley has recently graduated from the Federal University of Technology in Owerri with a degree in chemical engineering, and yet despite his efforts, he cannot secure a job in Nigeria, where connections, criminality, and corruption seem the best methods for getting ahead. As the *opara*, the oldest son, he feels tremendous shame that he cannot take care of his ailing father or help provide for his large family, and without a job, he cannot afford to marry. Trapped in poverty and enticed by the fleet of SUVs, well-dressed security guards, flat screen TVs, and designer clothes that belong to his uncle Boniface, also known as Cash Daddy, Kingsley decides to join Cash Daddy's team of Internet fraudsters. Using the "big English" of a college graduate, he composes artful e-mail messages that convince wealthy foreigners to wire large sums of cash to him, a complete stranger, in anticipation of the even greater sums of money that they will receive in return for their "investment." Adopting Kingsley's point of view, the novel explores the depravity and desire that drive young Nigerians to participate in Internet fraud schemes and describes the inner workings of these ploys, giving readers an insider's view of the mechanisms of the successful scam.

Though Africans account for only 4 percent of worldwide Internet users, the number of Africans on line has increased at an accelerated rate, 1,000 percent between 2000 and 2008 (Fair et al. 2009). The Internet has facilitated the creation of new spaces of transnational interaction and economic exchange, and Internet fraud scams represent, as Mathew Zook explains, an "unanticipated and aggravating derivative" of this new connectivity (2007, 66). Although Nigeria has been identified as the country from which 419 originated, the practice has spread across the globe, and the losses are huge. In 2006, it was estimated that more than $3,000,000 was lost to 419 Internet scams (Zook 2007).

Narratives about Internet fraud have also appeared across numerous sites of public culture in West Africa, including Ghanaian and Nigerian video movies, but unlike literary representations of 419, these popular narratives associate the success of Internet fraud with the intervention of witchcraft. In 2009 when I was in Ghana, stories about a particular type of Internet fraud, referred to as *sakawa*, were ubiquitous, appearing in newspapers, broadcast on radio programs, and circulating as rumors. The word *sakawa* generally refers to a type of magic or juju used by Internet scammers to penetrate the Internet through the computer and enable the success of their fraud schemes. But like the term "419," to which it is linked, sakawa sometimes functions in popular discourse as "an all-encompassing signifier" for the many forms of illicit behavior that rely "on dissimulation, illusion, or some other manipulation of the truth in order to facilitate gain or advantage" (D. J. Smith 2007, 20). Movies about sakawa, which are produced in Akan and English and include titles such as *Café Guys* (2002) and *Sakawa Boys* (2009), poached narratives from these other sites of public culture, cashing in on the curiosity and anxiety that fueled stories about sakawa. Socrate Safo's *Sakawa Boys* (2009) made almost $50,000 profit on the first of his four-part series. Other producers, eager to benefit from the popularity of sakawa narratives, quickly released their own movies. Several actresses from Safo's Movie Africa Productions released *Sakawa Girls* (2009), and *Agya Koo Sakawa* I and II (2009) by Barfour Awuah Production's appeared. Venus Film produced *The Dons in Sakawa, Parts 1–4* (2009), and Big Joe Productions made *Sakawa, Parts I and II* (2010). Other Ghanaian titles include *Sika Mu Sakawa* (2009) and *Sakawa 419* (2009).

The commercial success of these movies is tied to their ability to rapidly respond to and reimagine stories about Internet fraud and its supernatural sources, which are found in other sites of public culture. The movies deploy what Angela Ndalianis has described in

Hollywood films as "a logic of seriality" that emphasizes "the marketable aspects of stories rather than their 'originality'" (2004, 59). These serial forms of screen media craft an elaborate narrative web that reaches beyond the text of the single movie to include other movies, rumors, and media accounts. Sakawa movies dialogue with other sakawa movies as well as with current news stories and stories that circulate orally. Their topicality and immediacy make them irresistibly appealing to local audiences, who are also ensnared in this locally generated, narrative web.

The word *sakawa* derives from Hausa and translates into English as "to penetrate," or "to get into." Ghanaian newspaper articles identify several different types of sakawa crimes. The most common involve Internet fraud schemes: online shopping and cash advances with stolen credit card information, money transfers with hacked bank account numbers, and elaborate business deals conducted online and over the phone, in which the scammer assumes a fake identity and uses counterfeit documents and other bogus information to convince the so-called victim that if she or he deposits a large sum of money into a bank account, an even larger sum of money will be released to her or him.

The young men who engage in sakawa are said to employ "spiritual assistance," a phrase that describes various occult activities, including visiting shrines and performing the rituals demanded by the shrine priest or the *mallam*. Many sakawa boys, it is alleged, engage in blood-money rituals, known in Akan as *sika aduro*, to access wealth. They are told to kill family members or strangers, or in some instances to obtain blood, in exchange for money. The crimes are consistently said to be perpetuated by young men who drive flashy cars and, as stated by the journalist Muhammed S. S. Jawando (2009), spend their "ill-gotten wealth lavishly on women." These are men without the money to meet their family and social obligations, who lack the capital to be men, in effect. Without income, they cannot marry, build homes, support themselves, or assist their families.

Again and again, columnists connect the emergence of sakawa to the failures of the postcolonial state. In an article from *Ghanaweb*, Stephen Owusu (2009) writes:

> It is a common sight in Ghana to see the newly rich, thanks
> to sakawa, driving in Porsche, Hummer and Mercedes Benz
> cars all white in color. These things normally crop up when
> students cannot pay their fees, high rate of employment,

commodities becoming very expensive, people turning more
to pastors for a miracle and many more. It behooves on the
government to sit up and tackle this problem.

Comments made by Haruna Iddrisu, the Minister of Communications in Ghana, suggest that perhaps the Ghanaian government has taken notice and demonstrate, too, the reach and prevalence of Internet crime. At the launching of a state-private sector initiative to make broadband services available in the remote Bonsaaso Millennium Village Cluster in the Ashanti region of Ghana, the minister reminded his audience that the proper use of telecommunications would help eradicate poverty and promote wealth in Africa, and, according to a report by I. F. Joe Awuah Jr, in *Modern Ghana News*, he "warned students not to try to use the Internet for any criminal activity." Yet, as the movies point out, the youth who engage in Internet fraud do indeed escape poverty and create wealth, and they do so by seeking private sector business partners. Their "businesses," however, hijack official and legal networks. Much like piracy, Internet fraud attaches itself to and in a sense becomes a parody of the legitimate flows of capital through global telecommunications networks. It "corrupts," to borrow a term from Brian Larkin (2008), official and legitimate infrastructures.

Like other popular discourses about magic, wealth, and corruption, sakawa narratives provide an explanation for what seems the sudden and mysterious acquisition of wealth by young men. One producer explained that sakawa rumors emerged as information about 419 scams became more widely circulated. As people were becoming more and more educated about 419 e-mails, he said, the scam had gradually become less profitable. Still, it appeared that many young men were still making large sums of money rather too quickly, and their fast wealth incited rumors about the intervention of juju and magic in their lucrative cyber fraud schemes. According to this producer, sakawa narratives also explained why a rich person would fall for a 419 scam and send large sums of money to a complete stranger. Such a scam could only work with the intervention of magic.

Sakawa movies, then, reveal the hidden source of the affluence of the young men suspected of being fraudsters. They uncover the secret of the successful scam, and in this function much like recent academic studies of cyber fraud: they try to explain why a wealthy white person would fall for the improbable opportunities presented in 419 narratives. But whereas scholars have probed the particularities of the discourse of 419 to understand its rhetorical impact on those it victimizes (Zook

2007; Chiluwa 2009), video moviemakers in Ghana adopt the point of view of the scammers, describing the unemployment and poverty that drive young men to engage in sakawa and exposing and punishing their immoral crimes and their selfish consumption.

Like Nwuabani's literary text, these popular narratives criticize the conditions of bare life prevalent in the postcolony, the dire material circumstances that push unemployed men and women into Internet fraud. In this, the movies aim to represent the materiality denied by Frimpong-Manso's shiny surfaces and commodity aesthetics. They express what those movies hide: the profound ambivalence that results from the collision of dire poverty and excessive consumption as experienced virtually through global and local media images and observed, firsthand, in the pockets of prosperity and displays of commodities, like those found at the Accra Mall, that dot the urban landscape of the postcolonial city. Each movie devotes significant time to narrating the extreme economic hardships that drive young men to sakawa.

In the Akan-language movie *Café Guys*, Sammy and Kobi, both students at the University of Ghana, complain bitterly that though they value education, it no longer can feed them. Similarly, in the English-language feature *Dons in Sakawa*, the three protagonists Hakeem, Justin, and Mike have just graduated from the University of Ghana, but despite their high hopes and limitless aspirations, they are unable to secure employment and quickly find themselves struggling to get by. The movies' attention to disappointed male college students at the nation's top university, an institution established by Kwame Nkrumah to support the development of Ghana, emphasizes the failures of the postcolonial state to meet the ideals on which the nation was founded. The entire first part of Movie Africa's *Sakawa Boys*, made in English, emphasizes the dire poverty of Ato, Edem, and Fifi, the three young men who turn to the spiritualist Mallam Isaa to help them get money. Ato's mother, a plantain seller, has severe asthma and cannot afford the medicines she needs. Edem's sister, Dela, has a bad heart and needs an expensive surgery to live. Fifi is desperately in love with Fati, but because he has no money to keep her, she leaves him. Frustrated by their inability to take care of themselves and to fulfill their obligations to their families and loved ones, the boys are easy targets for Ajinkwa, the obscenely rich disciple of Mallam Issa who initiates them into what he calls "his business."

The disciple-recruiter is a common figure in all of the sakawa movies that I have been able to obtain copies of. His actions represent a vile perversion of the customary obligations of the prosperous patron to share his wealth instead of hoarding it selfishly. Under the guise of assisting his old school friends, the recruiter lures the uninitiated into immorality, corruption, and selfish consumption. He offers to teach the boys "line of work," and after a period of intense reflection, during which each boy considers the ramifications of what he is about to do in voice-over, Ato, Edem and Fifi, the three protagonists of *Sakawa Boys*, conclude that they have no choice but to accept Ajinkwa's offer to become followers of Mallam Issa and gain access to the occult powers that will allow them to procure the money they need to help their families. The movies emphasize that "free" choice is compromised by family and social obligations.

Each boy is required to survive an initial arduous ordeal and then to obey, without question or hesitation, the series of interdictions that Issa places before them. These tasks are referred to as the "work" the young men do and require the men to engage in extreme, antisocial acts that violate basic tenets of community. Sammy and Kobi, from *Café Boys*, are not allowed to bathe or touch water for three weeks. In other movies, the protagonists must eat garbage, collect menstrual blood from used sanitary napkins, have sex with mad and homeless women, or sleep in coffins. Although, initially, the young men resort to sakawa to help their families, the trials gradually sever the boys' links to their families and loved ones, becoming increasingly demanding and destructive and escalating to the taking of human life. Much like the "stories of evil rituals and occult practices in the pursuit of wealth" analyzed by Daniel Jordan Smith (2007), sakawa movies call attention to the tensions people confront in the contemporary, neoliberal world order where "individual desires increasingly conflict with widely shared values of social obligation" (162). The movies resolve this tension by erecting a moral binary between wealth acquired to meet social obligations and immorally gained money that is spent selfishly and lavishly on individual desires. In *Agya Koo Sakawa*, a movie made in Akan, Gyima is forced to kill his brother to keep his wealth. Ironically, Gyimah's wish to help his brother get established in the city is the main reason he falls prey to the occult. In *Sakawa Boys* the newly rich young men are not allowed to spend any of their sakawa money on homes or cars for their families; all of their wealth must be consumed selfishly, or only "for fun," as the mallam puts it. When Ato disobeys and buys a home for his mother, she is struck with a nearly fatal asthma attack and the house catches on fire. Similarly, in *The*

Dons in Sakawa, Hakim is granted immense wealth on the condition that he obey "the golden rule," which forbids him from giving money to his mother and sister or spending any of his money to feed them or maintain their health. If he breaks this rule, he will die. When Hakim's mother and sister become critically ill and the hospital refuses to treat them unless Hakim pays for their care, he is forced to either let them die or give up his life to save them. In the end, he pays for their care and dies. Hakim's decision to sacrifice his life for the well-being of his family represents his moment of personal redemption. The movie emphasizes the arduousness of his moral deliberation process, adopting melodramatic codes, such as an extreme close-up of extended duration of Hakim's tear-stained face, to intensify affect and prolong the viewer's encounter with his pain and anguish. This is not a choice made without loss.

The sakawa initiates, in all movies, either seek exorcism and redemption through a Pentecostal pastor, or die. In *Café Boys*, Sammy is saved through the intervention of his pastor, but Kobi, who violates the mallam's demand that he not let water touch his skin, dies an excruciating slow and gruesome death. He contracts a horrible skin ailment, his body bloated and covered in bloody and festering sores. The friends who periodically visit him to give his mother money say that he "has gotten rotten." The movie returns to the grotesque display of his body several times throughout the movie; the VCD cover also features the bloody body of Kobi. It functions as a visualization of abjection and suffering and invites pity and moral rectitude from the audience. The suffering body, in this instance, becomes a public display similar to that of the publicly tortured body as theorized by Foucault in *Discipline and Punish* (1995). In Foucault's analysis, public torture, which included the display of the tortured body, enacted the power of the state on the body. This spectacle used theatricality and visual intensity to express it power. Foucault writes: "Not only must people know, they must see with their own eyes. Because they must be made to be afraid; but also because they must be the witnesses, the guarantors, of the punishment, and because they must to a certain extent take part in it" (58). The crowd, then, was part of this performance of state power. In *Café Boys*, it is morality, and not the state, that marks the body, and through the exhibition of this suffering body, the consequences brought on by individual, immoral acts are made manifest publicly. The antisocial acts of the "criminal" unleash moral judgment on the body, and the audience is called as witness.

This affective display is similar to the revolting scenes in Nollywood movies described by Larkin (2008). It is meant to "scandalize and disgust" (Larkin 2008, 190), provoking a bodily response of revulsion from the audience.

These exaggerated assertions of moral authority seem to address deep cultural anxieties about neoliberal values that place individual desires above the basic needs of the family, community, and nation. The movies align the condemnation of greed and selfish accumulation with a critical look at patriarchy and the destructive and immoral power of Big Men. In sakawa movies, and especially those that incorporate blood money rituals, individual men gain wealth and power only by causing harm to others, and in particular to unsuspecting and vulnerable women.

In *Sika Mu Sakawa*, Fred, Frank, and Ampong must regularly abduct women, who are usually roadside merchants or prostitutes, and use their bodies in the rituals that produce their wealth. Ampong joins the shrine only by agreeing to sacrifice his sister. He takes her life while she sleeps, covering her body with a white, magic cloth. Under the white cover, she disappears, seemingly transported through the cloth to the shrine, where her body first morphs into a snake and then into its human form. But she is more zombie than human. She appears with sores and cuts on her arms and legs, and she does not speak or resist. On her hands and knees, she emits animal groans and vomits money. Her body, neither alive nor dead, has been transformed into a money-producing apparatus. In this grotesque allegory of capitalism, the movie enacts the extraction of wealth from human life. After this first ordeal, Ampong must take other women so that his Internet fraud delivers the vast sums of money he needs to feed his lifestyle. He meets, seduces, and promises to marry each of the several women he consumes. They die slow and painful deaths, developing bloody and cankerous sores. Ampong promises to help them, but abandons each to her suffering and death. In this instance, the display of the tortured and mutilated body invites pity for the victim and absolute moral denunciation for the perpetrator. It requires spectators to *dis*identify with Ampong.

Friends and family express their suspicions of the young and rich recruiter, and they always warn the young protagonist to be careful. The same people who express caution about wealth too quickly gained, however, willingly accept the houses, cars, and gifts that sakawa money buys them even when it is clear that their prosperity has been secured through immoral means. The movies position spectators in a similar zone of ambivalence. The narratives punish the protagonists who engage in the immoral acquisition of wealth and the selfish consumption such wealth buys. In *Sakawa Boys*, for example, Edem and Ajinkwa die while Ato and Fifi, faced with ever more impossible trials and interdictions, admit the errors of their ways and try to extricate themselves from the hold of Mallam Issa through the intervention of a powerful pastor.

Yet, the film, simultaneously, invites spectators to admire the riches had through Internet fraud and occult practices. The close affiliation between punishment and pity, desire and derision, and attraction and revulsion in the movies reiterates the "logic of conviviality" that Achille Mbembe (2001) has suggested is characteristic of the African postcolony. This logic ensnares both the powerless and powerful within the same episteme (110). Neither resisting nor assimilating to regimes of domination, video movies and other popular modes of expression are among "the myriad ways ordinary people guide, deceive, and toy with power instead of confronting it directly" (128). In this instance, videomakers capitalize on the ambivalence of their African audiences, offering them a virtual encounter with the wealthy and powerful and a narrative that imaginatively enacts and finally contains their desire with a strong assertion of moral clarity. This play with power never quite manages to develop into a full-blown political critique, and instead it remains coded as a moral lesson. Melodrama perfectly accommodates this logic. As Adejunmobi notes, melodramatic narratives "account for political and institutional failure by displacing such failures onto the realm of morality" (2010, 114). This morality, though not oppositional in the ways we expect, nonetheless does address the social and economic conditions and costs that have been concealed in the luscious movies of Frimpong-Manso. It questions neoliberal rationalities by exposing the poverty that leads to bad choices and, more urgently, the human costs of unbridled greed driven by capitalistic values.

A general consensus has emerged in the vast body of scholarship on magic, the occult, and witchcraft that suggests that magic should be understood as "a thoroughly modern cultural form" that reflects and attempts to make sense of the "experience of capitalist modernity" (D. J. Smith 2007, 37). The occult and witchcraft, much like Ponzi schemes and lotteries, "speak to the sense that the movements of capital are mysterious, inherently dubious, and that if one could only find means by which to domesticate these abstract forces, untold riches await" (38). In *A Culture of Corruption: Everyday Deception and Popular Discontent in Nigeria* (2007) Daniel Jordan Smith interprets witchcraft accusations and stories of the occult within the context of scarcity and corruption, suggesting that these and other narratives of magic practices be read as expressions of profound ambivalence about accumulation. On the one hand, they articulate discontent with the appropriation of wealth and power by a privileged few and illustrate "the continuing power of moralities that privilege people and obligations of social relationships above the naked pursuit of riches" (D. J. Smith 2007, 138). On the other hand, they "highlight the intimate connections between popular condemnation of the unequal accumulation of great wealth and the widely shared fantasies about being rich" (142). Following Smith, I read sakawa movies as articulations of this ambivalence; they articulate discontent about everyday corruption, punishing those characters who engage in dishonest practices to get rich or who use their wealth selfishly and immorally, and simultaneously these movies play to the audience's desire to have wealth.

The pleasures offered by sakawa movies, pleasures linked to their incredible commercial success, also derive from their capacity to visualize Internet enchantment and money magic. Ndalianis (2004) has described the historical lineage joining cinematic and magical spectacles and tricks. Following this long history, sakawa movies, and in particular the movies of Socrate Safo, create "magical illusions out of new technologies that are associated with the rational and scientific" in order to evoke amazement (228). Safo's video movies showcase fantastic visual tricks created by computer-generated special effects that make available to audiences the invisible magic of the Internet and its entanglements with the mysterious movement of immaterial forms of money. Birgit Meyer has written extensively on Ghanaian video movies as cultural forms inscribing Pentecostal vision, which allows spectators to see the hidden rituals and secret conventions of the occult. Informed by Pentecostal discourse, video movies represent the occult as "the machinations of the devil" (Meyer 2006, 441) and their appeal involves the pleasure and power spectators experience in adopting the view of God and gaining access into the operations of the invisible in everyday life. Sakawa movies have a similar revelatory dimension, but the mysteries and magics they claim to unveil involve particular iterations of invisibility: the flow of digital data through the Internet and of wealth from the rich to the poor.

The insights of Andrew Smith who, in a compelling analysis of 419 e-mail scams, understands the discourse of 419 within the broader historical context of globalization and late capitalism, seem pertinent. Smith suggests that Internet fraud schemes and magical practice operate according to a similar logic; both narratives reveal "hidden economic processes" and so "provide surrogate accounts of how value enters the world" (A. Smith 2009, 39). Though not discussed in Smith's article, sakawa movies perfectly demonstrate Smith's thesis. They promise to expose the magic of digital technologies and the mystery of de-materialized forms of money. Of course, the special effects conceal as much as they reveals, relying on the tricks of technology to expose technological trickery.

In many of the movies, an enchanted object, which is worn by the sakawa disciple, releases magic into the computer network. Ajinkwa, from *Sakawa Boys*, wears a large ring that has been blessed by the mallam to serve as a conduit between the supernatural and the everyday. A flash of light bursts from the ring, snakes into the computer through its keyboard and from there moves into cyberspace, although at this point in the movie, the camera does not follow the light into the virtual unknown. Instead, we watch as Ajinkwa reads a new e-mail message and then leaps from his chair because he has scored a "hit" and convinced a wealthy person in the West to wire a large sum of money into his bank account.

In this movie, it isn't until the boys undergo their initiation into sakawa that the virtual-supernatural realm is visualized. Each boy agrees to spend two weeks in a coffin to demonstrate his allegiance to the mallam. The day of the boys's release, Mallam Issa chants near each coffin, and his incantations appear to create an opening into the spiritual realm, signaled by a cross dissolve into a vast clearing. Here, each boy appears naked and veiled in white light. The boys' bodies seem to float in a space that looks like the surface of the moon (see fig 5.8). In the next shot, an animated skeleton appears and draws balls of fire from the air (see fig. 5.9). As the balls drop, they morph into coffins. The scene cuts back to the skeleton as he spins fire from nothing and sprinkles it into the coffins. Inside the coffins, the fire transforms into money (see fig. 5.10). For each boy who survives the ordeal, a coffin of money is created. This is the money each sakawa boy will now conjure from the Internet. These visualizations, created with digital effects software and by digital image manipulation, articulate what Harry Garuba calls the African animist mode of thought,

Figure 5.8. The virtual-supernatural realm (*Sakawa Boys 2*, 2009)

Figure 5.9. Skeleton casts fire (*Sakawa Boys 2*, 2009)

Figure 5.10. Fire morphs into money (*Sakawa Boys 2*, 2009)

"a process whereby 'magical elements of thought' . . . continually assimilate new developments in science, technology, and the organization of the world within a basically 'magical' worldview" (2003, 267). Keenly aware that their audiences have been influenced by the discourse of animism, which Garuba claims carries the authority of a cultural norm, videomakers have capitalized on the newness and strangeness of the Internet, explaining its power through reference to magic. More than that, the showy special effects, attractions in their own right, are meant to enchant viewers who will respond with wonder and amazement. Not because they believe that what they see is actually sakawa, but because the computer-generated images are stunning and their creation mysterious. As one young Ghanaian woman explained to me when I asked about the appeal of computer-generated images and effects, "We like how it looks. We want to know how it is done." *Sakawa Boys*, in this regard, is not too far from movies like *The Matrix* (1999); it, too, is intended to "evoke not only curiosity and wonder, but an aura of the mystical" (Ndalianis 2004, 227) in its visualization of the Internet.

Much like the 419 scam, these movies are products of globalization and its neoliberal and capitalist undergirding. They emerge from a global order in which the compression of space and time, as theorized by David Harvey (1989), brings into sharp relief the gaps between lack and plenitude that characterize the world in the period of late capitalism. Unlike the movies of Shirley Frimpong-Manso, here the gap is not obscured but brought into the narrative, described and criticized; it is the reason young men take up corrupt and immoral lifestyles. Sakawa movies offer a critique of the consumer desires provoked by Frimpong-Manso's movies. Through the idioms of witchcraft and magic, they reveal the uncanny underside of capitalism.

Conclusion

Jean-Marie Teno's lyrical documentary *Sacred Places* (2009) unfolds in the small, poor neighborhood of Saint Léon in Ouagadougou, Burkina Faso, during the 2007 FESPACO Pan-African film festival. It returns to an old conundrum: African cinema, like the many films shown at FESPACO, is not within the reach of African audiences. Teno tells us early in the film that he has come to St. Léon on the recommendation of a friend who scolded him for staying in fancy hotels during his time in Ouaga instead of experiencing its "paradise," and its music, literature, and cinema. Teno explains in voice-over that during his encounter with St. Léon, he has "rediscovered" the joy of sharing his work with this "remarkable audience," which he laments has been shut out of the festival since it discontinued the tradition of free open air film screenings. Adopting a subjective and self-reflexive style, the camera moves through this paradise, St. Léon, capturing its character and rhythms and meeting its central personalities: the djembefola, Jules César Bamouni; Nanema Boubakar, the owner of the local video parlor; and Abbo, the engineer, who calls himself a public writer and comes to the neighborhood each day to write a few thoughts in chalk on a large wall. The camera never presents itself as a distant, objective eye. People look directly into it as they walk by; children smile and stare as they run across its path. At various points, we hear Teno speak warmly to his interlocutors, and his voice-over narration reflects, throughout, on the film festival and the failed promises of African cinema.

Closed off from the high-priced film screenings, the residents of St. Léon frequent Boubakar's Ciné Club to watch pirated DVDs of Hollywood and Bollywood movies on a large television screen for about the equivalent of ten cents. Boubakar explains that all of his "film fans" want to see African films, and the people Teno interviews affirm that they love films like *Yaaba* (1989) and *Buud Yam* (1997). But these films don't appear often, and when they do, are far too expensive to see in a movie theater. Boubakar complains that a VHS tape of an African film can cost as much as twenty-five dollars, while a bootleg DVD of a Wesley Snipes film rents for as little as fifty cents. In the documentary's rhetoric, St. Léon functions as a metonym for ordinary Africans who have no access to serious African cinema, a cinema that purports to contain their history and culture. At the end of the film, Teno casts this paradox as metaphor: "The African filmmaker before his audience" is like "a guy who wants children with his beloved without ever touching her."[1] The filmmaker, in other words, longs for his films to be seen in Africa by Africans, but he is unwilling to do what he needs to do in order for Africans to have access to his films.

Though I am completely charmed by this beautifully shot and edited documentary, and by its subjects and the stories they tell, the project strikes me as strangely out of sync, or out of date, with what has been happening with video in African neighborhoods just like St. Léon for over thirty years. Haven't the popular video industries in Ghana and Nigeria offered one solution to the problems contemplated in *Sacred Places?* And in a documentary about African cinema and African audiences, why was there no mention made of African popular movies? I asked Teno these questions, and he told me that he captured what he saw, that Nollywood movies were not screened at the Ciné Club during the three weeks he was in St. Léon.[2] This explanation seems plausible, but African popular video, a cinema that does precisely what Teno wants African film to do, raises questions crucial to the documentary's central premise: namely, it troubles the claim that Africans have no access to their cinema. Boubakar tells Teno that "African directors and producers need to conquer this market." It is in the "ghetto," the name he uses to refer to his neighborhood, "where it's happening. We're the ones who love these films." And it seems that Ghanaian and Nigerian videomakers have offered filmmakers a model for how they might reach local audiences.

The residents of St. Léon, in response to Teno's prompts, describe the pleasures of cinema and their love not only of African film, but of the global popular, too (During 1997). An auto mechanic explains that he has always admired the strength and grace portrayed in martial arts films. A young woman says that she never misses a new Hindi film. Boubacar recalled loving action movies since he was a child, when he would risk a beating to sneak out to the cinema, and Jules César tells Teno that the video parlor is important to the neighborhood because "it gives the youth a chance to see something besides their routine."

These remarks sound nearly identical to the answers I received when I asked Ghanaian videomakers why they wanted to make movies, what kinds of movies they liked, and what movies shaped their sense of cinema. They recounted stories about watching Bollywood and Hong Kong movies as children and, as adults, being swept away by Hollywood films like *Titanic*. Most Ghanaian directors would mention Stephen Spielberg as a filmmaker whose work they admire. They did not describe themselves as griots or visionaries, but as lovers of movies, of good stories, and of entertainment. The makers of African popular video came to movies, first, as consumers of global, commercial cinema. Many of the first Ghanaian videomakers, like Bouba, were involved in the distribution of pirated global media before they started making movies. Videomakers have tapped this archive, translating and remaking global mass media, without apology, for local audiences with whom they have in common a cultural vocabulary.

While Teno's documentary is critical of the barriers that shut ordinary Africans out of FESPACO, *Sacred Places* enacts a similar exclusiveness, discounting locally made and watched movies. It is as if Teno does not recognize Nollywood as cinema because it isn't the African cinema of Sembene and Mambety, the pioneers whose words scroll across the black screen at the documentary's conclusion. Yet, these local, commercial industries have managed to thrive in Africa's "dime plus a dime" economy, the phrase Idrissa Ouedraogo uses in the documentary to describe the limited purchasing power of the local African market. Why not, at least, raise the topic of Nollywood with Ouedraogo? Perhaps Teno's silence is a response to the ambivalence that popular video movies generate for artists and scholars. Our political and aesthetic sensibilities, after all, are not shared by the videomakers. We bristle at the crass consumerism that fuels these industries, and yet, we want to praise the videomakers for their doggedness and drive and for creating a local African product for local African audiences.

This book has tried neither to uncritically celebrate African popular movies nor to view them from a disengaged and disapproving perspective. It aims to take popular video seriously as a subject of investigation, historicizing its development and analyzing the complexities and contradictions it engenders. It highlights the singularity of the movies and their incorporation into global processes, and it elaborates on the particular pleasures and engagements they produce. Though I do not describe the movies as "political" or "oppositional," language never used by the moviemakers or their audiences, I have argued that popular movies give expression to a morality, or an ethics, that is highly critical of the rationalities and ideologies of neoliberalism and capitalism. In this, the movies fulfill audiences' expectations for instruction and resolution. Melodrama, as a cultural form, best expresses this "politics." It distills the sociopolitical and displaces it onto the personal, constructing a morality rooted in but not limited to local context.

Akin Adesokan (2011) has written about an "aesthetics of exhortation" that shapes African popular movies, and he connects it to West African traditions of populism. He states, "A dramatic or narrative text is thought to be fundamentally about notions of good and bad conduct and, in exhortatory and didactic registers, subsumes every aspect of human relations—social, political, economic, and so on—to this basic theme" (82). This aesthetics, it seems to me, is also melodramatic and has been a feature of films produced by the Gold Coast Film Unit, the Ghana National Film Company, and, finally, commercial video movies. If popular movies refrain from criticizing the postcolonial African state for failing to provide health care and education for its citizens and from targeting the World Bank for its role in currency devaluation, we do find that corrupt and greedy individuals, the beneficiaries of these larger structural realities, are held up for criticism and condemnation.

This book has read Africa video movies as examples of the "new modes of self-writing" or "practices of the self" through which, Mbembe (2002) argues, Africans fashion their identities and engage with the world under processes of globalization. They motivate the imagination at the meeting of the local and global in at least two registers. They mobilize "a religious imaginaire" (270), as has been brilliantly detailed by Birgit Meyer in all of her many articles on Ghanaian movies and Pentecostalism. And, as this book has tried to suggest, they activate an "imaginaire of consumption" (Mbembe 2002, 271), providing audiences with opportunities to virtually attain desired goods and status in an economy of chronic scarcity, "an economy where desired goods are known, that may sometimes be seen, that one wants to enjoy, but to which one will never have material access" (271). It is the condition of impossibility that stimulates the imagination and new modes of self-formation through consumption, Mbembe argues, and, it seems that it is scarcity, too, that makes the consumer fantasies played out in many video movies appealing. As we have seen, however, popular movies simultaneously contain this desire by making visible, and calling spectators to witness, the human costs of greed and envy. While the movies probe the sources of wealth in an economy of scarcity and act out the fantasy of being rich, they also dramatize the death and violence brought about by the immoral accumulation of capital.

Adopting a historical approach to the study of video movies in Ghana, this book has only touched on the remarkable transformations that have occurred in the last decade. In Ghana, these changes have included the appearance of Akan-language movies, which now dominate the local market; the emergence of Kumasi as a second video-production city; the arrival of a high-priced multiplex in Accra, the Silverbird Cinema, that is linked to a transnational, African distribution circuit and of a cadre of directors who have abandoned the straight-to-VCD model of distribution for cinema release, hoping to ignite a renaissance of cinema going in Africa. Newcomers Shirley Frimpong-Manso, Leila Djansi, and Francis Gbormittah are making movies that blur the lines between movies made for local and global audiences. These are a few among the many exciting developments that need to be investigated and written about. There is much work to be done, and I hope this book, in some small way, might facilitate it.

Notes

Introduction

1. I have borrowed from Haynes's comprehensive literature reviews (2010a and 2010b) for several of the citations included in this chapter.

2. According to Haynes (2010a), these conferences include Modes of Seeing; The Video Film in Africa (2001), organized by Onookome Okome and Till Forester at the University of Bayreuth, Germany; the First International Conference on Hausa Films (2003), organized by the Center for Hausa Cultural Studies in Kano; The Nigerian Video/DVD Film Industry: Background, Current Situation, and International Prospects (2007) at the Open University in the UK; African Film: An International Conference (2007) organized by Mahir Şaul and Ralph Austen, University of Illinois, Urbana-Champaign; an academic conference and film festival, African Video Film Arts Festival (2007), organized by Foluke Ogunleye at Obafemi Awolowo University, Ile-Ife, Nigeria; and Nollywood and Beyond: Transnational Dimensions of the African Video Industry (2009), organized by Matthias Krings and Onookome Okome at Johannes Gutenberg University, Mainz, Germany. There have been the conferences organized by Kwara State University in July 2010, and two conferences in Lagos in 2011; one at the University of Lagos, called Reading and Producing Nollywood, and another at the conference at Pan-African University in July 2011. Both of the Lagos conferences were organized by Onookome Okome.

3. Documentaries include one on Ghana's video industry, *Ghanaian Video Tales* (2006), and the following on Nollywood: *Hollywood in Africa* (2002); *Nick Does Nollywood* (2004); *A Very, Very Short Story of Nollywood* (2005); *Nollywood Dreams* (2005); *Welcome to Nollywood* (2007); *This Is Nollywood* (2007); *Good Copy, Bad Copy* (2007); *Nollywood Convention* (2007); *Nollywood Babylon* (2008); and *Nollywood Lady* (2008).

4. I want to thank Carmen McCain for reminding me that the scholarly and international press's focus on English-language Nigerian videos has also eclipsed Nigerian video production in Hausa, Yoruba, and other languages (personal communication). In her research on Hausa video production in Nigeria, McCain has also mapped transnational circuits that link Northern Nigeria to Niger and Ghana, where a few Hausa-language movies have been made. These transnational networks have hardly been noticed by researchers.

5. Kenneth Harrow, the conference organizer, explained that the organizers did not receive one single proposal on popular video.

6. The gap between the networks taken up by popular video and those maintained by academic and official cultural forms in part explains the appearance of the eleven documentaries on African popular video (see note 3 above). The documentaries bridge the space dividing the distinct circuits followed by the different forms. They provide the "context" needed to understand the forms and in this way translate it, effectively re-creating it, for transnational audiences.

7. For these very reasons, Moradewun Adejunmobi argues that video movies, as "commercial forms of transnational cultural productivity," have the potential to "offer greater opportunity for autonomous voices from globally minoritized populations to engage in dialogue with local publics and outside dominant centers of cultural production, than do the non-commercial forms of cultural productivity" (2007, 12), such as African canonical cinema.

8. Both Kelani and Afolayan have screened their movies at FESPACO, and Kelani's *Thunderbolt* is distributed by California Newsreel (see http:// newsreel.org/video/THUNDERBOLT). Perhaps because his body of work conforms readily to the auteur criticism that has been dominant in African film criticism, Kelani continues to attract scholarly interest (Esonwanne 2008; Adesokan 2011; Haynes 2007b).

9. John McCall makes a related point when he writes that "the videos partake of a mix of local, national, and global discourses and aesthetics. They reproduce elements of Western cinema and indigenize those appropriations" (McCall 2002, 88).

10. A similar point has been made by Ginsburg et al. (2002); Ezra and Rowden (2006), and Adejunmobi (2007).

11. Brian Larkin in *Signal and Noise* (2008) also refers to Sundaram's work on pirate modernity, but in connection to the infrastructures of piracy out of which African video production has emerged.

12. Brian Larkin (2008) also focuses on noise, but his use of the concept is different from Ferguson's use of the term, which Larkin himself notes (275n10). Larkin describes noise as a material artifact, a mediating surface that is an effect of the pirate infrastructures of Africa's media environment.

Chapter 1: Mapping the Modern

1. It is also worth noting that *The Boy Kumasenu* was broadcast many times on Ghanaian television until as late as 1998.

2. Now streamed in full online, as part of the BFI's Colonial Film Archive, *The Boy Kumasenu* is likely to earn far more scholarly interest. The archive can be found here http://www.colonialfilm.org.uk/archives.

3. As the next chapter explains, private videomakers, armed with new, mobile, and easy to use video technologies, had been making video features since 1987, operating without the assistance of and beyond the reach of the state and giving Ghanaian audiences locally produced movies.

4. The earliest motion pictures brought to Ghana included lantern slide-shows at Azuma in Jamestown (Barber et al. 1997, 9) and shows sponsored by the Basel Mission trader George Geppert, who projected slides as part of Bible classes at the YMCA in the Christianborg neighborhood of Accra (Dadson, 1995a).

5. Cole's well-researched book includes many interviews with veteran actors of the concert party who describe the influence of these early cinema shows on the emergent Ghanaian concert party form. As will be discussed in later sections of the book, cinema and the concert party shared a circuit of influence, which shifted and modified over time. Hollywood characters and musical numbers were recreated by concert party actors while concert party types and themes influenced Ghanaian cinema, where they were continually remade to be picked up again by other cultural articulations. The concert party and cinema, at various points, shared performers and stages, and, at other times, competed for audiences.

6. The Cinematograph Act (or Quota Act) of 1927 promoted British films against Hollywood's prevalence in the domestic British market and the colonies.

7. The pamphlet reports that by 1955, 869 films had been censored and, of that number, 16 rejected.

8. Many of these films are part of the BFI's online Colonial Film Archive, which can be found at http://www.colonialfilm.org.uk/archives.

9. This is as reported in the brochure *Advance of a Technique: Information Services in the Gold Coast* (Accra, Gold Coast: Information Services, 1956).

10. In an interview with Dan Adjokatchcer (1995), Graham claimed that it was Grierson who recommended him for the position as head of the Gold Coast Colonial Film Unit.

11. In its use of documentary and narrative, the film borrows from and modifies a convention deployed in British empire films like *Sanders of the River* (1935). Jaikumar explains that imperial British cinema presented colonial subjects as objects of documentary footage while reserving narrative for the colonizers. The incorporation of actual documentary footage shot in Africa in a feature film was intended to portray "colonial subjects in a state of savagery or infancy and in need of assistance" (Jaikumar 2006, 109). Jaikumar points out that the narratives of these feature films, fabricated "with carefully constructed sets and continuity editing," normalized the social and racial hierarchies of colonialism (2006, 109), depicting the British colonizers as the carriers of order and history.

Although it does not include the stock documentary footage found in British empire films, *The Boy Kumasenu* does deploy ethnographic and narrative realist modes.

12. All layers of the soundtrack were added during postproduction, and this might suggest another point of affinity between Graham and Grierson, who also preferred dubbed sound and found bulky synchronous sound equipment intrusive to the documentary film process. For more discussion of this, see Brian Winston's *Claiming the Reel: The Documentary Film Revisited*. Graham adds sound to the film during the postproduction process even though the Gold Coast Film Unit had the ability to do simultaneous and synchronous sound and image recording.

13. See Christine Oppong 1974; Vellenga 1983; Abu 1983; Clark; Mann 1980; Harrell-Bond 1975; and Quayson 2000.

14. The narrator informs the spectator that Adobia is "a successful trader by day" and "by night enjoyed the protection of a wealthy lawyer," Mr. Mensah. The ideological investment required by the narrative implies that because she cannot be faithful to one man and takes Yaboa as a lover, Mr. Mensah's anger is justified. The implication is that she, and not he who fabricated charges against her, is to blame for her arrest, and she disappears from the film, a necessary deletion in the narrative of Kumsenu's journey to subjectivity.

15. West African Pictures was purchased by the state-owned Industrial Corporation in 1956. In 1962, the IDC was liquidated, and its film exhibition division was absorbed by GFIC.

16. Guided by Dr. Kwame Nkrumah's fusion of anticolonial, cultural-nationalist, and pan-African political philosophies, GFIC set out to achieve the following objectives: "To contribute to the economic, social, and political development of the country; to stimulate qualitative growth and change in all spheres of our national life; to promote the ethical state, personality, and culture of the African and to give him wide international exposure; to help remedy the harm the Western media, particularly film, has done and continues to do to the African through the presentation of distorted pictures and information about him and the manipulation of his mind; to entertain the people; and to protect the consciousness of the Ghanaian from the onslaught of foreign values and their manifestation of obscenity, violence, and vulgarity" (qtd. in Sakyi 1996, 2).

17. Several of my informants agreed that this shift might signify a loosening of connections between the University of Ghana School of Music and Drama and the film company, and perhaps might represent changes in the management of the company. Aryeety stepped down as managing director in 1980 and was replaced with his colleague R. O. Fenuku. The 1981 military coup orchestrated by J. J. Rawlings, who came

to be the head of state, initiated a "cultural revolution," through which, John Collins explains, "all the arts institutions in the country were rejuvenated and young men brought in to run them" (1996, 254). Shortly after the coup, thirty-one-year-old Haruna Attah became managing director of GFIC. Among the first class to graduate from NAFTI, Attah was something of an outsider. He was not, obviously, among those who were part of the Gold Coast Film Unit, and he was much younger than most of the filmmakers working at the company.

18. In an interview, Hesse described his work in this way: "The only time I didn't film Kwame Nkrumah was when he was asleep, when he was at home. You know I filmed his whole life."

19. This story was related to me by Mark Coleman and George Arcton-Tetty, both of whom worked at GAMA Film as film and video editors.

20. Ghanafilms released three other video movies the same year: *Baby Thief, Schemers,* and *The Other Side of the Rich.* In 1995 broadcasting was deregulated in Ghana, and the following year, GFIC divested. The sale of GFIC to TV Malaysia was contingent on the provision that the Malaysian consortium would facilitate the development of the film industry. TV Malaysia agreed to establish, within the GFIC infrastructure, a private TV station, TV3 Ghana, to compete with the state-owned Ghana Broadcasting Corporation and to use this station to promote and distribute new films. However, film production dwindled at GAMA Films as a result of TV3's emergence. As one GAMA filmmaker bemoaned: "Film studios became TV studios. Film production offices became TV marketing offices." Since 2004, GAMA Films has produced no features for theater release, and, instead, produces programming for the television station.

Chapter 2: Work, Women, and Worldly Wealth

1. Nick Teye, in an interview on July 31, 2000, told me that instability that followed the 1981 military coup worsened an already dire situation. Teye, who between 1979 and 1988 was responsible for obtaining films and arranging film exhibitions for GFIC, explained that the curfew imposed after the coup, from 1982 until 1986, restricted cinema showings, and the already meager exhibition returns GFIC took from film exhibitions dropped dramatically. As will be discussed in the next chapter, in 1995, the Rawlings government embarked on a Broadcasting Liberalization Policy, which resulted in a joint ownership agreement between TV3 Malaysia and the Ghanaian government, and in 1996, GFIC became the Ghana-Malaysia Film Company (GAMA Film Company Ltd). TV3 Malaysia, holding seventy percent of the company's equity, established the

first independent television station in Ghana, TV3. Under the aegis of GAMA Films, film exhibition and production in Ghana came to a complete halt. The founding of TV3 was followed by a general liberalization and privatization of television broadcasting in the county. The Ghana Broadcasting Corporation, the national television company established in 1968, now competes with privately owned stations such as Metro TV, Fontomfrom TV, and TV Africa-Ghana. These stations, although offering some local programming, primarily broadcast serials, soap operas, and movies from the US, South Africa, India, and Brazil. The availability of satellite television has furthered Ghanaians' access to independent and international programming.

2. Munir Captan, interview with author, May 25, 2000.

3. As quoted in the *Mirror*, October 8, 1988.

4. Ghanaian newspapers from this period, including *Daily Graphic* and the *Mirror*, published many advertisements for these and similar video exhibition outlets.

5. Asonzeh F.-K. Ukah suggests that in Nigeria the use of VCRs and video cassettes by Pentecostal pastors provided "publicity for the new technology and stimulated interest in the purchase of VCRs" (2003, 212).

6. The conversion from film to video projection in cinema halls signals the start of a gradual transformation from public cinema exhibition to private home viewing and, related to this, from the production of video movies for cinematic space to the production of video media forms, features burned to video compact discs, for the TV or computer monitor. The significance of this shift is discussed in later chapters.

7. In their study of the role of small media in the Iranian revolution, Annabelle Sreberny-Mohammadi and Ali Mohammadi point out that because video can be "the source of multiple points of production and distribution" (1994, 27), it easily subverts import duties and regulations, censorship boards, piracy laws, and other forms of government control.

8. As reported in the *Mirror*, Oct. 8, 1988.

9. Sam Ankrah shared this with me in an interview on February 16, 2000, at his home in Accra, Ghana. Unfortunately, Ankrah did not have a copy of this video, and I was not able to find it in any of the many video shops in Accra or Kumasi.

10. This information was passed to me by Nana Bosomprah, whom I interviewed in July 1998. Socrate Safo and Samual Ankrah have confirmed this information.

11. In later years, the storage of videos fell to commercial duplicators and video distributors, who for obvious reasons held on to and continued to print profitable videos. Although the shelves of a commercial video outlet are by no measure an acceptable substitute for a proper cinema

archive or video library, at least some effort was made to retain some of the older videos.

12. In this chapter, information about videos that I was unable to find copies of, (including the original *Zinabu, Morbor, Cult of Alta*, and *Unconditional Love I* and *II*) has been compiled from censorship records, newspapers articles, and personal interviews. My analysis of *Zinabu* also draws on Akuffo's 1999 remake of the 1987 original, which, according to Akuffo, is meant to be a replica; it uses the original script, the same crew and cast and attempts to re-create the scene and shot compositions of the first *Zinabu.*

13. This is the case in *Unconditional Love, Sasa,* and *Shoeshine Boy.*

14. Another early occult video is *Sasa.*

15. This is a point persuasively made by Adejunmobi (2002) in an analysis of Nigerian videos.

16. The phrase "kalabule work" refers to illegal, illicit, or otherwise immoral work. Nugent (1995) alleges that the widespread use of the term "kalabule" in public discourse is a symptom of the shift in dominant ideologies about wealth.

17. William Akuffo, interview with author, February 15, 2000. Information verified by Chris Hesse, interview with author, February 16, 2000.

18. Two years later, after Ansah brings the film back to Ghana to exhibit it, Dadson reported that "in some parts of the country a little over 30 million cedis has been realized out of which 21 million cedis has gone into taxes, hiring of theaters and operational expenses" ("How Fares *Heritage*?" *Mirror,* January 28, 1989).

19. Many of the first videomakers were forced to rent cinema space, at privately owned cinemas, to exhibit their features. Munir Captan, who owned a string of cinemas in Ghana, already had video projection equipment installed in his theaters because he had been projecting pirated videos for several years. The first video to be projected at a theater owned by GFIC was *Ayalolo* (1990), a feature made by Sediku Buari, who was well established as a musician. Buari was also responsible for selling the first video projection machines to GFIC.

Chapter 3: Professional Movies and Their Global Aspirations

1. According to a 1999 UNESCO report, the number of television sets per one thousand inhabitants increased by thirteen in Africa between 1970 and 1997.

2. As Larkin and other scholars of African culture have noted, the occult has become a popular idiom used to explain "why vast sections of society live in poverty while a tiny elite accumulate fantastic sums of

money" (2008, 108) and to criticize the immense disparities of wealth produced by late capitalism. Professional videomakers, by refusing to portray or to explore themes linked to the occult and blood money, further turned away from the scarcity and deprivation that, in many of the first features, lured otherwise moral characters into illicit acts of consumption.

3. My attention to these so-called professional movies does not, quite deliberately, revisit the large body of research on the representation of the occult in Ghanaian movies, nor does it rehearse Meyer's analyses of Ghanaian videos as a Pentecostal form of cultural expression. Instead, my intention is to move the critical conversation forward by historicizing and analyzing video movies that scholars have tended to overlook. Professional movies performed their professionalism, in part, through difference. They defined themselves against the occult videos that, for many scholars, represent the dominant form of West African popular videos.

4. Film and videomakers employed by Ghana Film Industry Corporation (GFIC), such as William Sefa, a cameraman, and Mark Coleman, an editor who graduated from the National Film and Television Institute (NAFTI) in 1984, worked for independent video producers on the side. Coleman, in fact, edited *Zinabu II* as well as other early movies at the editing studio at GFIC.

5. It is worth mentioning that many of the actors who participated in the first productions, including Bob Smith Jnr., Fred Amugi, Wakefield Akuaku, and Regina Pornortey, had received training and had worked in film, theater, and television before appearing in independent video features. They brought their expertise with them to these projects, becoming collaborators in the movies. Most importantly, the label "amateur" itself when applied to Akuffo and Safo and others needs to be questioned. As was explained in Chapter 2, the first video movie producers were not complete novices in the field of visual media. Most were already involved in some capacity in commercial film or video distribution and exhibition. William Akuffo was importing, distributing, and exhibiting films for many years before he made his first video feature. Mr. Safo gained experience with video technology while working in a video parlor that made and screened "actualities," neighborhood events videotaped for commercial exhibition.

6. Only after independent producer Sidiku Buhari had screened his video *Ayalolo* for large audiences at the Captan theaters did GFIC grudgingly permit him to screen the video at its Rex Theatre. The video's success convinced GFIC to accommodate video movies.

7. Assuming full and personal responsibility for distributing his movie to each movie theater where it would be screened had the advantage of preventing his VHS tape from being copied illicitly and his movie from

being pirated. It also allowed the producer to do his own, independent tally of ticket sales at the film theater so that he was certain to receive his fair share of gate proceeds from each screening.

8. Initially, 30 percent of gate proceeds went to producers and 70 percent to the film company. But because private film houses were giving producers as much as 60 percent, producers pushed and were able to secure 55 percent. As attendance at theaters dwindled, however, GAMA Films instituted a 50/50 split.

9. As quoted in the *Mirror*, October 8, 1988.

10. Brian Larkin has written on the infrastructure of video reproduction generated by media piracy in Nigeria. He observes that piracy and its infrastructure "show how the parallel economy has migrated onto center stage, overlapping and interpenetrating with the official economy, mixing legal and illegal regimes, uniting social actors, and organizing common networks" (2008, 240). Since the early years of the industry, when the first Ghanaian videomakers exploited the pirate exhibition infrastructure to show their features, the pirate and legitimate video economies have been entangled. Locally produced videos were projected in the same small venues as pirated foreign films copied onto video cassettes.

11. Established in 1990 in Opera Square in central Accra, Hacky Films copied and rented pirated foreign movies and media years before it began to reproduce local video movies legitimately. When I visited Hacky Films in 1998, a large selection of Hollywood, Kung Fu, Nigerian, and Ghanaian video cassettes shared shelf space in Mr. Hackman's air-conditioned store.

12. Mr. Boateng, for instance, saved money and avoided high tariffs on the importation of finished video cassettes by importing rolls of blank video tape, or "pancakes," and cassette casings separately and assembling them in his stores in Ghana.

13. *Price of Love* was the first video to be shown on GTV, but *Step Dad* was the first video movie that GBC bought the rights to exhibit, with a conditional time to broadcast. Hence, *Price of Love* was shown earlier than *Step Dad*, which was broadcast on March 6 to commemorate the independence celebrations that year.

14. According to many producers, TV3 typically agreed to purchase rights for Ghanaian movies only if they bought them for fourteen years, and TV3 paid independent producers less than $200. Metro TV also showed Nigerian movies on television, and many of these movies were shown illegally.

15. In 2009, Mr. Nyantakyi, director of programming at GAMA Film, reiterated the point. He said that the company also was not prepared to make certain compromises with quality and content, including making anything at all similar to "those witchcraft films."

16. In my 1999 interview with him, Othman insisted that he had no interest in producing or even broadcasting witchcraft movies. But, according to Birgit Meyer (2001), he told her that he in fact was very interested in showing movies that visualized occult forces if that is what audiences wanted. I don't know how to explain this discrepancy. It is important to note that GAMA Films did not make any movies that took up occult or witchcraft themes. GAMA's purchasing of broadcast rights from private producers seemed more driven by profit than ideology. In other words, TV3 broadcast a range of local movies, some about witchcraft and some not. According to independent producers, the company's primary concern was maximizing profit. If they could get your film from you cheaply, they would, no matter what your movie was about.

17. Dramas and soap operas were the overriding genre of media available on television in the sudden surge of global media broadcast on Ghanaian television in the 1990s and into the next decade, on both public and private stations (Adu-Gyimah 2003; Nuviadenu 2004). Among these programs were the American soap operas *Bold and the Beautiful* and *Days of Our Lives;* the South African drama series *Generations;* and South American telenovelas such as *Maria de Los Angeles, La Usurpadora,* and *Acupulco Bay.* GTV, Metro TV, and TV3 all featured weekly, evening films, which were typically out-of-date Hollywood films or American made-for-TV movies.

18. Censorship records indicate that in 1991, only five video movies were viewed by the board. In 1992, twenty-seven movies were submitted for approval and in 1993, the number jumped to fifty-two. Even allowing for the fact that many producers did not submit their video movies for certification, the escalation in the numbers of movies is remarkable.

19. The movie featured experienced actors Kwesi Koomson, Doris Sackitey, Dzifa Gomashie, and Edinam Atatsi. The crew included Mr. William Sefa, a camera operator who had worked at GFIC since its inception, and Mark Coleman, a graduate of NAFTI and employee of GFIC, to edit the movie.

20. The movies were: *Ghost Tears* (1992); *Lover's Blues* (1993); *Step Dad* (1993); and in 1995 *Lovin' You, True Love, Lady's Choice,* and *Sacrifice.*

21. The only video movies not to have been made in English after 1991, to the best of my knowledge, were *Sika Sunsum* (1991) and *Kananna* (1992), made in Akan and produced by Kofi Yirenkyi and Kofi Owusu. Owusu told me that the movies were not as profitable as English-language productions.

22. After widely publicized discussion and debate, the conference delegates, whose numbers included Ghana's first lady, Nana Rawlings, adopted the landmark Beijing Declaration and Platform for Action, a written commitment to "advance the goals of equality, development and peace for all women everywhere in the interest of all humanity" and a

detailed plan of action for reaching this end. The declaration can be found at http://www.un.org/womenwatch/daw/beijing/platform/declar.htm.

Chapter 4: Tourism and Trafficking

1. Arjun Appadurai's call for the construction of ethnographies that "incorporate the complexities of expressive representation" (1996, 64) indexes the larger shift Gikandi outlines.

2. The letter is quoted below.

> Excellencies, gentlemen, and responsible citizens of Europe:
> It is our great honor and privilege to write to you about our trip and the suffering of the children and youth in Africa. We offer you our most affectionate and respectful salutations. In return, be our support and our help.
> We beseech you on behalf of your love for your continent, your people, your families, and above all your children, whom you cherish more than life itself. And for the love of God, who has granted you all the experience, wealth, and power to ably construct and organize your continent. We call upon your graciousness and solidarity to help us in Africa. Our problems are many: war, sickness, hunger, lack of education. We beseech you to excuse us for daring to write this letter to you, important people whom we truly respect. It is to you, and to you only, that we can plead our case.
> And if you find that we have sacrificed our lives, it is because we suffer too much in Africa. We need your help in our struggle against poverty and war.
> Be mindful of us in Africa. There is no one else to turn to.

James Ferguson (2006) also discusses this letter.

3. Hamid Naficy's *An Accented Cinema* (2001), Ella Shohat and Robert Stam's *Multiculturalism, Postcoloniality, and Transnational Media* (2003), and Elizabeth Ezra and Terry Rowden's *Transnational Cinema* (2006), among many others, validate this claim.

4. The movies I have obtained are listed here. *Mamma Mia Italiana*, directed by Bob Smith Jnr. (Ghana and Italy, 1995); *Double Trouble (Mamma Mia Part Two)*, directed by Bob Smith Jnr. (Ghana and Italy, 1998); *Black Is Black: Mamma Mia 3*, directed by Bob Smith Jnr. (Ghana and Italy, 2000); *Love Brews in Toronto*, directed by Pius Famiyeh (Ghana and Canada, 2000); *Back to Kotoka*, directed by Socrate Safo (Ghana and the Netherlands, 2001); *Wild World: If Wishes Were Horses*, directed by Bob Smith Jnr. (Ghana and Italy, 2002); *Wild, Wild World: Wild World 2*, directed by Bob Smith Jnr. (Ghana and Italy, 2004); *See You, Amsterdam*, directed by Ashong Katai (Ghana and the Netherlands: HM Films Production,

2003); *Amsterdam Diary*, directed by Socrate Safo (Ghana and the Netherlands: Movie Africa Productions, 2005); *Koofori in London*, directed by Paa Kofi Mannoh (Ghana and UK, 2005); *Idikoko in Holland*, directed by Augustine Abbey (Ghana and the Netherlands, 2005); *Otolege*, directed by Albert Kuvodu (Ghana and the Netherlands, 2005); *London Got Problem*, directed by Albert Kuvodu (Ghana and UK, 2006); *Coming to Ghana*, directed by Bob Smith Jnr. (Ghana and USA, 2005); *U Gotta Go Home: Coming to Ghana II*, directed by Bob Smith Jnr. (Ghana and USA, 2007); *Love in America*, directed by Socrate Safo (Ghana and USA, 2008); *Run Baby Run*, directed by Emmanuel Apea (Ghana and UK, 2008); *Agya Koo in Libya*, directed by Jones Agyemang (Ghana and UK, 2009); *Abrokyire Bayie*, directed by Albert Kuvodu (Ghana and UK, 2009).

5. At the time of writing, a DVD of a Ghanaian movie sold exclusively for home viewing costs about seven euros.

6. A far more monologic and overtly political movie than most, its uncharacteristic narrative reflects the uncharacteristic conditions of its production and distribution. Nana Ama, a Ghanaian nurse, enters Amsterdam with illegal documents, which she thought she had acquired legally and believed to be authentic. With no other choice, because, as she tells the immigration officer, she has sold everything to come to Holland, she flees the airport and begins to build a life for herself in Amsterdam as an illegal alien. As usual, the central character makes several romantic and melodramatic detours, but in the end, she finds the good Ghanaian Mike, who happens to be a doctor and, like Ama, came to Europe in search of better opportunities. They decide to fulfill their duties as citizens of Ghana and go back home, where, Nana Ama assures him, "the government is doing everything it can to improve the condition of medical facilities in the country."

7. Bob Smith's *Mamma Mia* series delivers a Christian message that Socrate Safo's videos do not. Kwabena's wife advises him not to forget her or God while he is abroad and to pray and fast. When life in Italy has become unbearable, Dabo prays to Jesus Christ for help and guidance, and, immediately, two Ghanaian men and their children appear. Members of the Ghanaian church in Verona offer Dabo lodging and help him find work. Throughout the video, Dabo asks God to fend off the evil of the witches whom Kwabena blames for trying to sabotage his efforts. Indeed, Safo's videos about life in Europe seem self-consciously critical of Christianity, ridiculing hypocritical pastors who commit adultery and self-proclaimed born-again Christians who pray to God for money.

8. In Ghana, Kwabena organizes two beauty pageants, one held near the pool of his hotel and the second at the beach, in order to find the perfect wife. These long segments, which feature gorgeous, sexy, and very

scantily dressed women who dance, one at a time, before their judges, make up more than half of the movie. Smith explained that aside from the economic benefits, such segments appeal to audiences because of the music and the dance. Cheap to produce, requiring little investment in crew, sets, light, or sounds and allowing him to pay reasonable artist fees to actors who are only dancing, these dance segments appeal to Ghanaian audiences who, Smith claims, play them, again and again like music CDs or music videos.

Chapter 5: Transcultural Encounters and Local Imaginaries

1. The average exchange rate in 2002 was 2,669.30 cedi to one US dollar. The Nigerian VHS sold for about 7,000 cedis.

2. Largely as a result of the lobbying efforts of industry stakeholders, the Minister for Information dissolved the Cinematograph Exhibition Board of Control. In 2010 a new board was established under the Development and Classification of Film Bill, a law intended to replace the Cinematograph Act of 1861.

3. The committee also created an official copyright label indicating to consumers, producers, and copyrights officials that the recording to which the label is affixed has been registered with the copyright office and reproduced legally. Videos without the copyright label are assumed to be sold in violation of copyright law. Producers, upon registering their product with the copyright office, can request the number of stickers needed to validate as many copies of the video as they intend to produce.

4. In 2004, a distributor could purchase the Ghanaian rights to a Nigerian film for about $1,000, while to produce a Ghanaian feature, a producer would have to invest, up front, at least $7,500.

5. The enforcement of copyright protections in Ghana falls largely to individual producers because the state lacks the resources to effectively police copyright infringement. Whereas a Ghanaian producer might attempt to prosecute a video pirate operating in Ghana by bringing a complaint before the Copyright Office, a producer located outside Ghana, in Nigeria or elsewhere, would likely not know that his video was being pirated in Ghana, and even if he did, he probably would lack the resources or will to travel to Ghana to file a complaint.

6. Available in Asia since at least 1996, the video compact disc, or VCD, has been widely used as a storage and retrieval device for content produced for other, more expensive and high-end formats. In West Africa, however, the VCD has become the primary format for not only the distribution of movies, but for their production and original release. The advantages of the VCD are many: VCDs are much cheaper to

manufacture than VHS cassettes and DVDs, and they are compatible with VCD players, most DVD players, and personal computers. Compared to a videocassette, a video compact disc is a more robust technology, one that more effectively tolerates heat and dust, and that, unlike a VHS tape, can be replicated, or copied without generational loss. Because of this, the VCD is often perceived to offer higher sound and image quality than VHS, the quality of which is significantly diminished as a result of duplication and generational loss.

7. The producer delivers his master digital tapes to one of the two VCD plants that have opened in Ghana, and the plant sends the tape, using an international courier service such as DHL, to Singapore or China, where another factory stamps out a glass master. Ten days later, the glass master arrives at the plant in Ghana, where it is used to replicate thousands of VCDs.

8. Backed by sponsorship from Key Soap, *Mama* (1999) takes up the cause of child homelessness. In anticipation of the expense of making a movie in two countries, Mensah explained that he and Williams chose to make a movie about homeless children because they hoped "a message film" with a humanitarian focus would appeal to a commercial sponsor. In *Mama*, Ufoma, a beautiful and successful government employee, gives up her job and relationship to establish a home for street children.

9. But, it is also the case that many Nigerian producers, equally constrained by finances, have released videos of comparable quality to low-budget Ghanaian movies, and in recent years, several Ghanaian moviemakers have been able to release movies with very high production values.

10. Prior to directing these movies, Nanor released *Expectations* (1999), a movie produced in Ghana, but edited in Nigeria.

11. The producers agreed to sponsor those segments of the movies made in their respective countries and to hire and pay their own cast and crew. Each producer would then market and distribute the movie and collect revenues earned in his own country. In *Asimo, The Visitor*, and *Time* big men win wealth through immoral dealings with the occult and sacrifice the lives of their loved ones for money and power. Disapproving parents interfere in their sons' relationships with women who are too poor or from the wrong ethnic group in *Lost Hope* and *Web*.

12. Tyler Perry is a Hollywood filmmaker whose films feature and target African Americans. Titles includes *Why Did I Get Married?* (2007) and *For Colored Girls* (2010).

13. See http://www.accramall.com/.

14. Owned by the Silverbird Group, a Nigeria-based media and real estate company, the Silverbird Cinema in Accra has state of the art projection and Dolby digital surround sound.

15. I obtained this information in an e-mail interview with Albert Mensah, general manager for Silverbird Theatres, January 28, 2011. Mr. Mensah estimated that over twenty thousand patrons watched the movie at the Silverbird in Accra. Tickets prices at Silverbird vary. On weekends, an adult ticket costs GhC15.00, or about fifteen dollars, and a student or child admission is about twelve dollars. Weekdays, an adult ticket costs thirteen dollars, and a student ticket can be purchased for ten dollars.

Conclusion

1. The metaphor compares the African man with the African filmmaker. The woman, following the logic of the metaphor, stands in for Africa, and the children the man desires are the African audiences. The metaphor represents African men as cultural producers, here filmmakers, while women remain symbolic. The documentary reflects a similar gender divide. The one woman who is interviewed by Teno in *Sacred Places* is not named, and, unlike the many men who speak as gender-less African producers of culture, she speaks as a female consumer of cinema, explaining that she rarely goes to the Cine Club because the environment is not safe for women.

2. Although Nollywood movies might not have been available in Ouagadougou in 2007, they were available there in 2009, according to Carmen McCain, who found pirated copies of Ghanaian and Nigerian movies dubbed in French in Ouaga's central market. Two Nigerian video movies were screened at FESPACO that same year, competing in the marginal TV/Video Film category, and not as feature films (McCain 2011).

Films and Videos

Aboa Bone. 2000. Directed by Kofi Yirenkyi. Ghana: Nankani Electronic Image Ltd. and Starlight Motion Pictures. In English. VHS.

Abrokyire Bayie. Two parts. 2009. Directed by Albert Kuvodu. Ghana and UK: June Productions. In Akan and English. VCD.

Abyssinia. 1985. Directed by John Owusu. Ghana: Produced by Charles Allen Gyimah. In Akan. VHS.

Agony of Christ. 2008. Directed by Frank Rajah Arase. Ghana. Venus Films. In English. DVD.

Agya Koo in Libya. 2009. Directed by Jones Agyemang. Ghana and UK: E and E Productions. In Akan. VCD.

Agya Koo Sakawa. Two parts. 2009. Directed by James Aboagye. Ghana: Miracle Films. In Akan. VCD.

Amenu's Child. 1950. Directed by Sean Graham. Produced by Sean Graham and Basil Wright. Gold Coast: The Gold Coast Film Unit. In English. 16mm. Black and white. For additional information see http://www.colonialfilm.org.uk/node/6730.

Amsterdam Diary. Two parts. 2005. Directed by Socrate Safo. Ghana and Holland. Movie Africa Productions. In English. VCD.

Asem. 2001. Directed by Kenny McCauley. Ghana: Miracle Films. In Akan. VCD.

Asimo. 1999. Directed by Ifeanyi Onyeabor and Dugbartey Nanor. Ghana: Miracle Film and Igbo Motion Pictures. In English. VHS.

Ayalolo. 1990. Directed by Sidiku Buari. Ghana: Sid Studio and Film Works. VHS.

Aya Minnow. 1987. Directed by T. A. Daniels. Ghana: Ghana Film Industry Corporation. In English. 35mm. Black and white.

Back Home Again. 1995. Directed by Kofi Nartey. Ghana and UK. In English. 35mm.

Back to Kotoka. 2001. Directed by Socrate Safo. Ghana and Netherlands: Movie Africa Productions. In English. VHS.

Beyoncé: The President's Daughter. 2006. Directed by Frank Rajah Arase. Ghana: Venus Films. In English. VCD.

Beyonce II. 2007. Directed by Frank Rajah Arase. Ghana: Venus Films. In English. VCD.

Big Time. 1989. Directed by Ramesh Jai. Ghana: Screen Winner Productions. In English. VHS.

Black Is Black: Mamma Mia 3. 2000. Directed by Bob Smith Jnr. Ghana and Italy: R.A.P. In English. VHS.

Boy Kumasenu, The. 1952. Directed by Sean Graham. Produced by Sean Graham and Basil Wright. Gold Coast: The Gold Coast Film Unit. In English. 35mm. Black and white. For more information, go to http://www.colonialfilm.org.uk/node/332.

Burma: West African Troops Cross the Maturahari River. 1944. GB. War Office Directorate of Public Relations. In English. 35mm. Black and white. For more information, go to http://www.colonialfilm.org.uk/node/2605.

Buud Yam. 1997. Directed by Gaston Kaboré. Burkina Faso and France: Car-Cine Production and Cinecom Production. In Mossi. 35mm.

Café Guys. Two parts. 2002. Directed by Uriel Adjin-Tetty. Ghana: Creative Mindz Production. In Akan. VCD.

Checkmate. 2010. Directed by Shirley Frimpong-Manso. Ghana: Sparrow Productions. In English. DVD.

Clando. 1996. Directed by Jean-Marie Teno. Camaroon, France, Germany: Arte; Films du Raphie. In French.

Coming to Ghana. 2005. Directed by Bob Smith Jnr. Ghana and USA: R.A.P. In English. VCD.

Contact: The African Deal. 1973. Directed by Giorgio Bontempi. Ghana and Italy: Ghana Film Industry Corporation and Ital Victoria. 35mm.

Cult of Alata. 1989. Directed by William Akuffo. Ghana: World Wide Motion Pictures. In English. VHS.

Dark Sands. 1999. Directed by Lambert Hama. In English. GAMA Films. Ghana. VHS.

Debut for Dede, A. 1992. Directed by Tom Reibero. Ghana: Ghana Film Industry Corporation. In English. VHS.

Deliverance from the Powers of Darkness. 1990. Directed by Samuel Ankra. Ghana.

Doing Their Thing. 1972. Directed by Bernard Odjidja. Ghana: GFIC.

Dons in Sakawa. 2009. Directed by Moses Ebere. Ghana: Venus Film. In English. VCD.

Double Trouble: Mamma Mia Part Two. 1998. Directed by Bob Smith Jnr. Ghana and Italy. R.A.P. In English. VHS.

Europe by Road. 2004. Directed by Ikenna Ezeugwu. Produced by Ikuku Christopher. Nigeria: Time Entertainment. In English. VCD.

Everyone's Child. 1996. Directed by Tsitsi Dangaremgba. Zimbabwe: Media for Development Trust.

Expectations. 1999. Directed by E. Dugbartey Nanor. Ghana: Miracle Films. In English. VHS.

Fight TB at Home. 1946. Colonial Film Unit. GB.

For Colored Girls. 2010. Directed by Tyler Perry. USA: Lionsgate. 35mm.

Genesis Chapter X. 1979. Directed by Tom Ribeiro. Ghana: Ghana Film Industry Corporation. In English. 35mm. Color.

Ghost Tears. 1992. Directed by Socrate Safo. Ghana: Movie Africa Productions. VHS.

Glamour Girls. 1994. Directed by Kenneth Nnebue. Nigeria. In English VHS.

Hamile the Tongo Hamlet. 1964. Directed by Terry Bishop. Produced by Sam Aryeetey. Ghana: The Ghana Film Industry Corporation. In English. 35mm. Black and white.

Heritage Africa. 1988. Directed by Kwaw Ansah. Ghana: Film Africa Production. 35mm.

His Majesty's Sergeant. 1984. Directed by Ato Yanney. Ghana: Film Afrique, Reo Cinema, Film Lines, and Vision Motion Pictures. In English. 35mm.

Hot Fork. 2010. Directed by Socrate Safo. Ghana: Movie Africa Productions. In English. VCD.

Idikoko in Holland. 2005. Directed and produced by Augustine Abbey. Ghana and Netherlands. In Akan and English. VCD.

I Told You So. 1970. Directed by Egbert Adjeso. Ghana: Ghana Film Industry Corporation. In English. 35mm. Black and white.

Jennifer: So Lovely, So Deadly. 1998. Directed by Nick Narh Teye. Ghana: GAMA Films. In English. VHS.

Juju. 1985. Directed by King Ampaw. Ghana: Reinery Verlag & Filmproduktion in Association with Afro Movies Ltd. and North German Television. In English. 16 mm.

Kananna. 1992. Directed by Kofi Yirenkyi. Ghana: Graceland Motion Pictures. In Akan. VHS.

Koofori in London. 2005. Directed and produced by Paa Kofi Mannoh. Ghana and UK. In Akan and English. VCD.

Kukurantumi the Road to Accra. 1983. Directed by King Ampaw. Ghana: Reinery Verlag & Filmproduktion in Association with Afro Movies Ltd. and North German Television. In English. 35mm.

Lady's Choice. 1994. Directed by Socrate Safo. Ghana: Hacky Films and Movie Africa. In English. VHS.

La Noire de . . . 1966. Directed by Ousmane Sembene. In French. Senegal and France: Filmi Domirev and Les Actualités Françaises.

Life and Living It. 2007. Directed by Shirley Frimpong-Manso. Ghana: Sparrow Productions. DVD.

London Got Problem. 2006. Directed by Albert Kuvodu. Accra, Ghana; London, England.

Lost Hope. 2000. Directed by Ifeanyi Onyeabor. Ghana: Miracle Films. In English. VHS.

Love Brewed in the African Pot. 1980. Directed and produced by Kwaw Ansah. Ghana. In English. 35mm.

Love Brews in Toronto. 2000. Directed by Pius Famiyeh. Ghana and Canada. In English. VHS.

Love from Asia. 2007. Directed by Ugo Ugboh. Nigeria: DERACO Productions. In English. VCD.

Love in America. 2004. Directed by Socrate Safo. Ghana and New York: Movie Africa Productions. In English. VCD.

Lover's Blues. 1993. Directed by Socrate Safo. Ghana: Hacky Films and Movie Africa. In English. VHS.

Lovin you. 1995. Directed by Socrate Safo. Ghana: Hacky Films and Movie Africa. In English. VHS.

Mama. 1999. Directed by Opa Williams. Ghana: HM Films Production. In English. VHS.

Mamma Mia Italiana. 1995. Directed by Bob Smith Jnr. Ghana and Italy: Routes Africa. In English. VHS.

Menace. 1992. Directed by Rex Quartey. Accra, Ghana: Paragon Pictures. VHS.

Mobor. 1989. Directed by William Akuffo. Accra, Ghana: World Wide Motion Pictures. VHS.

Motorcycle Diaries, The. 2004. Directed by Walter Salles Jr. Argentina: Film Four. In Spanish. 35mm.

Mr. Ibu in London. 2004. Directed by Adim Williams. Produced by Chukwuka Emehonwu. Nigeria and UK. In English and Nigerian Pidgin. VCD.

Mr. Mensah Builds a House. 1955. Directed by Sean Graham. Accra: Gold Coast Film Unit. In English. 35mm. Color. For more information, go to http://www.colonialfilm.org.uk/node/615.

Nkrabea. 1992. Directed by C. B. Baffoe Bommie. Ghana: Amahilbee Productions. VHS.

No Tears for Ananse. 1965. Directed by Sam Aryeetey. Ghana: Ghana Film Industry Corporation. In English. 35mm. Black and white.

Otolege. 2005. Directed by Albert Kuvodu. Produced by Albert Kuvodu and Adelaide Cole. Ghana and Netherlands. In English. VCD.

Passion of Christ. 2004. Directed by Frank Rajah Arase. Ghana: Venus Films. In English. VCD.

Perfect Picture. 2009. Directed by Shirley Frimpong-Manso. Ghana: Sparrow Productions. In English. DVD.

Police Officer I. 1995. Directed by Godwin Kotey. Hitline Films. VHS.

Police Officer II: The Tiger of Mwamba. 1995. Directed by Godwin Kotey. VHS.

Police Officer III: Shwiimemee. 2002. Directed by Godwin Kotey. Aphrik Motion Pictures Production. VHS.

Pretty Woman. 1990. Directed by Garry Marshall. Silver Screen Partners. Touchstone Pictures. 35mm.

Price of Love. 1993. Directed by Socrate Safo. Ghana: Hacky Films and Movie Africa. In English. VHS.

Rage: Ripples III. 2003. Directed by Veronica Quarshie. Ghana: Princess Films. In English. VHS.

Run Baby Run. 2008. Directed by Emmanuel Apea. Ghana and UK: Revele Films. In English. DVD.

Sacred Places. 2009. Directed by Jean-Marie Teno. Burkina Faso and France: Les Films du Raphia. In French.

Sacrifice. 1994. Directed by Socrate Safo. Ghana: Hacky Films and Movie Africa. In English. VHS.

Sakawa. Two parts. 2010. Directed by Richmond Aframe. Big Joe Production. Ghana: In Akan. VCD.

Sakawa 419. 2009. Directed by Jones Agyemang. Miracle Films. In Akan and English. Ghana. VCD.

Sakawa Boys. Four parts. 2009. Directed by Socrate Safo. Movie Africa Productions. Ghana. VCD

Sakawa Girls. Two parts. 2009. Directed by Kafui Dzivenu. Ghana: Blema Production. In English. VCD.

Sanders of the River. 1935. Directed by Zoltan Korda. Produced by Alexander Korda. London Film Productions.

Sasa. 1990. Directed by George Lomoty. Ghana: Telestar Film. VHS.

Scent of Danger. 2000. Directed by Godwin Kotey. In English. Ghana. VHS.

Scorned. 2008. Directed by Shirley Frimpong-Manso. Ghana: Sparrow Productions. In English. DVD.

See You, Amsterdam. 2003. Directed by Ashong Katai. Ghana and Netherlands: HM Films Production. VHS.

Shadows from the Past I: Ripples. 2000. Directed by Veronica Quarshie. Ghana: Princess Films. In English. VHS.

Shadows from the Past II: Ripples II. 2000. Directed by Veronica Quarshie. Ghana: Princess Films. In English. VHS.

Shoeshine Boy. 1992. Directed by Nana King. In English. Astron Production. Ghana. VHS.

Sika Mu Sakawa. 2009. Directed by Evans Kumi Wademor. Ghana: Miracle Films. In English and Akan. DVD.

Sika Sunsum. 1991. Directed by Kofi Yirenkyi. Ghana: Graceland Motion Pictures. In Akan. VHS.

Six Hours to Christmas. 2010. Directed by Shirley Frimpong-Manso. In English. Ghana: Sparrow Productions. DVD.

Song of Ceylon. 1934. Directed by Basil Wright. Produced by John Greirson. GPO Film Unit.

Stab in the Dark. 1999. Directed by Veronica Quarshie. Ghana: Princess Films. In English. VHS.

Stab in the Dark II. 1999. Directed by Veronica Quarshie. Ghana: Princess Films. In English. VHS.

Step Dad. 1993. Directed by Socrate Safo. Ghana: Movie Africa Productions. In English. VHS.

Sting in a Tale. 2009. Directed by Shirley Frimpong-Manso. Ghana: Sparrow Productions. In English. DVD.

Theresa, the Story of a Nurse in Training. 1955. Directed by John Hollingsworth and Sean Graham. Accra: Gold Coast Film Unit. In English. 35mm. Black and white.

Thorns in My Home. 2000. Directed by Yaw Firempong-Boakye. Ghana: GAMA Film. In English. VHS.

Time. 2000. Directed by Ifeanyi Onyeabor. Ghana: Miracle Films. In English. VHS.

True Love. 1995. Directed by Socrate Safo. Ghana: Hacky Films and Movie Africa. In English. VHS.

Tsotsi. 2005. Directed by Gavin Hood. UK and South Africa: UK Film and TV Production Company PLC; Industrial Development Corporation of South Africa; The National Film and Video Foundation of SA. In Zulu, Xhosa, Afrikaans, and English. 35mm.

Twin Lovers. 1995. Directed by Veronica Quarshie. Ghana: Pirofilms. In English. VHS.

Twists and Turns. 2005. Directed by Albert Kuvudo. Produced by Albert Kuvudo and Adelaide Cole. Ghana and Netherlands. In English. VCD.

U Gotta Go Home: Coming to Ghana II. 2007. Directed by Bob Smith Jnr. Ghana and USA: R.A.P. In English. DVD.

Unconditional Love I and II. 1989. Directed by Socrate Safo. Ghana: Movie Africa Productions. In English. VHS.

The Visitor. 1979. Directed by Tom Ribeiro. Ghana: GFIC, Musicians Union of Ghana: Mick Fleetwood, and Micky Shapriro.

Viva Riva! 2010. Directed by Djo Munga. Democratic Republic of the Congo: uFilm; France: Cofinova 6; and Belgium: Formosa Productions. In French and Lingala.

Weaving in Togoland. 1948. Gold Coast Colonial Film Unit.

Web. 2000. Directed by Zack Orji. Ghana: Alexiboat Productions. In English. VHS.

Wedlock of the Gods. 2007. Directed by Frank Rajah Arase. Ghana: Venus Film. In English. VCD.

Why Did I Get Married? 2007. Directed by Tyler Perry. USA: Lionsgate.

Wild, Wild World: Wild World 2. 2004. Directed by Bob Smith Jnr. Ghana and Italy: R.A.P. In English. VCD.

Wild World: If Wishes Were Horses. 2002. Directed by Bob Smith Jnr. Ghana and Italy: R.A.P. In English. VCD.

Wild World 3: What a World! 2004. Directed by Bob Smith Jnr. Ghana and Italy: R.A.P. In English. VCD.

Yaaba. 1989. Directed by Idrissa Ouedraogo. Burkina Faso, Switzerland, and France: Arcadia Films, Télévision Suisse Romande, Les Films de l'avenir, and Thelma Film AG. In Mòoré. 35mm.

Zinabu II. 1999. Remake of 1987 original. Directed by William Akuffo. Accra, Ghana: World Wide Pictures. In English. VHS.

References

Abu, Katherine. 1983. "The Separateness of Spouses: Conjugal Resources in an Ashanti Town." In *Female and Male in West Africa*, edited by Christine Oppong, 156–68. London: Boston: Allen and Unwin.

Abu-Lughod, Lila. 1993. "Finding a Place for Islam: Egyptian Television Serials and the National Interest." *Public Culture* 5 (3): 493–514.

———. 1995. "The Objects of Soap Opera: Egyptian Television Serials and the Cultural Politics of Modernity." In *World Apart: Modernity through the Prism of the Local,* edited by Daniel Miller, 190–210. London: Routledge.

———. 2002. "Egyptian Melodrama: Technology of the Modern Subject?" In *Media Worlds: Anthropology in New Terrain,* edited by Faye D. Ginsberg, Lila Abu-Lughod, and Brian Larkin, 115–33. Berkeley: University of California Press.

Achebe, Chinua. 1975. *Morning Yet on Creation Day: Essays.* Studies in African Literature. London: Heinemann Educational.

Adejunmobi, Moradewun. 2002. "English and the Audience of an African Popular Culture: The Case of Nigerian Video Film." *Cultural Critique* 50:74–103.

———. 2007. "Nigerian Video Film as Minor Transnational Practice." *Postcolonial Text* 3 (2). http://postcolonial.org/index.php/pct/article /view/548/405.

———. 2010. "Charting Nollywood's Appeal Locally and Globally." *Film in African Literature Today* 28:106–21.

Adesokan, Akin. 2004. "'How They See It': The Politics and Aesthetics of Nigerian Video Films." In *African Drama and Performance*, edited by John Conteh-Morgan and Tejumola Olaniyan, 189–97. Bloomington: Indiana University Press.

———. 2011. *Postcolonial Artists and Global Aesthetics.* Bloomington and Indianapolis: Indiana University Press.

Adjokatcher, Dan. 1995. "Produced and Directed by Sean Graham." *Mirror,* September 30.

Adu-Gyimah, Ama Serwah. 2003. "Broadcasting in Ghana: An Overview of Changing Times." MA thesis, University of Leeds.

Advance of a Technique: Information Services in the Gold Coast. 1956. Accra: Department of Information Services.

Agbese, Aje-Ori. 2010. "The Portrayal of Mothers-in-Law in Nigerian Movies: The Good, the Bad & Oh, So Wicked." *African Literature Today* 28:84–105.

Agorde, Wisdom S. 2007. "Blood Masculinities: The Triad of Men's Violences in *Time:* A Ghanaian Occult Video Film." *Postcolonial Text* 3 (2). http://postcolonial.org/index.php/pct/article/view/516/413.

Agovi, Kofi Ermeleh. 1992. "Joe de Graft." In *Twentieth-Century Caribbean and Black African Writers, First Series,* edited by Bernth Lindfors and Reinhard Sander, 134–41. Detroit, MI: Wayne State University Press.

Ajibade, Babson. 2007. "From Lagos to Douala: Seeing Spaces and Popular Video Audiences." *Postcolonial Text* 3 (2). http://postcolonial.org/index.php/pct/article/view/524/418.

Akyeampong, Emmanuel. 1996. *Drink, Power, and Cultural Change: A Social History of Alcohol in Ghana, c. 1800 to Recent Times.* Portsmouth, NH: Heinemann.

Allman, Jean, and Victoria Tshjian. 2000. *"I Will Not Eat Stone": A Women's History of Colonial Asante.* Portsmouth, NH: Heinemann; Oxford: James Currey; Cape Town: David Philip.

Alvaray, Luisela. 2008. "National, Regional, and Global: New Waves of Latin American Cinema." *Cinema Journal* 47 (3): 48–65.

Ampofo, Akosua Adomako. 2008. "Collective Activism: The Domestic Violence Bill Becoming Law in Ghana." *African and Asian Studies* 11 (7): 395–421.

Anderson, Benedict. 1983. *Imagined Communities: Reflections on the Origin and Spread of Nationalism.* London: Verso.

Ansah, Kwaw. 2000. "On Ghanaian Theatre and Film." Interview by Kofi Anyidoho. In *FonTomFrom: Contemporary Ghanaian Literature, Theatre, and Film,* edited by Kofi Anyidoho and James Gibbs, 301–14. Amsterdam: Rodopi.

———. 2002. "Kwaw Ansah (Ghana)." Interview by Nwachukwu Frank Ukadike. In *Questioning African Cinema: Conversations with Filmmakers,* edited by Nwachukwu Frank Ukadike, 3–17. Minneapolis: University of Minnesota Press.

Appadurai, Arjun. 1996. *Modernity at Large: Cultural Dimensions of Globalization.* Public Worlds, Vol. 1. Minneapolis: University of Minnesota Press.

———. 2001. *Globalization.* A Millennial Quartet Book. Durham, NC: Duke University Press.

Armes, Roy. 2006. *African Filmmaking: North and South of the Sahara.* Bloomington: Indiana University Press.

Asamoah-Okae. 1987. "Filmmaking Pangs." *Mirror,* September 5.

Aveh, Africanus. 2000. "Ghanaian Video Films of the 1990s: An Annotated Select Filmography." In *FonTomFrom: Contemporary Ghanaian Literature, Theatre and Film,* edited by Kofi Anyidoho and James Gibbs, 283–300. Amsterdam: Rodopi.

Awuah, Joe, Jnr. 2009. "Don't Use Internet for Sakawa." *Modern Ghana News*, November 9. http://www.modernghana.com/news/247919/1/dont-use-internet-for-sakaw.html.

Bakari, Imruh, Mbye B. Cham, and British Film Institute. 1996. *African Experiences of Cinema*. London: BFI Pub.

Barber, Karin. 1987. "Popular Arts in Africa." *African Studies Review* 30 (3): 1–78.

Barber, Karin, John Collins, and Alain Ricard. 1997. *West African Popular Theatre*. Bloomington: Indiana University Press; Oxford: James Currey.

Barlet, Olivier. 2000. *African Cinemas: Decolonizing the Gaze*. New York: Zed Books.

Barrot, Pierre, ed. 2009. *Nollywood: The Video Phenomenon in Nigeria*. Oxford: James Currey; Bloomington: Indiana University Press.

Bastian, Misty L. 1993. "'Bloodhounds Who Have No Friends': Witchcraft and Locality in the Nigerian Popular Press." In *Modernity and Its Malcontents: Ritual and Power in Postcolonial Africa*, edited by Jean Comaroff and John Comaroff, 129–66. Chicago: University of Chicago Press.

———. 2001. "Vulture Men, Campus Cultists and Teenaged Witches: Modern Magics in Nigerian Popular Media." In *Magical Interpretations, Material Realities: Modernity, Witchcraft and the Occult in Postcolonial Africa*, 71–96. London: Routledge.

Bauman, Zygmunt. 2004. *Wasted Lives: Modernity and Its Outcasts*. Cambridge: Polity Press.

Bhabha, Homi K. 1994. *The Location of Culture*. London: Routledge.

Boafo-Arthur, Kwame. 1999. "Ghana: Structural Adjustment, Democratizaton, and the Politics of Continuity." *African Studies Review* 42 (2): 41–72.

Bourdieu, Pierre. 1985. "The Market of Symbolic Goods." *Poetics* 14:13–44.

Brown, Wendy. 2003. "Neo-liberalism and the End of Liberal Democracy." *Theory and Event* 7 (1): 1–25. http://muse.jhu.edu/journals/theory_and_event/v007/7.1brown.html.

Burton, Julianne. 1997. "Film Artisans and Film Industries in Latin America, 1956–1980: Theoretical and Critical Implications of Variations in Modes of Filmic Production and Consumption." In *New Latin American Cinema, I: Theory, Practices and Transcontinental Articulations*, edited by Michael T. Martin, 157–84. Detroit, MI: Wayne State University Press.

Butler, Judith. 1990. *Gender Trouble: Feminism and the Subversion of Identity*. New York: Routledge.

———. 1993. *Bodies That Matter: On the Discursive Limits of "Sex."* New York: Routledge.

Chatterjee, Partha. 1993. *The Nation and Its Fragments: Colonial and Post-colonial Histories*. Princeton: Princeton University Press.

Chiluwa, Innocent. 2009. "The Discourse of Digital Deceptions and '419' Emails." *Discourse Studies* 11:635–60.

Clark, Gracia. 1994. *Onions Are My Husband: Survival and Accumulation by West African Market Women*. Chicago: University of Chicago Press.

———. 1999. "Negotiating Asante Family Survival in Kumasi, Ghana." *Africa* 69 (1): 66–85.

———. 2001. "Gender and Profiteering: Ghana's Market Women as Devoted Mothers and 'Human Vampire Bats.'" In *"Wicked" Women and the Configuration of Gender in Africa*, edited by Dorothy L. Hodgson and Sheryl A. McCurdy, 293–311. Portsmouth, NH: Heinemann; Oxford: James Currey; Cape Town: David Philip.

Cole, Catherine M. 2001. *Ghana's Concert Party Theatre*. Bloomington: Indiana University Press.

Cole, Catherine M., Takyiwaa Manuh, and Stephan Miescher, eds. 2007. *Africa after Gender?* Bloomington: Indiana University Press.

Cole, Jennifer, and Lynn M. Thomas, eds. 2009. *Love in Africa*. Chicago: University of Chicago Press.

Collins, John. 1997. *Highlife Time*. Accra: Anansesm Publications.

Comaroff, Jean, and John Comaroff. 2002. "Alien Nation: Zombies, Immigrants and Millennial Capitalism." *South Atlantic Quarterly* 101 (4): 772–99.

"Commercial Video Operators: What People Say." 1987. *Mirror*, October 8.

Creed, Barbara. 1993. *The Monstrous-Feminine: Film, Feminism, Psychoanalysis*. London: Routledge.

Curtin, Michael. 2003. "Media Capital: Towards the Study of Spatial Flows." *International Journal of Cultural Studies* 6 (2): 202–28.

Dadson, Nanabanyin. 1987a. "Diary from Ouagadougou: Part One." *Mirror*, March 7.

———. 1987b. "Diary from Ouagadougou: Part Two." *Mirror*, March 11.

———. 1987c. "Kwaw Ansah: To Film and Back." *Mirror*, October 10.

———. 1987d. *"Zinabu:* A Pioneering Film." *Mirror*, August 1.

———. 1988. "'I Told You So' Gives a Clue." *Mirror*, May 14.

———. 1989. "How Fares Heritage?" *Mirror*, January 28.

———. 1995a. "Ghana Goes to Watch 'Cine.'" *Mirror*, July 29.

———. 1995b. "The Pattern of Local Film Production Continues." *Mirror*, August 19.

———. 1995c. "Rundown of Ghanaian Films." *Mirror*, August 26.

Dal Yong Jin. 2007. "Transformation of the World Television System Under Neoliberal Globalization, 1983 to 2003." *Television and New Media* 8 (3): 179.

Dawson, Ashley. 2010. "Cargo Culture: Literature in the Age of Mass Displacement." *WSQ: Women's Studies Quarterly* 38 (1&2): 178–93.

de Lauretis, Teresa. 1984. *Alice Doesn't: Feminism, Semiotics, Cinema.* Bloomington: Indiana University Press.

———. 1987. *Technologies of Gender: Essays on Theory, Film, and Fiction.* Bloomington: Indiana University Press.

Desai, Jinga. 2004. *Beyond Bollywood: The Cultural Politics of South Asian Diasporic Film.* New York: Routledge.

Diawara, Manthia. 1992. *African Cinema: Politics and Culture.* Bloomington: Indiana University Press.

———. 1998. "Toward a Regional Imaginary in Africa." In *The Cultures of Globalization,* edited by Fredric Jameson and Masao Miyoshi. Durham, NC: Duke University Press.

———. 2010. *African Film: New Forms of Aesthetics and Politics.* Munich, Germany; New York: Prestel.

Dobler, Gregor. 2008. "From Scotch Whisky to Chinese Sneakers: International Commodity Flows and New Trade Networks in Oshikango, Namibia." *Africa* 78 (3): 410–32.

Dogbe, Esi. 2003. "Warped Identities: Dress in Popular West African Video Films." *African Identities* 1 (1): 95–117.

Dovey, Lindiwe. 2009. *African Film and Literature: Adapting Violence to the Screen.* Film and Culture. New York: Columbia University Press.

During, Simon. 1997. "Popular Culture on a Global Scale: A Challenge for Cultural Studies?" *Critical Inquiry* 23 (4): 808–33.

Esonwanne, Uzome. 2008. "Interviews with Amaka Igwe, Tunde Kelani, and Kenneth Nnebue." *Research in African Literatures* 39 (4): 24–39.

Ezra, Elizabeth, and Terry Rowden. 2006. *Transnational Cinema: The Film Reader.* New York: Routledge.

Fair, Jo Ellen, Melissa Tully, Brian Ekdale, and Rabiu K. B. Asante. 2009. "Crafting Lifestyles in Urban Africa: Young Ghanaians in the World of Online Friendship." *Africa Today* 55 (4): 29–49.

Ferguson, James. 1999. *Expectations of Modernity: Myths and Meanings of Urban Life on the Zambian Copperbelt.* Perspectives on Southern Africa 57. Berkeley: University of California Press.

———. 2006. *Global Shadows: Africa in the Neoliberal World Order.* Durham, NC: Duke University Press.

Flitterman-Lewis, Sandy. 1987. "Psychoanalysis, Film, and Television." In *Channels of Discourse: Television and Contemporary Criticism,* edited by Robert Clyde Allen, 172–210. Chapel Hill: University of North Carolina Press.

Foucault, Michel. 1995; 1977. *Discipline and Punish: The Birth of the Prison.* Translated by Alan Sheridan. New York: Vintage Books.

Friedberg, Anne. 1993. *Window Shopping: Cinema and the Postmodern.* Berkeley: University of California Press.

Garritano, Carmela. 2000. "Women, Melodrama, and Political Critique: A Feminist Reading of *Hostages, Dust to Dust,* and *True Confessions.*" In *Nigerian Video Films,* edited by Jonathan Haynes, 165–91. Athens: Ohio University Press.

Garuba, Harry. 2003. "Explorations in Animist Materialism: Notes on Reading." *Public Culture* 15 (2): 261–85.

Gifford, Paul. 2004. *Ghana's New Christianity: Pentecostalism in a Globalizing African Economy.* Bloomington: Indiana University Press.

Gikandi, Simon. 2001. "Globalization and the Claims of Postcoloniality." *South Atlantic Quarterly* 100 (3): 627–58.

———. 2004. "African Literature and the Colonial Factor." In *The Cambridge History of African and Caribbean Literature. Volume 1,* edited by F. Abiola Irele and Simon Gikandi, 379–97. Cambridge: Cambridge University Press.

Ginsburg, Faye. 1993. "Aboriginal Media and the Australian Imaginary." *Public Culture* 5 (3): 557–78.

———. 1994. "Embedded Aesthetics: Creating a Discursive Space for Indigenous Media and Cultural Activism." In *Between Resistance and Revolution: Cultural Politics and Social Protest,* edited by R. Fox and O. Starn, 118–44. London: Routledge.

———. 1999. "Shooting Back: From Ethnographic Film to the Ethnography of Media." In *A Companion to Film Theory,* edited by Toby Miller and Robert Stam, 295–322. London: Blackwell.

Ginsburg, Faye D., Lila Abu-Lughod, and Brian Larkin, eds. 2002. *Media Worlds: Anthropology on New Terrain.* Berkeley: University of California Press.

Grierson, John. 1948. "The Film and Primitive Peoples." In *The Film in Colonial Development: A Report of a Conference,* 9–15. London: British Film Institute.

Gugler, Josef. 2003. *African Film: Re-Imagining a Continent.* Bloomington: Indiana University Press.

Guillory, John. 1995. *Cultural Capital: The Problem of Literary Canon Formation.* Chicago: University of Chicago Press.

Gunning, Tom. 1990. "'Primitive' Cinema: A Frame-Up? or, the Trick's on Us." In *Early Cinema: Space, Frame, Narrative,* edited by Thomas Elsaesser and Adam Barker, 95–103. London: British Film Institute.

———. 1995. "An Aesthetic of Astonishment: Early Film and the (In) Credulous Spectator." In *Viewing Positions: Ways of Seeing Film,* edited by Linda Williams, 114–33. New Brunswick: Rutgers University Press.

————. 2004. "An Aesthetic of Astonishment: Early Film and the (In) credulous Spectator." In *Film Theory and Criticism*, edited by L. Braudy and M. Cohen, 862–76. New York: Oxford.

Hansen, Miriam. 1991. *Babel and Babylon: Spectatorship in American Silent Film*. Cambridge, MA: Harvard University Press.

Harrell-Bond, Barbara. 1975. *Modern Marriage in Sierra Leone: A Study of the Professional Group*. The Hague: Mouton.

Harrow, Kenneth W. 2007. *Postcolonial African Cinema: From Political Engagement to Postmodernism*. Bloomington: Indiana University Press.

Harvey, David. 1989. *The Condition of Postmodernity: An Enquiry into the Origins of Cultural Change*. Oxford, England; New York: Blackwell.

Hasty, Jennifer. 2005. *The Press and Political Culture in Ghana*. Bloomington: Indiana University Press.

Haynes, Jonathan. 1995. "Nigerian Cinema: Structural Adjustments." *Research in African Literatures* 26 (3): 97–119.

————, ed. 2000. *Nigerian Video Films: Revised and Expanded*. Athens: Ohio University Press.

————. 2003a. "Africans Abroad: A Theme in Film and Video." *Africa e Mediterraneo: Cultura e Società* 25:22–29.

————. 2003b. "Mobilising Yoruba Popular Culture: Babangida Must Go." *Africa: Journal of the International African Institute* 73 (1): 77–87.

————. 2005. "Nollywood; What's in a Name?" *Guardian*, July 3. http://www.odili.net/news/source/2005/jul/3/49.html.

————. 2007a. "Nollywood in Lagos, Lagos in Nollywood Films." *Africa Today* 54 (2): 131–50.

————. 2007b. "TK in NYC: An Interview with Tunde Kelani." *Postcolonial Text* 3 (2). http://postcolonial.org/index.php/pct/article/view/659/409.

————. 2007c. "Video Boom: Nigeria and Ghana." *Postcolonial Text* 3 (2). http://postcolonial.org/index.php/pct/article/view/522/422.

————. 2010a. "A Literature Review: Nigerian and Ghanaian Videos." *Journal of African Cultural Studies* 22 (1): 105–20.

————. 2010b. "What Is to Be Done? Film Studies and Nigerian and Ghanaian Videos." In *Viewing African Cinema in the Twenty-First Century: Art Films and the Nollywood Video Revolution*, edited by Mahir Şaul and Ralph A. Austen. Athens: Ohio University Press.

Haynes, Jonathan, and Onookome Okome. 2000. "Evolving Popular Media: Nigerian Video Films." In *Nigerian Video Films: Revised and Expanded*, edited by Jonathan Haynes, 51–88. Athens: Ohio University Press.

Hayward, Jennifer Poole. 1997. *Consuming Pleasures: Active Audiences and Serial Fictions from Dickens to Soap Opera*. Lexington: University Press of Kentucky.

Heath, Stephen, and Gillian Skirrow. 1977. "Television: A World of Action." *Screen* 18 (2): 7–59.

Hilderbrand, Lucas. 2004. "Grainy Days and Mondays: Superstar and Bootleg Aesthetics." *Camera Obscura* 57:57–91.

Hjort, Mette, and Duncan J. Petrie. 2007. *The Cinema of Small Nations.* Bloomington: Indiana University Press.

Hoefert de Turegano, Teresa. 2004. "The International Politics of Cinematic Coproduction: Spanish Policy in Latin America." *Film & History: An Interdisciplinary Journal of Film and Television* 34 (2): 15–24.

Iwabuchi, Koichi. 2002. *Recentering Globalization: Popular Culture and Japanese Transnationalism.* Durham, NC: Duke University Press.

Jaikumar, Priya. 2006. *Cinema at the End of Empire: A Politics of Transition in Britain and India.* Durham, NC: Duke University Press.

Jameson, Fredric. 1981. *The Political Unconscious: Narrative as a Socially Symbolic Act.* Ithaca, NY: Cornell University Press.

Jaques, Pierre-Emmanuel. 2006. "The Associational Attractions of the Musical." In *The Cinema of Attractions Reloaded,* edited by Wanda Strauven, 281–88. Amsterdam, Netherlands: Amsterdam University Press.

Jawando, Muhammed S. S. 2009. "Sakawa Boys Invade Ghanaweb." *Ghanaweb,* April 6. http://www.ghanaweb.com/GhanaHomePage/feature/artikel.php?ID=160084/.

Johnson, Lemuel. 1998. *Shakespeare in Africa (and Other Venues): Import and the Appropriation of Culture.* Trenton, NJ: African World Press.

Jones, A. Creech. 1948. Introduction to *The Film in Colonial Development: A Report of a Conference,* 4–8. London: British Film Institute.

Jørgensen, Anne Mette. 2001. "Sankofa and Modern Authenticity in Ghanaian Film and Television." In *Same and Other: Negotiating African Identity in Cultural Production,* edited by Mai Palmberg and Maria Eriksson Baaz, 119–41. Uppsala, Sweden: Nordiska Afrikainstitutet.

Julien, Eileen. 2006. "The Extroverted African Novel." In *The Novel, Volume I: History, Geography, and Culture,* edited by Franco Moretti, 667–700. Princeton, NJ: Princeton University Press.

———. 2007. "When a Man Loves a Woman: Gender and National Identity in Wole Soyinka's *Death and the King's Horseman* and Mariama Bâ's *Scarlet Song.*" In *Africa after Gender?,* edited by Catherine M. Cole, Takyiwaa Manuh, and Stephan F. Miescher, 205–22. Bloomington: Indiana University Press.

Kosher, Khalid. 2003. "New African Diasporas: An Introduction." In *New African Diasporas,* edited by Kahlid Kosher, 1–16. London: Routledge.

Larkin, Brian. 2000. "Hausa Dramas and the Rise of Video Culture in Nigeria." In *Nigerian Video Films: Revised and Expanded,* edited by Jonathan Haynes, 209–42. Athens: Ohio University Press.

————. 2002. "The Materiality of Cinema Theatres in Northern Nigeria." In *Media World: Anthropology in New Terrain*, edited by Faye D. Ginsberg, Lila Abu-Lughod, and Brian Larkin, 319–36. Berkeley: University of California Press.

————. 2004. "Degraded Images, Distorted Sounds: Nigerian Video and the Infrastructure of Piracy." *Public Culture* 16 (20): 289–313.

————. 2008. *Signal and Noise: Media, Infrastructure, and Urban Culture in Nigeria.* Durham, NC: Duke University Press.

Lionnet, Françoise, and Shu-mei Shih. 2005. *Minor Transnationalism.* Durham, NC: Duke University Press.

Mann, Kristin. 1980. *Marrying Well: Marriage, Status and Social Change among the Educated Elite in Colonial Lagos.* Cambridge: Cambridge University Press.

Manuh, Takyiwaa. 1995. "Women, State and Society under the PNDC." *Women's Studies with a Focus on Ghana: Selected Readings*, edited by Prah Mansah. Schriesheim, Germany: Books on African Studies.

————. 2007. "Doing Gender Work in Ghana." In *Africa after Gender?*, edited by Catherine M. Cole, Takyiwaa Manuh, and Stephan Miescher, 125–49. Bloomington, Indiana: Indiana University Press.

Masters, Ian. 2006. *Media Training Needs Assessment: Ghana 2006.* London: Scriptnet.

Mbembe, Achille. 2001. *On the Postcolony.* Studies on the History of Society and Culture [Notes provisoires sur la postcolonie]. Vol. 41. Berkeley: University of California Press.

————. 2002. "African Modes of Self-Writing." Translated by Steven Rendall. *Public Culture* 14 (1): 239–73.

————. 2004. "The Aesthetics of Superfluity." *Public Culture* 16 (3): 373–405.

McCain, Carmen. 2011. "FESPACO in a Time of Nollywood: The Politics of the 'Video' Film at Africa's Oldest Festival." *Journal of African Media Studies* 3 (2): 241–61.

McCall, John C. 2002. "Madness, Money, and Movies: Watching a Nigerian Popular Video with the Guidance of a Native Doctor." *Africa Today* 49 (3): 78.

————. 2007. "The Pan-Africanism We Have: Nollywood's Invention of Africa." *Film International* 5 (4): 92–97.

McCaskie, T. C. 1983. "Accumulation, Wealth and Belief in Asante History: I. To the Close of the Nineteenth Century." *Africa* 53 (1): 23–43.

————. 1986. "Accumulation, Wealth and Belief in Asante History: II. To the Close of the Twentieth Century." *Africa* 56 (1): 2–23.

McClintock, Anne. 1997. "'No Longer in a Future Heaven': Gender, Race and Nationalism." In *Dangerous Liaisons: Gender, Nation, and*

Postcolonial Perspectives, edited by Anne McClintock, Aamir Mufti, and Ella Shohat, 89–112. Minneapolis: University of Minnesota Press.

Menon, Nivedita. 2005. "Between the Burqa and the Beauty Parlor? Globalization, Cultural Nationalism, and Feminist Politic." In *Postcolonial Studies and Beyond*, edited by A. Loomba et al. Durham, NC: Duke University Press.

Meyer, Birgit. 1998. "The Power of Money: Politics, Occult Force, and Pentecostalism in Ghana." *African Studies Review* 41 (3): 15–37.

———. 1999. "Popular Ghanaian Cinema and 'African Heritage.'" *Africa Today* 46 (2): 93–114.

———. 2001. "Money, Power, and Morality: Popular Ghanaian Cinema in the Fourth Republic." *Ghana Studies* 4 (3): 51–67.

———. 2002. "Occult Pentecostalism, Prosperity and Popular Cinema in Ghana." *Culture and Religion* 3 (1): 67–87.

———. 2003. "Visions of Blood, Sex and Money: Fantasy Spaces in Popular Ghanaian Cinema." *Visual Anthropology* 16 (1): 15–41.

———. 2004. "'Praise the Lord': Popular Cinema and Pentecostalite Style in Ghana's New Public Sphere." *American Ethnologist* 31 (1): 92–110.

———. 2006. "Religious Revelation, Secrecy and the Limits of Visual Representation." *Anthropological Theory* 6 (4): 431–53.

———. 2008. "Powerful Pictures: Popular Christian Aesthetics in Southern Ghana." *Journal of the American Academy of Religion* 76 (1): 82–110.

———. 2010. "Tradition and Colour at Its Best: 'Tradition' and 'Heritage' in Ghanaian Video-movies." *Journal of African Cultural Studies* 22 (1): 7–23.

Mishra, Vijay. 2001. *Bollywood Cinema: Temples of Desire*. New York: Routledge.

Mitchell, Timothy. 2000. "The Stage of Modernity." In *The Question of Modernity*, edited by Timothy Mitchell, 1–34. Minneapolis: University of Minnesota Press.

Mulvey, Laura. 1989. *Visual and Other Pleasures: Theories of Representation and Difference*. Bloomington: Indiana University Press.

Naficy, Hamid. 2001. *An Accented Cinema: Exilic and Diasporic Filmmaking*. Princeton, NJ: Princeton University Press.

Ndalianis, Angela. 2004. *Neo-Baroque Aesthetics and Contemporary Entertainment*. Cambridge, MA: MIT Press.

Newell, Stephanie. 1997. *Writing African Women: Gender, Popular Culture, and Literature in West Africa*. London: Zed Books.

———. 2000. *Ghanaian Popular Fiction: 'Thrilling Discoveries of Conjugal Life' and Other Tales*. Oxford: James Currey; Athens: Ohio University Press.

————. 2005. "Devotion and Domesticity: The Reconfiguration of Gender in Popular Christian Pamphlets from Ghana and Nigeria." *Journal of Religion in Africa* 35 (3): 296–323.

Nugent, Paul. 1995. *Big Men and Small Boys and Politics in Ghana.* Accra: Asempa.

Nuttall, Sarah, and Achille Mbembe, eds. 2008. *Johannesburg: The Elusive Metropolis.* Durham, NC: Duke University Press.

Nuviadenu, Kekeli K. 2004. "Media Globalization and Localization: An Analysis of the International Flow of Programs on Ghana Television (GTV)." PhD diss., Howard University.

Nwaubani, Trisha Adaobi. 2009. *I Do Not Come to You by Chance.* New York: Hyperion.

Ogunleye, Foluke, ed. 2003. *African Video Film Today.* Manzini, Swaziland: Academic Publishers.

Okome, Onookome. 2000. "*Onome:* Ethnicity, Class, Gender." In *Nigerian Video Films: Revised and Expanded,* edited by Jonathan Haynes, 148–64. Athens: Ohio University Press.

————. 2007a. "Introducing the Special Issue on West African Cinema: Africa at the Movies." *Postcolonial Text* 3 (2): 1–21. http://jounrals.sfu.ca/pocol/index.php/pct/article/view/766/433.

————. 2007b. "Nollywood: Spectatorship, Audience and the Sites of Consumption." *Postcolonial Text* 3 (2). http://postcolonial.org/index.php/pct/article/view/763/425.

————. 2007c. "Women, Religion and the Video Film in Nigeria: Glamour Girls and End of Wicked." *Bayreuth African Studies Series* 82:161–85.

Okome, Onookome, and Jonathan Haynes. 1995. *Cinema and Social Change in West Africa.* Jos, Nigeria: Nigerian Film Institute.

Ong, Aihwa. 1999. *Flexible Citizenship: The Cultural Logics of Transnationality.* Durham, NC: Duke University Press.

Oppong, Christine. 1974. *Marriage Among a Matrilinial Elite: A Family Study of Ghanaian Senior Civil Servants.* Cambridge: Cambridge University Press.

Oppong, Joseph. 2004. "Ghana: Internal, International, Transnational Migration." In *Migration and Immigration: A Global View,* edited by Maura Toro-Morn and Marixsa Alicea, 81–95. Westport, CT: Greenwood Press.

Owusu, Maxwell. 1996. "Tradition and Transformation: Democracy and the Politics of Popular Power in Ghana." *Journal of Modern African Studies* 34 (2): 307–37.

Owusu, Stephen Atts. 2009. "'Sakawa' Hysteria Ghana's 419." *Ghanaweb,* May 26. http://www.ghanaweb.com/GhanaHomePage/features/artikel.php?ID=162565/.

Papastergiadis, Nikos. 2000. *The Turbulence of Migration: Globalization, Deterritorialization, and Hybridity.* Oxford: Polity Press.

Parish, Jane. 1999. "The Dynamics of Witchcraft and Indigenous Shrines among the Akan." *Africa: Journal of the International African Institute* 69 (3): 426–47.

———. 2000. "From Body to Wallet: Conceptualizing Akan Witchcraft at Home and Abroad." *Journal of the Royal Anthropological Institute* 6:487–500.

Parker, Andrew, Mary Russo, Doris Sommer, and Patricia Yaeger, eds. 1992. *Nationalisms and Sexualities.* New York: Routledge.

Pearson, George. 1948. "The Making of Films for Illiterates in Africa." In *The Film in Colonial Development: A Report of a Conference.* London: British Film Institute.

Quartey, Rex. 1982. "Film in a Revolution." *Mirror,* August 6.

Quayson, Ato. 2000. *Postcolonialism: Theory, Practice, or Process.* Cambridge: Polity Press.

Radhakrishnan, R. 1992. "Nationalism, Gender, and the Narrative of Identity." In *Nationalisms and Sexualities,* edited by Andrew Parker et al., 77–95. New York: Routledge.

Reynertson, A. J. 1970. *The Work of the Film Director.* New York: Communication Arts Books.

Rice, Tom. 2010. "The Boy Kumasenu." *Colonial Film: Moving Images of the British Empire, 2010.* http://www.colonialfilm.org.uk/node/332 (accessed June 2011).

Rosen, Philip. 2001. *Change Mummified: Cinema, Historicity, Theory.* Minneapolis: University of Minnesota Press.

Rouch, Jean. 2003. *Ciné-Ethnography.* Translated and edited by Steven Feld. Minneapolis: University of Minnesota Press.

Sakyi, Kwamina. 1996. "The Problems and Achievements of the Ghana Film Industry Corporation in the Growth and Development of the Film Industry in Ghana." Master's thesis, University of Ghana.

Sama, Emmanuel. 1996. "African Films Are Foreigners in Their Own Countries. In *African Experiences of Cinema,* edited by Imruch Bakari and Mbye B. Cham, 148–56. London: British Film Institute.

Sassen, Saskia. 2001. *The Global City: New York, London, Tokyo.* 2nd ed. Princeton, NJ: Princeton University Press.

Şaul, Mahir, and Ralph A. Austen. 2010. *Viewing African Cinema in the Twenty-First Century: Art Films and the Nollywood Video Revolution.* Athens: Ohio University Press.

Sexton, Jamie. 2002. "Greirson's Machines: *Drifters,* the Documentary Film Movement and the Negotiation of Modernity." *Canadian Journal of Film Studies* 11 (1): 40–59.

Shaw, Deborah. 2011. "Babel and the Global Hollywood Gaze." *Situations* 4 (1). http://ojs.gc.cuny.edu/index.php/situations/article/view /742/1203.

Shohat, Ella, and Robert Stam. 2003. *Multiculturalism, Postcoloniality, and Transnational Media.* New Brunswick, NJ: Rutgers University Press.

Sinclair, John, Elizabeth Jacka, and Stuart Cunningham. 1996. *New Patterns in Global Television: Peripheral Vision.* Oxford: Oxford University Press.

Simone, AbdouMaliq. 2001. "On the Worlding of African Cities." *African Studies Review* 44 (2): 15–41.

———. 2006. "Pirate Towns: Reworking Social and Symbolic Infrastructures in Johannesburg and Douala." *Urban Studies* 43 (2): 357–70.

Singer, Ben. 2001. *Melodrama and Modernity: Early Sensational Cinema and Its Contexts.* New York: Columbia University Press.

Smith, Andrew. 2009. "Nigerian Scam E-mails and the Charms of Capital." *Cultural Studies* 23 (1): 27–47.

Smith, Daniel Jordan. 2007. *A Culture of Corruption: Everyday Deception and Popular Discontent in Nigeria.* Princeton, NJ: Princeton University Press.

———. 2009. "Managing Men, Marriage, and Modern Love: Women's Perspectives on Intimacy and Male Identity in Southwestern Nigeria." *In Love in Africa,* edited by Jennifer Cole and Lynn M. Thomas. Chicago: University of Chicago Press.

Smith, Hilda Lan. 2010. "6 Hours to Christmas." *Ghana News.* October 15. http://www.modernghana.com/lifestyle/1663/16/0396-hours-to-christmas039.html.

Smyth, Rosaleen. 1979. "The Development of British Colonial Film Policy, 1927–1939, with Special Reference to East and Central Africa." *Journal of African History* 20 (3): 437–50.

———. 1988. "The British Colonial Film Unit and Sub-Saharan Africa, 1939–1945." *Historical Journal of Film, Radio and Television* 12 (2): 285–98.

———. 1992. "The Postwar Career of the Colonial Film Unit in Africa, 1946–1955." *Historical Journal of Film, Radio and Television* 12 (2): 163–77.

Spivak, Gayatri Chakravorty. 1999. *A Critique of Postcolonial Reason: Toward a History of the Vanishing Present.* Cambridge, MA: Harvard University Press.

Sreberny-Mohammadi, Annabelle, and Ali Mohammadi. 1994. *Small Media, Big Revolution: Communication, Culture, and the Iranian Revolution.* Minneapolis: University of Minnesota Press.

Stratton, Florence. 1994. *Contemporary African Literature and the Politics of Gender.* New York: Routledge.

Sundaram, Ravi. 1999. "Recycling Modernity: Pirate Electronic Cultures in India." *Third Text* 47: 59–65.

Sutherland-Addy, Esi. 2000. "The Ghanaian Feature Video Phenomenon: Thematic Concerns and Aesthetic Resources." In *Fon Tom From: Contemporary Ghanaian Literatures, Theatre and Film*, edited by Kofi Anyidoho and James Gibbs, 265–82. Amsterdam: Rodopi.

Tcheuyap, Alexie. 2011. *Postnationalist African Cinemas*. Manchester, UK: Manchester University Press.

Teer-Tomaselli, Ruth, Arrie de Beer, and Herman Wasserman. 2007. "South Africa as a Regional Media Power." In *Media on the Move: Global Flow and Contra-flow*, edited by Daya Kishan Thussu. London: Routledge.

Thussu, Daya Kishan, ed. 2007. *Media on the Move: Global Flow and Contra-flow*. Communication and Society. London: Routledge.

Tsikata, Dzodzi. 2009. "Women's Organizing in Ghana since the 1990s: From Individual Organizations to Three Coalitions Development." *Development* 52 (2): 185–92.

Tuomi, Krista. 2007. "Organisational Shifts in the Feature Film Industry: Implications for South Africa." *Transformation* 63:68–91.

Turner, Terence. 1991. "The Social Dynamics of Video Media in an Indigenous Society: The Cultural Meaning and the Personal Politics of Video-making in Kayapo Communities." *Visual Anthropology Review* 7 (2): 68–76.

———. 1992. "Defiant Images: The Kayapo Appropriation of Video." *Anthropology Today* 8 (6): 5–16.

———. 1995. "Representation, Collaboration, and Mediation in Contemporary Ethnographic and Indigenous Media." *Visual Anthropology Review* 11 (2): 102–6.

———. 2002. "Representation, Politics, and Cultural Imagination in Indigenous Video: General Points and Kayapo Examples." In *Media Worlds: Anthropology in New Terrain*, edited by Faye D. Ginsberg, Lila Abu-Lughod, and Brain Larkin, 75–89. Berkeley: University of California Press.

Twum-Baah, K. A. 2005. "Volume and Characteristics of International Ghanaian Migration." In *At Home in the World? International Migration and Development in Contemporary Ghana and West Africa*, edited by Takyiwaa Manuh, 55–77. Accra, Ghana: Sub-Saharan Publishers.

Ugor, Paul. 2009. "Small Media, Popular Culture, and New Youth Spaces in Nigeria." *Review of Education, Pedagogy, and Cultural Studies* 31 (4): 387–408.

Ukadike, Nwachukwu Frank. 1994. *Black African Cinema*. Berkeley: University of California Press.

————. 2003. "Video Booms and the Manifestations of 'First' Cinema in Anglophone Africa." In *Rethinking Third Cinema*, edited by Anthony R. Guneratne and Wimal Dissanayake, 126–43. New York: Routledge.

Ukah, Asonzeh F. K. 2003. "Advertising God: Nigerian Christian Videofilms and the Power of Consumer Culture." *Journal of Religion in Africa* 33 (2): 203–31.

Vasudevan, Ravi. 2001. "The Politics of Cultural Address in a 'Transitional' Cinema: A Case Study of Indian Popular." In *Reinventing Film Studies*, edited by Christine Gledhill and Linda Williams, 130–64. London: Arnold; New York: Oxford University Press.

Vellenga, Dorothy Dee. 1983. "Who Is a Wife? Legal Expressions of Heterosexual Conflicts in Ghana." In *Female and Male in West Africa*, edited by Christine Oppong. London: George Allen.

Wendl, Tobias. 2001. "Visions of Modernity in Ghana: Mami Wata Shrines, Photo Studios and Horror Films." *Visual Anthropology* 14 (3): 269–92.

————. 2007. "Wicked Villagers and the Mysteries of Reproduction: An Exploration of Horror Movies from Ghana and Nigeria." *Postcolonial Text* 3 (2). http://postcolonial.org/index.php/pct/article/view/529/420.

"Who's Kidding with Video Centres." 1998. *Mirror*, April 16.

"Why We Must Ban Video Operators." 1998. *Mirror*, May 16.

Wilks, Ivor. 1975. *Asante in the Nineteenth Century: The Structure and Evolution of a Political Order*. Cambridge: Cambridge University Press.

Winston, Brian. 1995. *Claiming the Reel: The Documentary Film Revisited*. London: British Film Institute.

Yang, Mayfair Mei-hui. 2002. "Mass Media and Transnational Subjectivity in Shanghai: Notes on (re)Cosmopolitanism in a Chinese Metropolis." In *Media Worlds*, edited by Faye D. Ginsburg, Lila Abu-Lughod, and Brian Larkin. Berkeley: University of California Press.

Yanney, Ato. 1988. "To Be or Not to Be a Filmmaker." *Mirror*, August 22.

Zook, Matthew. 2007. "Your Urgent Assistance Is Requested: The Intersection of 419 Spam and New Networks of Imagination." *Ethics, Place and Environment* 10 (1): 65–88.

Index